The

LOVE

They

LOST

The
LOVE
They
LOST

Living with the Legacy of
Our Parents' Divorce

STEPHANIE STAAL

DELACORTE PRESS

Grateful acknowledgment is made for permission to reprint the following:

An excerpt from *What We Talk About When We Talk About Love,* by Raymond Carver. Published by Alfred A. Knopf, a division of Random House, Inc.

An excerpt from "Lost in Translation" by James Merrill. From SELECTED POEMS 1945–1985, by James Merrill. Copyright © 1992 by James Merrill. Reprinted by Alfred A. Knopf, a division of Random House, Inc.

An excerpt from *Composing a Life* by Mary Catherine Bateson. Copyright © 1989 by Mary Catherine Bateson. Used by permission of Grove/Atlantic, Inc.

An excerpt from "Autobiography" from COLLECTED POEMS by Thom Gunn. Copyright © 1994 by Thom Gunn. Reprinted by permission of Farrar, Straus and Giroux, LLC. Also, from JACK STRAW'S CASTLE by Thom Gunn. Reprinted by permission of Faber and Faber Ltd.

An excerpt from "East Coker," copyright 1940 by T.S. Eliot and renewed 1968 by Esme Valerie Eliot, reprinted by permission of Harcourt, Inc. Also from "East Coker," from *The Four Quartets* from COLLECTED POEMS 1909–1962 by T.S. Eliot. Reprinted by permission of Faber and Faber Ltd.

Published by
Delacorte Press
Random House, Inc.
1540 Broadway
New York, New York 10036

Library of Congress Cataloging-in-Publication Data

Staal, Stephanie.
The love they lost: living with the legacy of our parents'
divorce / Stephanie Staal.
p. cm.
ISBN 0-385-33409-5
1. Adult children of divorced parents—Psychology.
2. Adult children of divorced parents—Mental health.
3. Adult children of divorced parents—Attitudes. I. Title.

HQ777.5 .S7 2000
306.89—dc21   00-038366

Includes bibliographical references.

Book design by Lynn Newmark

Manufactured in the United States of America.
Published simultaneously in Canada.

September 2000

10 9 8 7 6 5 4 3 2 1

BVG

ACKNOWLEDGMENTS

I WOULD FIRST LIKE to give my heartfelt gratitude to all the men and women who let me into their lives, so generously giving their time and energy to participate in this project. Your candor, your stories, and your spirit were constant sources of inspiration for me along the way, and without each and every one of you, this book could never have been written.

Likewise, this book would never have been more than just a kernel of an idea if not for my agent, Tanya McKinnon, whom I can't possibly thank enough . . . for her brilliant skills as an agent, for her on-target insight as a reader, for her unfailing enthusiasm, for her sharp wit and dedication, and, finally, for being more than a super-agent, but also a wonderful friend. I would also like to thank Mary Evans for her much appreciated wisdom and general good cheer.

Thanks to my editor, Tom Spain, for his consistent support and ineffable patience and for allowing me the freedom to explore my vision for this book; in addition, I would like to thank Kathleen Jayes and Andie Nicolay for all their assistance.

To Tasha Blaine, who read several drafts of the manuscript, for the invaluable editorial input, for the hours of probing conversation and for basically keeping me sane. To Barbara Messing, Lorena

Shih, Kristen Buckley, and Jason Anthony, I would like to extend special thanks for their friendship, advice, comfort and help throughout. I am also greatly indebted to the many people who helped get the word out during the research phase, especially Justin Hall, Ed Han, Karen Ginsberg, and Lynn Riordan. And thanks to Richard Simon, who has an uncanny knack for titles.

I would like to give special recognition to my mother and father who, despite the painful nature of this book's subject, never flagged in offering me their love and support, for which I am forever grateful. I know my decision to write this book was difficult for them, and even though their version of events would most certainly differ from mine, they respected my need to tell my own story. I love and admire you both. Thanks also to my baby sister, Caroline, whose maturity, intelligence, sense of humor, and compassion never fail to amaze me, and to my grandfather, for being my friend and biggest supporter, always. And to my grandmother, who passed away the day after I sold this book on proposal, but who lives on in everything I do and am, thank you for believing in me and for teaching me the art of kindness.

Finally, to John, for putting up with me during the process of writing this book; for making me laugh even when I was at my crankiest and most irritable; and for being the all-around incredible person you are, I give you my thanks, my love.

CONTENTS

INTRODUCTION

WHEN I WAS THIRTEEN, my parents divorced.

For a long time, that was all that needed to be said. I accepted the prevailing wisdom that parents divorce, children adjust, end of story. I even took pride in my easy ability to handle crises, which I viewed as a clear by-product of my parents' divorce. I was prepared for things to fall apart and could calmly respond to any difficult situation on my own: food poisoning in a foreign country, a missed plane I needed to catch, a business meeting gone wrong. But as I got older, the prospect of love and loss—the hurt of a failed relationship or possible rejection from a partner—sent me into a tailspin. It wasn't until I was struggling through my own personal attachments as an adult that the fallout from my parents' breakup began to become apparent.

Like most children of divorce, I spent much of my adolescence caught up in dealing with the day-to-day negotiating myself between two parents who were not especially fond of each other. I blindly steered my way through what has now become familiar territory, that landscape of single parenthood and divided loyalties so carefully mapped out in the public consciousness. What I didn't realize until I left home was that, in the process, I had built my own emotional topography, one that could not be left behind, no matter how far I tried to run away from the past.

For my generation, divorce has taken on the social proportions of a Great Depression, a World War II, or a Vietnam in influencing our lives. Divorce struck in the privacy of our own homes, shaking our beliefs about family to the core. We saw affection wither into nasty words, kisses replaced by custody battles. We knew too much about how relationships end before our own relationships had even started. As adults, we must now live with the legacy of our parents' divorce. For many of us, the past walks alongside the present, and as we get older and enter into our own relationships, we are reliving issues from our parents' divorces, issues we never fully examined, either because we were too young or because we had no one to turn to for support.

Never before has divorce been such a common experience, traveling across families with a breathtaking swiftness during the short span of our childhoods. We were born as the divorce rate started its climb to dizzying heights during the mid-sixties, doubling within a decade. By 1979, the overwhelming incidence of divorce had morphed into popular entertainment, with *Kramer vs. Kramer*—Hollywood's version of parental breakup—a critical and commercial phenomenon. Not long after, social scientists estimated that only 50 percent of children could expect to grow up with two parents living in the same house. By the eighties, as our parents continued to divorce, the top two rated television shows—*The Bill Cosby Show* and *Family Ties*—portrayed cozy nuclear families. As a child, I rushed home from school to watch *The Brady Bunch* reruns; by my early twenties, I was sitting in a darkened theater watching *The Brady Bunch Movie*, laughing along with the rest of the audience as what I had once viewed as the perfect family—albeit a blended one—became the stuff of satire. Even though the divorce rate has slowed its phenomenal climb in recent years, the outlook on marital success, let alone marital bliss, remains gloomy. In 1990, the Census Bureau recorded roughly 2.4 million marriages and 1.2

million divorces, leading to the much-repeated prediction that one out of two unions will eventually dissolve. The ratio persists, hanging over every trip to the altar. By 1998, one out of every ten adults was divorced, not including those who had remarried, and almost one out of three children under the age of eighteen was living with only one parent. The "traditional," two-parent family had emerged as the new endangered species of choice, the latest spotted owl.

Growing up, we all learned the tough lessons that in families, the binds of love can be weak, and in romance, fairy tales rarely come true. The culture of divorce has permeated our generation to such an extent that even those with married parents have been affected. Marriage is no longer perceived as something that lasts forever. In this intensifying climate of uncertainty, more couples, whether products of divorce or not, live together before getting married and wait longer before tying the knot, if they choose to marry at all. In fact, it is now considered foolish to rush into marriage without first knowing a partner intimately, without having ferreted out every conceivable point of incompatibility before going to the altar.

We are America's first divorce generation.

Such a label carries consequences. As a group, children of divorce have been studied at length, with varying degrees of alarm and acceptance. We have been seductively reduced to a series of poignant images and a few easy catchwords. We have been told that, after our parents divorce, we bounce back, or bounce sideways, or bounce straight into trouble. The experts—many of whom, as far as I can tell, never grew up in a broken home—juggle statistics and conduct in-depth trials in a search to pin down this raging bull, divorce. Some conclude that we are better off, saved from growing up with two parents strained by tension and misery. Others conclude, with a note of doom, that we suffer such deep emotional scars from our parents' divorce that we continue to be adversely affected years, sometimes decades, later, as if having divorced parents was supposed to be an awkward stage one grows out of, like puberty.

I'm not saying the experts are wrong, only that they provide one perspective, that of observer peering from the outside in. Their function is to prod, poke, and analyze, to scrunch and whittle their observations to fit into an interpretation, a definitive answer. They are often compelled to label divorce in black-and-white terms. For those of us who are living with the aftermath of divorce, however, their conclusions offer little guidance to understanding the blueprints our parents gave us as we build our own lives.

Divorce may be everywhere we turn, yet for many adult children of divorce there remains a silence on the issues we want most to hear about. From inside our world of experience, the view is not the same. Experts try to measure the effects of divorce through school performance, criminal records, psychological tests, but we know the final price of our parents' divorce is paid when we make our own attempts at love and security. It is not enough to say, as many experts do, that children of divorce are themselves more likely to divorce. The anxiety that crackles through so many of our relationships cannot be dismissed as a simple matter of cause and effect. Of course divorce continues to shape our behavior, for divorce is all we know. It's a part of who we are. That much is obvious. The hard part is to figure out how to move forward while living with the past. Through frank discussions with adult children of divorce, this book will trace some of the specific ways in which our emotional makeup today is informed by our parents' divorce of yesterday. This book is for us.

When I first started to scour bookstores and libraries for literature geared toward adult children of divorce, I essentially came up empty-handed. Eager to find out if others were dealing with similar issues, I discovered instead only that talking about divorce is messy business. I quickly determined that while much has been written on children of divorce, most books fall into one of three categories: dense psychological studies, politically imbued tracts, or popular books that either exaggerate or diminish the aftershocks.

By now, I have read books on divorce written by sociologists, psychologists, historians, feminists, conservatives, and divorced parents; yet few give a real glimpse into the ongoing influence of divorce, how the experiences of childhood translate into those of adulthood, how the old fears and defenses rise once we're faced with forming our own families. Amidst all the righteous fury and mud-slinging, discussions about divorce have become, for lack of a better term, divorced from real life, stuck in this endless round of "divorce is good," "divorce is bad." We rarely emerge from the data as real people trying to find our way through our own lives. We are not given room for either the ambivalence so many of us feel about our parents' divorce or the passage of time to show how our emotions from childhood replay in different ways once we become adults.

That divorce has become such a loaded issue is not surprising. Concepts of marriage and family—as reflections of society as a whole—have always crossed swords to some extent, but as the number of children living in divorced homes multiplied, the debate over family exploded, stoked by both hot tempers and a growing body of cold empirical data. Amidst the growing political backlash of "family values," divorce has been blamed for everything from promiscuity to teenage pregnancy, from substance abuse to stunted growth among today's youth. Yet, despite our sheer numbers, children of divorce remain the centerpiece of the discussion, not active participants. It is not about us, not really. In the public debate, we serve primarily as the psychological antidote for a new generation of families contemplating divorce, proof as to why parents should *not* divorce. The debate hardly ever addresses the more relevant issue of our struggle to deal with the repercussions of our parents' divorce in our adult lives; rather, our fears and concerns, if they're mentioned at all, form an ending, not a starting point, for investigation.

After wading through books and numerous studies on divorce, this is what I realized, the one true thing: Those of us who have lived through divorce can't possibly squeeze the light and shadow of our lives into a model, or a graph, or a chart. We long for stories, not theory. We crave a forum to share our experiences, not open them up for judgment. Stories—yours and mine—are what guide us, forming what author Jill Ker Conway calls our "inner life plots," and it is only through stories that many of us gain true insight into our own lives. We may be struggling in our intimate relationships, but when we hear of others' struggles we realize that we are not alone.

As I began to speak with others about the emotional impact of their parents' divorce on their romantic lives today, similar themes came forth again and again, described in similar language: *I have built up walls, rarely letting anyone in. I have trouble living in the moment, and often find myself wondering how things will end, even as they start. I feel like the rug could be pulled out from underneath me at any time. I constantly set up tests, forcing people to prove their love to me. I have a hard time trusting. I am so scared of being abandoned.* The memories still shimmer so close to the surface, and many of those I interviewed told their stories in raw language, their voices betraying the toll of remembering. I found that our parents and our partners tap into a shared vein of emotion. As one woman said about her first serious boyfriend breaking up with her in college, "It was more than a failed relationship. It was like reliving my dad leaving. That's when all the hurt that I felt as a child started to come out."

For many of us, bad memories of parental conflict shadow our intimate relationships, often reawakening our childhood fears and defenses as we grapple with the adult issues of trust and commitment. The popular concepts of love and family have been shattered over the past decades, and a generation influenced by divorce is now struggling to piece together its own definitions from an intimate knowledge of their darker opposites. It's not an easy task, to perform this awkward crabwalk of finding what we want, based on what we don't want. We are constantly plagued by questions. Even after living with her boyfriend for five years, one woman summed it up like this: "I'm always asking him, 'Are we okay? Is this right?

Is this how it is supposed to work? Are we too close? Are we not close enough?' I don't know." She shrugged her shoulders, palms up. "I have no frame of reference to work from."

In the end, through both written surveys and personal interviews, I heard the experiences of 120 adult children of divorce, ranging in age from their early twenties to their early forties. All of the respondents' names have been changed for the purposes of this book. Although the group I interviewed is a self-selected one, found through newspaper ads, postings on the Internet, and word of mouth, they form a diverse sampling, coming from a variety of ethnic, geographic, and social backgrounds and professions. Some grew up in major cities and others in small towns. Some of their parents divorced before the children were born, and others divorced just as their kids were leaving for college. Some are already married and have children of their own. My only criterion was that their parents divorced while the children were still technically dependents, a focus I chose not because I believe we suffer any more or less than those who are older when their parents split up, but because of the special circumstances that arise when we as children see our parents divorce.

Many of those I interviewed raised the valid question of how to separate the divorce as an isolated event from what followed— everything from our parents' behavior to changes in our economic situation. The answer is, we can't. Divorce is not a cleanly defined experience bracketed by the filing and signing of papers. From our perspective, divorce is mainly about the division of a home, and as such, it unleashes complicated family dynamics and personalities, difficult situations, tough decisions, and finally, conflicting emotions. All the various elements that come into play before, during, and after the divorce rise and fall in a continuous and unique sound track of experience.

Every story of divorce is complex, each as unique as a fingerprint. The why is not hard to articulate—irreconcilable differences, infidelity, emotional or physical abuse—but the how is ours alone.

We each attach different meanings to our parents' divorce; as adults, we feel its lasting emotional impact according to how the divorce changed our childhood. In some cases, divorce liberated us from an unhappy home life. As thirty-two-year-old Timothy, whose parents divorced when he was eight, remembers, "My father was at that point an alcoholic, although a functional one, and he had a long and not very well-hidden history of dating women on the side. Had my parents not divorced, I would have turned out to be a complete, instead of just a partial, basket case," he jokes. "No, seriously, it would have been a terrible thing for all parties involved if they had stayed together. So I'm glad this possible world did not become actual. Nasty divorces can be harmful to the children involved, but then so can unhappy marriages."

Of course, not all divorces rob children of consistent support, and indeed many parents are able to build an equally, if not *more,* stable framework after they split apart. Among all the contradictory findings on the effects of divorce on children, almost all researchers agree that certain conditions must exist to protect a child's well-being: the presence of a caring custodial parent and a cordial relationship between both parents. Children who grow up in such an environment can usually emerge into adulthood with their self-esteem intact. But for those who continue to suffer from distress associated with the divorce—for instance, a parent who became severely depressed, ferocious fights over child support, or an abusive stepparent—the damage goes much deeper.

These are rather obvious, if vague, prescriptions for emotional health; in reality, the impact of our experiences is much more manifold, and therefore much harder to measure, than what is provided by this simple checklist. "When I think of home, I think of my mom being there, cooking and caring for me. I have that," says one twenty-eight-year-old woman. "My relationship with my mother would never have been the same if my parents hadn't divorced and that has made me who I am today. We have one of the best mother-daughter relationships I've seen—total honesty, support, and friendship—yet she's also a true mother to me. But also, when I go to my friends' houses, and see complete families with dads they respect, I see that what I have is really only half a home."

Despite the particulars of our parents' breakup, whether we were two years old or eighteen when it happened, regardless of who had custody or the nature of the subsequent changes, one fact remains constant: Divorce plants a splinter in our minds, and in response, we assemble our identities around it. When we forge ahead in our own intimate relationships, the splinter twists, and we are often forced to reassess our old scripts of behavior and challenge the lessons learned from our parents' breakup.

I have written this book to examine divorce not as a problem or a panacea but as a theme that permeates our lives, molding our outlook and behavior in intimate relationships. As a result, I feel compelled to give a few caveats: Since I only spoke with children of divorce, I do not present the parents' perspective; I suspect that if they had also been interviewed, the parents would have come up with different accounts, perhaps radically different ones. In addition, the events recounted here are seen through the eyes of retrospect and articulated in the voice of memory, which are prone to interpretation and lapses.

Finally, I don't have any answers. I am not a therapist or a social scientist. I do not pretend to offer any solutions, prescriptions, or policy recommendations. Nor do I try to break down the people with whom I spoke into percentages who do this and percentages who do that. These tasks belong in the realm of social science, where experts who have spent years studying the subject are much more qualified to fill this role than I am; indeed, many such books already line the shelves for those who are looking for such an analysis of divorce. Most of all, I am not here to state whether children of divorce are any better or worse off than they would have been otherwise, an endeavor I consider an entirely fruitless exercise in "what if"; obviously, not all divorces are the same, and not all situations I discuss apply to all divorces. And, although I don't explore the experiences of children whose parents remained unhappily married, I believe they may suffer similar effects as children of divorce.

Instead, first and foremost, this is a book of lives. While divorce plays a major part, acting as the common defining quality among those I interviewed, these people speak also of the other threads that make up a life, creating who they are. Stories allow for the roundness of character and personalities, the unexpected event, the influence of cultural norms, and a wide range of emotions. Stories offer more insight into the past and guidance in the present than our rank on a psychological scale. When we hear divorce described in the language of experience, in terms of how others found their way through similar situations and obstacles in their lives and relationships, we come a little bit closer to understanding ourselves. Only then can an honest dialogue begin, one that finally includes our voices too.

In his short story collection *Laughable Loves*, Milan Kundera writes "Man passes through the present with his eyes blindfolded. He is permitted merely to sense and guess at what he is actually experiencing. Only later when the cloth is untied can he glance at the past and find out what he has experienced and what meaning it has had."

I have now spent over half my life as a "child of divorce," and although time passes, the emotions from my youth have flared up with an irrational regularity. Sometimes the trigger is something as silly as a sentimental commercial, and a longing bursts deep inside, a hunger that has no name. Every once in a while, just when I feel that I have safely tucked away my parents' divorce as part of the past, that I have separated myself from their story, the old fears surface in different disguises: the fear of making the same wrong decisions my parents made; the fear of relying on someone, only to get hurt. As a child, I was battling with my parents and their hostility toward each other. As an adult, I am mostly battling with myself. I am still realizing what my parents' divorce means to my own life, the filter it placed across my vision. Only recently have I been able to connect the dots in my mind, to clearly see how the fact that I stumble over the words "I love you" travels a straight path back to a childhood where I witnessed love betrayed; how the sudden dips of melancholy are recesses carved long ago. I am finally untying the blindfold; though the process is slow, the knots get looser the more I work on them.

To understand where we're going though, we first need to look at where we've been. Remembering is difficult, and while we can't escape the hurt that comes with dredging up the past, I also know there is a certain reassurance that comes from talking with others, from sharing and comparing experiences. And when we do, a sudden space springs up between us and our own behavior, allowing a precious chance to gain perspective. Ultimately, I hope this book will offer a series of such spaces. Perhaps the stories we tell will lead others to see the motivations behind certain actions, hang-ups, and beliefs. When things fell apart during childhood, we put them back together as best we could, without the hand of age or experience. There are often cracks in the remaking, some so thin and faint we can hardly see them. Once we expose our emotional fault lines, though, we can work on sealing those cracks. We can drain some of those memories of their power, lessen the sway they still hold over our lives. For, while we cannot choose our past, we can choose our future.

I

Splitsville

There was a time when I thought I loved
my first wife more than life itself. But now
I hate her guts. I do. How do you explain
that? What happened to that love? What
happened to that love, is what I'd like to
know. I wish someone could tell me.

**—Raymond Carver, *What We Talk
About When We Talk About Love***

1

The Reluctant Heart

Home is where one starts from. As we grow older
The world becomes stranger, the pattern more
   complicated
Of dead and living. Not the intense moment
Isolated, with no before and after
But a lifetime burning in every moment

— T. S. Eliot, *The Four Quartets*

A COUPLE OF YEARS AGO, my mother went to the twenty-five-year reunion of her graduate school class, held on the very same university campus where she and my father first met. She tells me how, as she roamed through the reception, weaving among all those almost-recognizable faces peering nervously at name tags and clutching sweaty cocktails, she bumped into three old friends. The four of them had lost touch over the years, and with so much catching up to do, they got off to an awkward start. The conversation moved slowly, touching upon all the usual bases of idle chitchat, until suddenly they found the hook that broke through the proverbial ice.

"We almost had to laugh," my mom mused wonderingly, "because we were all divorced."

"Mom." I sighed, a little petulantly. "Who *isn't* divorced?"

The brief extent of this exchange illuminates the gap in perception between my mother and me when it comes to divorce: Both my parents grew up during the fifties, when divorce was relatively unusual; they married during the early seventies as the divorce rate started to hit its peak, and divorced during the eighties. For them, divorce was a difficult choice; for me, divorce is a fact of life.

Our parents are the architects of the culture of divorce we live in today. To some extent, every generation wrestles with the legacy inherited from the one before, and with our parents' generation, millions of couples—more than ever before—entered into marriages that disintegrated to the point that divorce seemed like the best way out. I know splitting up was often a painful process for them—sometimes devastating—but while our parents endured their divorces armed with the resources of age and experience, we were confronted with new and complicated emotions before we were fully capable of understanding them. For those of us who bore witness to the wave of divorce that engulfed our parents, their breakups defined our childhood, leaving imprints that may last a lifetime.

I can name the date when my mother and sister moved out, and my family as a whole ceased to exist; the boundaries of the emotional reverberations of my parents' divorce, however, are more difficult to identify. After the age of thirteen, I never again lived under the same roof with my mother and sister. Unlike the overwhelming majority of children whose parents separate, I remained with my father, living in the house we once shared as a family. Yet nothing was the same. The rooms rang with loss, reducing my home to four walls from which to escape, not seek refuge. The holidays and weekends turned into days dissected into hours claimed by each parent. Protected by a carefully constructed armor of indifference, I sailed through these changes, my emotions tightly self-contained. I never once allowed myself to miss having two parents as one unit, residing in one home. Why would I? I knew my parents had been unhappy together, so it was for the best, really, that they were apart.

I never engaged in any of the *Parent Trap* fantasies that my parents would reunite; on the contrary, the mere thought of having them in the same room, tense and silent, sent me into a panic.

After I left home, I spent the next eight years trying to get as far away as possible from the memories of childhood. At seventeen, I packed up a large duffel bag with most of my belongings and moved across the country to attend college, without ever looking back. In the years that followed, I zigzagged from coast to coast, spent time living abroad, and eventually landed in a three-hundred-square-foot apartment in New York City, furnished mainly with leftovers I collected off the street. During those early years of being on my own, I had convinced myself that I had outgrown my parents' divorce, and whatever losses I had sustained had been taken care of by time.

Here's the thing, though: Time flirts with us, flashing what could have been, what should have been, what was. When a parent dies, children are at least given the pretense that they will travel through the five stages of grief in accepting the death: Denial. Anger. Bargaining. Disorganization. Acceptance. But with divorce, there is no rubric detailing how we should act or feel, especially as we get older. Lacking the finality of death, divorce can start to mimic a film negative. We become hooked on what's missing, where blank spaces have replaced substance.

At some point, as I crossed the line from childhood to adulthood, the experience of divorce was no longer limited to my past and present, but began to infect my future as well. It became harder to put a finger on my feelings, to relate the confusion, the wariness, the lingering sadness to my parents' divorce. A year or so out of college, my "tough girl" façade from childhood started to slip. Small slips at first. I would see a mildly sad movie and, surrounded by the safe cloak of darkness in the theater, dissolve into tears. I skipped through relationships, ending them abruptly for the most minor of transgressions. I constantly felt anxious, worried about my future, yet never fully satisfied when things appeared to be going well. Every decision, from my relationships to my career, was harnessed by my own ambivalence. What if I'm hurt? What if I'm making the wrong choices? What if, just *what if,* I am starting down a path that will take me back to those empty rooms of childhood? These questions swirled in my head, leaving me paralyzed. Strange as it may sound, it wasn't until I left home that I started to acutely feel the effects of growing up in a divorced home.

Apparently, my experience is not unusual. In a 1995 study of adult children of divorce, researchers noted what seemed to be a contradictory finding: At the age of twenty-three, some of their subjects appeared to be *more* negatively affected psychologically by their parents' divorce than they were at the age of eleven. On the basis of this finding, the researchers suggested that the "developmental challenges of adolescence and young adulthood may have reinvoked certain vulnerabilities for the divorced group, evinced by deleterious effects of the aftermath of divorce in their early twenties." This increased vulnerability could be due to a variety of reasons, from a "continued or renewed sense of parental loss" to more tangible factors such as a decrease in economic status resulting in fewer educational opportunities.

In other words, going out on our own is scary, especially if we don't feel that we have been launched from a firm base of support. The pressures of adapting to being on our own and realizing our actions now have serious implications can leave us feeling confused and exposed. As adults, we have entered the opaque sphere of our own potential mistakes, with only the past as our guide. And for many of us, the suppressed emotions from our parents' divorce are sprung loose once we face the prospect of our own relationships.

"My father always blamed their divorce on *Cosmopolitan* magazine," says twenty-eight-year-old Denise, whose parents divorced when she was two. "I think it goes a little deeper than that. My mom just recently admitted to me that she was pregnant when she got married. I actually already knew because, interestingly enough, she had filled out one of those surveys in a magazine, and I had picked it up to read and saw what she had written. It made me really sad when I found that out. Empty." She pauses. "My mom always said the best thing she ever did in her life was to have my brother and me, but I still feel like I don't want to get married. I don't want to have kids and have them go through what I went through."

Our fears in love are often dictated by the past, sometimes without our being fully aware of it. Our parents' divorce offers a powerful lens through which to view both parental and romantic love, two types of love that are more intertwined than they may appear at first. The raw power of a child's love is fragile, and the literary canon is filled with perceptive stories about the feverish bond that develops between parent and child and how the nature of that bond affects the ability to love in adulthood. In his epic tale *Remembrance of Things Past*, Marcel Proust depicts the exquisite pleasure of a young boy waiting for his mother's kiss, his small world hinging on his parent's affection and care; as the narrator subsequently grows older and searches for women to love, the memory of his mother's kiss inspires his every pursuit. Proust illustrates a simple truth: Across the distance of years, the moments of hurt and longing from youth continue to instruct us in the present, surging to the forefront during adulthood with renewed and explosive force, particularly if we never confronted our emotions the first time around.

And so, adult children of divorce often speak of a void that cannot be filled, an empty space that continues to expand and contract during our daily lives. As thirty-three-year-old Tammy, whose parents divorced when she was five years old, remembers, "I thought it meant I no longer had a father, which in many ways turned out to be true. I have never known, and probably never will, what it means to have a father. My father never took the time to get to know me, and I don't think my mother has ever fully realized the impact this had on me. She always assumed that I would be fine if I had her, food, clothing, good grades, a job. But there's a big hole in my life. I still struggle to accept love, to trust love and maintain relationships. I am always seeking, and never finding, 'home.' "

So many of us share Tammy's search for home, but haunted by our parents' divorce, we can easily lose our way. Without a cohesive memory of family history that encompasses both the happy and sad times, the balance shifts. A fight that ends in an announcement of divorce is perceived on a much larger scale than an argument followed by reconciliation; the former emerges as a brutal cautionary tale that shapes our actions, the latter a minor blip in the vast network of a relationship. For so many of us, our parents' divorces continue to live on today—not only in our need to juggle our divided families—but in our fear of intimacy and other lingering defenses developed during childhood.

The Fear of Intimacy

This is what I have left of the relationship that brought me into the world: I have photos, incomplete stories, and the bits and pieces of my own memory. When it comes to my parents' marriage and divorce, there are too many things I simply don't know and probably never will. Oh, I have my own perceptions, my own theories of what went wrong. I can throw out key words like "infidelity" and "incompatibility" when discussing the demise of their marriage, and I can envision my parents as they are today and reconstruct how they must have clashed over a decade ago. But I can't pinpoint when their relationship crossed over some invisible trip wire, shutting their love down. I will never truly understand the depth of the frustration, disappointment, and unhappiness they felt when they were together; by the same token, I doubt they will ever really understand my feelings when they divorced. The three of us stand on opposite sides of this divide of age and experience, although I want nothing more than to reach out and bring us all together.

Our family stories serve as our defining armor as we go out into the larger world, and our parents provide our most salient role models as we enter into our own relationships. These stories ground us in an identity, a family, a future role. When parents divorce, however, they leave us with fractured narratives and loose ends that we carry with us into adulthood. After viewing the events of our parents' breakup within the limited scope of youth, many of us find that as adults, we lack the facts to see the parts of the past as a meaningful whole. "It really bothers me that my parents won't say why they divorced. They just don't want to talk about it. They'll say, 'It was so long ago' or 'I don't remember.' They just brush it off," says thirty-year-old Leslie, whose parents divorced when she was five. "It's just confusing and it makes it hard to put the pieces together."

When I rewind the reels of my imagination, back to a beginning before I was born, here's what happens: Things go a little haywire. My parents start moving faster and faster, the years coming off, the lines on their skin disappearing into youth. My mother's hair grows longer, her hemlines shorter, while my father's hair loses its gray. Faster and faster they move, like two separate blurs growing ever brighter until they stand still, frozen. The year is 1968, the place Los Angeles, and on a college campus filled with thousands of students, my parents' lives are about to intersect. They have no choice really; by some weird twist of fate, they have ended up with the exact same class schedule, and although their faces have grown vaguely familiar to each other, they have never exchanged a word. That, of course, is about to change.

California. I see endless horizons of blues and golds, but on this particular afternoon when my parents meet for the first time, I am told the skies performed a rare trick, turning dark, ominous, then ripping open with rain. I see my mother waiting inside one of the academic buildings, her black hair falling smoothly into the shadowy small of her back. She fidgets, shifting her books from one hip to the other as she checks her watch, wondering whether she should try to wait out the rain before heading over to her next class. She sighs, staring out a window, and at that moment, my father comes up behind her. Maybe he hears her sigh and decides to be chivalrous. Maybe he has been waiting for an opportunity to strike up a conversation with this girl from his classes. Maybe he is just in a good mood. Whatever the reason, he smiles at her and offers to get an umbrella out of his car. My mother nods gratefully, watching as he scurries out of sight, a book held uselessly over his head to fend off the raindrops. He returns a few minutes later, umbrella tucked under his arm, oblivious or simply not caring that his clothes are drenched, that water is dripping down his face, his legs, into his shoes. As he hands her the umbrella, their eyes meet, filled with expectation.

This romantic picture I once pasted together from photographs, scraps of information, and a large dose of fantasy sits lodged in my imagination like a foreign object. It makes me squirm to conjure up my parents—the same two people who haven't spoken to each other since an agonizing dinner after my college graduation—as twenty-year-olds in the first flush of infatuation. After spending most of my life viewing them apart, it doesn't feel natural to put them together. They are two puzzle pieces that no longer fit, and perhaps never did.

Like many of us who saw our parents divorce, the question for me now comes down to why. Not why my parents divorced exactly, but why the hell they ever got together in the first place. Looking back, their differences are so obvious: My mother's temper moved like a passing storm, striking quickly and with furious force, and afterward, the cause of her outburst was soon forgotten. When she was in a good mood, she was the fun parent, the player of practical jokes and the teller of wild tales, always ready to laugh. My father, on the other hand, never played games, not even board games, because he thought they were silly. He was unflappable, and unlike my mother, he never lost his temper in an explosion of anger. While his steady manner was often reassuring, his emotions sometimes seemed buried so far beneath the surface that he appeared distant and slightly out of reach. Whereas I could giggle with my mother on the bed as we watched *Dynasty*, my father was the responsible parent, the one who would patiently sit down with me for hours to go over my homework or spend his Sunday afternoons teaching me how to build model airplanes.

So, knowing my parents the way I do, I was curious to flesh out the beginning of their relationship so that I might separate truth from childish fiction; to grasp a better understanding of what happened to their marriage, I needed to know about its earlier years. This was a bold move on my part. For the past thirteen years my parents and I had carefully danced around the issue of their divorce, rarely acknowledging there even *was* a life before their breakup. It seems sort of ridiculous, our refusal to speak of an event that had such an influence in shaping our lives, and I would think so too if I hadn't been a willing participant in the silence.

That's why I nervously picked up the phone one night and in a rush asked my mother to tell me how she met my father. I can still remember the experience clearly: My mother hedges, but after some prodding gives me the facts. No frills.

Same class schedule. Rain. Umbrella.

"But what was it like?" I ask, trying to dig deeper.

Her tone gets businesslike, with a touch of wariness; like a reluctant interviewee, she chooses her words carefully, neatly skirting emotion.

"We went out a lot with friends," she says, not really answering my question. "We studied together." With a note of finality, she adds, "He was definitely the pursuer. He was very aggressive." She changes the subject, and I let it go, feeling as if I have violated some unspoken pact.

When I call my father and ask for his version of events, I can tell from the drawn-out pause that follows how unwilling he is to relive this particular memory.

"It was more than thirty years ago," he says finally. I wait for him to continue. "I think she mumbled something to me after class about a study group."

He doesn't remember anything about an umbrella.

"All I know is she made the first move," he grumbles.

End of discussion.

I hang up the phone, feeling something that falls between anger and resignation. Just another reminder that my parents' antagonism runs so deep that even this, the supposed blissful beginning of their relationship, is revised and contested, turning into an endless round of finger-pointing and blame. Instead of admitting that at one time their feelings had been different, each of them prefers to paint their courtship as an insidious form of trickery on the other's part.

Some things I do know. I know my parents continued to date for three years after college, even though they had moved to different cities three hours apart. Despite their convenient amnesia, I know they were in love, or at least thought they were. My father used to keep a bundle of old letters from my mother hidden away in a briefcase, along with his birth certificate and passport. I found them while nosing around one afternoon when I was still in elementary school. Kneeling on the floor of my father's study, I devoured these letters, embarrassed by all the *I miss you*s and *I can't wait to see you again*s, but also reassured: Parents who love each other must love me.

I know that in 1971, my parents got married in a quiet ceremony. I used to flip through a blue album that stood on the bookshelf in our living room and study the photos. They show my mother looking radiant as she stands on the steps of City Hall, her hair pulled up in an Audrey Hepburn–like bun, dressed in a long, slim white shift dotted with yellow daisies. My father towers beside her, suited in white shirt and white pants, black horn-rimmed glasses propped on his nose. His hand rests on my mother's elbow. Posing for the picture, white smiles flashing, the two of them appear to be consumed by the glow of youth and possibility. I know that within two years I had been born and my parents had both found jobs on the East Coast. My father sold his convertible, trading it in for a more family-oriented Peugeot, and he drove it across the country while my mother and I flew ahead of him.

Those old letters have long since been thrown away, along with my parents' wedding rings. The album that once contained the photos from their wedding and honeymoon has been dismantled, and the pictures now lay bundled in an old shoebox in my apartment because no one else wanted them; sometimes, when I look through them, they seem like artifacts from someone else's history.

I have, in some ways, become a stranger in my own life.

Divorce strikes at the heart of our identity. No matter how hard we try, we can't escape the fact that we are, according to the rules of biology, the product of both parents. But when the two people who created us then break the vows of love that once held them together, we can't help but feel displaced. The rationale behind our discomfort is not so hard to grasp: If our parents no longer love each other, and on some level we belong to both of them, where does that leave us? We lose our sense of continuity, the comfort of family as anchor, and in its place we are usually left with the disturbing fact that we can't even picture our parents as a couple, let alone believe they were ever in love. Says one twenty-eight-year-old woman, whose parents divorced when she was five, "I really don't see how my parents found the fifteen minutes of agreement it must have taken to conceive me."

For twenty-seven-year-old Tom, whose parents divorced when he was two, having divorced parents has always been a characteristic of his life, like having blue eyes or brown hair. Only as he's grown older and started to learn more details about his parents' marriage has he started to fully feel the effects of growing up with his life split in two:

"Divorce" was never in my language. I remember my dad would cry every time he put us on a plane. And when I was little, I never really understood it. I always thought, "What's the big deal? We'll be back again next summer." See, that's what I mean when I say it was never in my language. My parents were just divorced—no big deal. And really I think I felt that way because the reaction from people when I told them pretty much confirmed this notion. I grew up at a time when a lot of people were going through divorce—or were already divorced. "Oh, your parents are divorced? Okay, next?" I've never known a world where two people were there for me at the same time. One life was always very separate from the other, and no one ever questioned the fact that these two lives were separate.

Then, a few years ago, I became acquainted with my aunt. We used to meet for dinner and get drunk and talk about the past. I never knew her growing up at all, then suddenly she is telling me all these things that I had never thought to question. She told me that my dad fell in love with one of his students and that's why my parents got a divorce. I had never thought of my stepmother in that way until then. I guess it sort of made me mad to hear that. But what are you going to do? People make decisions and you have to live with it.

My parents have never liked each other. They couldn't even eat in the same room at my graduation. How could these people ever have been in love? A few years ago, I got into a big fight with my mom. I told her to imagine how it feels to be the product of two people who hate each other. To her credit, she tried to get a relationship going with my dad. She wrote him a letter and I think they talked once or twice on the phone—but so much time has gone by now. They haven't talked since, as far as I know. Where do you go?

For many of us, like Tom, our parents' divorces take on a new dimension once we reach adulthood. We are faced with what psychoanalyst Erik Erikson describes as an "identity crisis"—the more or less conscious struggle, through reflection and observation, to put together a sense of self and determine our role in society. Figuring out why our parents married and why they broke apart becomes more urgent as we determine who we are and where we're going. Without a firm grasp of our parents' romantic past, we are left not only with a fuzzy conception of self, but without a vision of intimacy for the future. As Erikson points out, these two ideas of identity and intimacy are linked. He writes "It is only when identity formation is well on its way that true intimacy—which is really a counterpointing as well as a fusing of identities—is possible." Until we gain a firm sense of our own identity, we do not have a solid foundation for love.

It's not merely coincidence that my desire to learn more about my parents' marriage grew as I started to contemplate my own relationships, and their reticence to speak about their relationship only reminded me how many vital pieces were missing from my knowledge. While my parents are reluctant to give me even the most basic details of their courtship and marriage, however, I know a great deal about how my grandparents fell in love. Every time I used to visit them as a child, I would ceremoniously dig through a dusty steamer trunk that sat hidden on the top shelf of their bedroom. Inside, among all the old letters and mementos, there was a gray blouse and skirt—utterly plain, almost bordering on drab—that I used to try on as if they were the most dazzling evening gown.

This outfit had served as my grandmother's wedding dress. When I was young, I constantly begged my grandparents to repeat the history that whispered in its musty fabric: How they had met while they were both enlisted in the Royal Air Force during World War II. How, after a whirlwind romance of three weeks, my grandmother traded in too many of her treasured ration coupons to buy something new to wear, such a luxury during the scarcity of war— the gray blouse and skirt—and they were married. How, almost a year later, my grandmother gave birth to my aunt in a London hospital as bombs rained down from the sky. As the three of us sat around their dining room table, my grandparents recounted these anecdotes in easy tandem, spinning a single story sanded by so many years together. I thought their union was the pinnacle of romantic drama, a way of embracing life in the face of death. But more than that, their story gave me a sense of my own place within the family, a small link in an unbroken chain that extended from the past into the present and beyond.

Nevertheless, my grandparents' relationship wasn't one that provided instruction in the everyday workings of a marriage; while their courtship is part of my history, it wasn't the union that directly produced me. With my parents' divorce, a link in my family chain was broken, creating a crucial distance between my grandparents' story and mine. As one thirty-year-old man says, "Between my parents they have had five marriages, and they have all sucked. The only role models I have are my grandparents, who have been married for fifty-five years and are joined at the hip, in a healthy way. They each perform the role they should be performing. They have formed a trust and a respect for each other that's wonderful, and I think, 'Why can't I learn from them?' I think I can't because I feel like they are from a different era and that kind of relationship doesn't exist anymore."

Our parents' marriages provide us with the primary model of intimacy that we internalize and refer to for comparison when we get older. When parents divorce—and particularly if they don't remarry—we are left to invent intimacy on our own terms, without any ongoing examples to guide us. In theory, this can be liberating, allowing us to conduct relationships without the binds of preordained guidelines. But in reality, it's often an intimidating prospect. "It's kind of like, if you're taught how to waltz, and so is your partner, it's very easy, and it's a beautiful dance. But if neither one of you know how to waltz, it doesn't matter if the music is playing—you're not going to do it gracefully," says one thirty-three-year-old man. "If you're lucky, you find someone who sees things the way you do, and you can kind of fake it and spin around, but chances are you are going to step on the other person's foot."

Twenty-five-year-old Frank still keeps a photograph of his parents standing side by side in front of a clapboard house, his mother holding him in her arms and the family dog lying at their feet. Only a few weeks after the picture was taken, when he was a little over a year old, his mother took her belongings and moved out, taking Frank and the dog with her. "They had a fight, but I don't know what it was about," he says. "I saw my father every other weekend, and I never really thought about it. My mom always reminds me of this story: I was watching *The Brady Bunch* when I was around five years old, and I came into her room and asked, 'Moms and Dads can actually live together?' " He laughs. "I guess I didn't feel a loss, but I mean, I had nothing to compare it to. And that's a problem that comes up today: When a couple gets into a fight, I can't say to myself, 'Oh, Mom and Dad used to fight and did this.' I never had the day-to-day experience of seeing my parents working together as a team. How did they resolve problems? When did they hold hands? When did they go out for coffee? All the daily stuff that people can take for granted on how to lead a relationship is missing for me," he says. "So I've been asking more questions lately about what preceded the divorce—how they met and, you know, silly stuff like that. Now that I'm doing my own dating, I want to know more about it."

Unlike Frank, even those of us who have five, ten, or fifteen years of observation filed away in our memory still face the same guesswork, the same holes in our education. I can still remember a time when I was young enough to be slightly in awe of my parents. Together, they formed a walking picture of not only adulthood but couplehood: Chatting at the dinner parties they used to throw at our house, outlined in the crisp lines of suit and dress. Coming backstage, arms linked, after my solo during the sixth-grade choral recital in a swish of winter coats. Wedged between these glossy images, I also remember my mother sitting on the stairs, crying with her head buried in her arms after an argument with my father that I didn't witness. I remember the two of them arguing loudly in the middle of a department store, although I can't remember why. Because these images haven't been updated in the past decade, they sway from idyllic to catastrophic, and I'm not sure anymore whether they are real or simply misperceptions. Who is there to tell me otherwise? While I know both my parents as individuals, I have little conception of them as husband and wife, and what few clear memories I have serve mainly as evidence of a relationship gone awry.

While my friends whose parents are still together can now view their parents' marriages through adult eyes, picking some characteristics they may want to repeat in their own relationships and rejecting others, I am working with rather limited material. After all, when parents separate, the story of their marriage ends, and the story of their divorce begins. My vision of my parents' marriage is frozen through the eyes of a thirteen-year-old and will never really evolve beyond that. Today I find myself comparing my current relationships according to my spotty memories of their marriage, and I realize that I don't know the boundaries of a good relationship: Is a disagreement a sign that the relationship will fail? Is a moment of genuine affection an indication that it will succeed? The markers for how a relationship progresses are not obvious to me.

If we transform past experience into maps for the future, many of us find that this road to marriage is overshadowed by the dead end of divorce. Says twenty-eight-year-old Dawn, whose parents separated when she was seven, "Growing up, I used to play with a cousin whose parents were also divorced. She and I would fantasize about our lives as adults, and we would always say, 'Oh, I'm going to have kids, but I don't need a husband. I don't plan to get married.' My aunt overheard us once, and she said, 'You don't want to do that.' But for me, it was so natural that the default family unit was the one-parent household. I really thought, 'Oh, I can do this on my own; I can be a single parent,' because that's what I knew. It made me think having a two-parent household was not the preferred unit."

As an adult, Dawn's recollections of her parents' divorce have taken on added significance, her memory raising warning flags in her own search for intimacy. "I know that my parents used to have these knock-down-and-drag-out fights, but it wasn't until I was twenty-three or twenty-four that those memories really came back—things my father said to my mother, how he insinuated she was having an affair, which was not true, but a way to legitimate his own bad behavior," she says. "I started to remember some of the ugly, awful things he said, which I knew were bad then, but I couldn't process them. When it really hit me, the complete disregard and just abuse my father gave to my mother, it upset me so much. I have not been able to trust a lot of men in my life because I keep replaying those arguments over and over again where my father is the offender." She pauses. "Now that both my parents are remarried, and I've gotten past the possibility of being an unwed teenage mother, both of them are like, 'So, when are you going to get married?' My mom keeps telling me, 'I want you to get married and be happy.' She doesn't even associate marriage with divorce anymore, but I do. I just keep saying, 'There's no one on the horizon.' I don't know if I could ever share anything with anyone. Whether I was meant to be married or not—I just wish I knew. It's the unknown that drives me crazy."

Thirty-seven-year-old Joan, whose parents divorced when she was twelve, says an absence of positive role models for intimate relationships has been the greatest consequence of her parents' divorce. She admits to rushing into marriage when she was twenty-six, lured by the promise of stability she believed it would offer her; she divorced two years later. "I think I was trying to recreate what I lost when my parents divorced, but I went about it entirely the wrong way. I met my husband, got engaged, and we were married, all within fourteen months," she says. "But I knew right away that it was a mistake. We bought a house, and I was depressed and miserable, losing tons of weight. I was in no position to be married, and so I put a halt to it pretty quickly. Marriage is nothing like it's portrayed on television. I think I was in love with the idea of getting married, without having a clue of the work. Relationships in general are murder, and I've just kind of had to struggle and formulate my own ideas—and that's the worst, not having any models for a decent, loving relationship. Even at this age, I haven't found one yet."

Although the years of observing her parents apart have revealed their incompatibilities, when her mother first sat Joan down on the couch one afternoon and told her she and Joan's father were separating, it was an utter shock. For many years, the reasons for her parents' divorce remained a mystery. "It took my father more than two decades to really talk about the divorce," she says. "He was not from the touchy-feely generation, and when my parents got divorced, they were the first ones in the neighborhood. It was a big, big deal back then. The local rinky-dink paper used to list who was getting divorced. They would have obituaries, weddings, and then all the names of who was getting divorced. And people saw that— in the paper! It was really ridiculous. And nobody talked about therapy. Nobody talked about counseling. We didn't get any of those things." She adds, "Years later, my mom is still saying, 'I don't know why he left.' They didn't really get over it, and they're not really honest about it either. My father actually started dating my stepmother during the separation, and he literally kept her a secret for five years before introducing her to us."

As Joan points out, we only know as much about what happened between our parents as they are willing to divulge, and once they split apart, their own recollections are usually wrapped up in hurt and resentment. Without an open dialogue with our parents about their divorce, our lives are brutally severed into before and after with little connection between them. Explains twenty-six-year-old Todd, whose parents divorced when he was eighteen, "I almost don't remember family life before the divorce. I know it was very strained. My father was often short-tempered, and sometimes he'd stick in snide comments about my mother. Of course, this was not all the time, but it's what stays in my mind." His family handled the breakup in different ways. "My mother's family was very support-ive in just talking about it openly. But my father's family was split. My grandparents and some aunts would talk about it, but when the family was gathered in large groups for holidays, no one ever men-tioned anything about my mother. No one expressed concern for her. Conversations about my mother were nonexistent, and I think that was one of the most painful parts of the divorce for me."

Once we have lost the thread of common history that generally binds our families together, the past comes under scrutiny and is available for revision. In a shifting game of rancor and blame, our parents can offer up two different versions of their marriage and di-vorce, fueled by their unresolved feelings toward their breakup. "When my dad first told me about the divorce, he said my mom wasn't in love with him anymore, and he couldn't provide her with the money she wanted in life. My mom said that she couldn't take it anymore—the struggling," explains twenty-three-year-old Lance, whose parents divorced when he was fourteen. "But over time, they have both changed their stories. Now and then my mom says stuff like, 'Well, what do you want me to do? My husband walked out and left me with three kids.' So who knows for sure?"

When our parents remain tangled in antagonism, unwilling or unable to discuss their divorce free of anger and resentment, it makes it more difficult to release our own emotions involving their breakup. Divorce effectively paralyzes our family relations. Thirty-six-year-old Emily, whose parents divorced when she was eleven, explains how her decision to get married during her mid-twenties sparked an unexpected response from her mother that circled back to her parents' divorce:

> When I decided to get married, my mother was the first per-son I called to tell. My fiancé and I didn't have any plans to have a big family affair—we were just going to City Hall—and honestly, it never occurred to me that my mother would

want to be there. And so, it turned into this four-hour marathon, very upsetting, with tears all around, and she accused me of holding the divorce against her because I didn't consult her about my plans to make sure she could come; I was punishing her. It was really awful stuff for her to be saying to me because it really had nothing to do with her. It had to do with my wedding. I remember sitting on the bed, shocked. I just didn't think she would want to make this major trip out to go to City Hall for a quiet ceremony, and that assumption was drawn into this whole other network of negativity, of punishment and grudges. She came in the end, and we all went to a nice restaurant afterward, but it really made me think.

It's like the divorce was some defining negative watershed in my parents' lives and everything that's happened afterward somehow reflects back on the divorce. My dad will avoid the issue at all costs, or play the role of complete outraged, innocent victim. My mother still seems to feel very guilty about it. I don't think she's gotten past the point of being defensive to say, "It happened this way, and I'm sorry you guys had to suffer." I think it would be good for her to say that, it would clear the air, and it might make it easier for me to accept her on some levels. It might bring us closer together to get past those points, but I don't know how to do it. It seems to be their unresolved issues, and I can't say or do anything to progress the discussion to another level. Sometimes I feel like if I could have a conversation with my parents, like the one we're having now, it might change things.

Like Emily, an overwhelming number of those I interviewed said they have never spoken of their parents' divorce, either to friends or within the family. Even in a culture where divorce is such a common experience, so many of our families didn't have the language to talk about divorce in a constructive way—either when it happened or years later. Divorce is a traumatic event, earning a ranking of four out of six on the American Psychiatric Association's stress scale, yet how many of us, taking cues from those around us growing up, remain caught up in a code of silence? And at what cost? For our silence gains a volume that mere words never could.

The Fear of Feeling

When I was fourteen, my father deposited me in a counselor's office, a tiny room with plants creeping across the windowsill and two rose-colored upholstered chairs squarely facing each other in the middle of the floor. I sat down in one of those itchy chairs, across from a middle-aged woman with short, graying hair. She nodded at me and shuffled some papers. After we exchanged a few pleasantries, she got down to business.

"How do you feel about your parents' divorce?" she asked, her legs crossed.

"Fine," I answered. "I mean, I was upset in the beginning, but now I've accepted it." I didn't know where to put my hands, so I clasped them in my lap. I smiled sagely. "People get divorced. It happens. You move on. I don't think it's my fault or anything." Just in case she wasn't convinced, I added, "I'm fine, really." She tried again, engaging in several permutations of this first exchange. "Are you sad? Does it bother you? Are you angry?" She vainly searched for an entry, and at every poke, I parried with my stock phrase— "I'm fine." Sixty minutes ticked by, and when my father finally knocked on the door, I immediately jumped up to leave. I felt very pleased with myself. I had acted mature, reasonable, and in control. I never went back.

By then, my parents had been divorced for a year, and in typical adolescent fashion, I was convinced that I could take care of myself, thank you very much. Mine has never been an openly expressive family, and perhaps things would have been different if we were. As it turns out, my parents were not equipped to deal with the emotional fallout of their divorce, to tackle it head-on without their own feelings getting in the way, and by association, neither was I. There were no provocative questions, no reassurances that everything would be okay. I stepped into this vacuum of feeling and focused on the details, like where I would spend my vacations and holidays. My parents rarely fought; in fact, they hardly acknowledged each other's existence, except with the occasional nasty comment or slight issued for my ears only. And life moved on, as it does, except that somewhere, I was left behind. After a childhood of shoving my emotions aside as a way to protect myself from hurt, I find myself still resorting to the same defenses at the slightest threat. For me, the preferred option is always flight—not fight. I don't mean fighting in the aggressive sense, but in the sense of standing up for the validity of my feelings or the value of a relationship. To not care is to feel safe. So for years, I've been "fine," precisely because I never learned how to deal with my emotions in any other way.

Pretending that everything is fine is an alluring option to a child presented with the chaos of divorce. Some of us actively sought out ways to avoid our emotions, either by spending more time with friends or involving ourselves in extracurricular activities or school; others isolated ourselves in a protective cocoon. As children, we are remarkably adept at putting up fronts and façades. Teenagers in particular are eager to hide their feelings and present the illusion of normalcy in order to fit in with their peers. As one woman remembers, "My mom sent me to counseling as a part of the custody battle, but other than that, I never talked about my parents' divorce. I was living it. I just wanted to be a kid and when I wasn't in the middle of their fighting, I blocked it out and tried to be like everyone else."

So many of us found ourselves caught up in a masquerade of emotion. I fiercely guarded from the outside world what was unfolding in my home after my mother moved out. For months, I told my friends that she was away on a business trip, and when I could no longer pretend that was the case, I admitted my parents had divorced, then quickly changed the subject. If they asked about it, I would shrug my shoulders and say it was no big deal. Part of it was that teenage instinct to blend in, but another part was fear. I wasn't sure what would happen if I let my bravado slip. "There is kind of this unwritten rule that you want to make everything look okay, so you pretend everything is great," agrees thirty-year-old Leslie. "And instead you start internalizing a lot of the bad things that are happening. You grow sort of used to hiding how you really feel about things. I became very good at hiding my emotions, which makes it difficult when I'm in a relationship, and the other person always wants to know why I'm hiding what I'm feeling."

Deflecting the emotional impact of divorce can be useful for children, temporarily giving us space until we have reached a point where we can handle it with more maturity and reflection. The danger, however, comes when avoidance turns into a way of life, when one puts these painful emotions on hold for years.

Until just recently, thirty-two-year-old George refused to talk about his parents' divorce at all, regarding the subject as simply too painful to bring up. When he forces himself to speak about it, his emotions seep through, beyond his control. The tremble in his voice reveals the toll it takes on him not only to remember, but to put those memories into words. "I don't know why I'm such an emotional wreck," he apologizes. "I guess I don't like talking about it, but it makes it easier to bring these things out in the open." He pauses, then adds, "I guess I should have been talking about it over the years."

George's parents battled the terms of their divorce in court for seven years, the length of their marriage. They separated when he was two, so he has no recollection of them as a couple and only a vague understanding of why they split up. One of George's earliest memories of his parents together consists of the two of them screaming at each other during the weekend exchange of the kids, with his mother trying to slam the door in his father's face and his father shoving his foot in the doorway to stop her. Thirty years later, his parents still can't be civil to each other. When I ask him how he responded to their hostility growing up, he pauses for a long time. "You know, when you're a little kid, you just sort of have to go along with it, until they stop and you can edit things yourself," he says. "I'm sure I would have been tremendously different if my parents hadn't divorced. I would have been more open emotionally, which I'm not really. It's hard for me to be really close to people. I have a lot of friends, but I'm not really that close to any of them. I don't show a lot of feelings. I don't know why—maybe because I hid my emotions at a young age."

Many children who grew up in an environment where their emotional security was under siege learned to cope by keeping their emotions in check; feeling was simply a door best kept shut. But the grief, longing, and hurt from childhood don't disappear because we lock them away, and yet, as children, that's the way many of us were left to cope with complicated emotions: to ignore them and hope they pass. This tactic of avoidance can work for years, sometimes decades, but in the interim, these emotions, continue to smolder inside, finding ways to work through to the surface in our thoughts and behavior as adults.

For thirty-year-old Theresa, whose parents divorced when she was six, the painful emotions she kept under tight control as a child started to spill out once she left home at eighteen. Until then, Theresa had concentrated her energies on getting good grades and excelling at her extracurricular activities. "I have always done things to create diversions for myself," she explains. "I would just exhaust myself and then sleep. It was a way to measure out the days. I taught myself to be stoic, to disengage from the situation until it didn't feel real. My mind tried to accommodate this, but in general, I had bad stomach problems." All her hard work paid off, and she entered a selective college honors program, but as she remembers it, "My life fell apart for the next three years. Suddenly I was free, and I didn't know what to do with myself. Everything had always been study, bury yourself in something else, and I couldn't do that anymore." In retrospect, she says, "I see my early twenties as being this time when I was just floundering. I think it was when the effects of everything that had happened to me as a kid were coming out every other second. I was a disaster because I had always held so much in."

Almost immediately, Theresa got involved in some bad romantic relationships to ease her sense of isolation, moving in with someone two weeks after she started school. "I wasn't even sure I liked him, but I didn't want to be alone," she says. "I lived with him, then broke up with him, and within a week I had another boyfriend." She lived with her next boyfriend for a year; when they separated, it brought up the same sense of abandonment she felt when her father left, sending her into such a deep depression that she dropped out of school. "My mother would call me up and we would talk for hours every day," she says. "So I didn't have any friends, and I didn't know what was wrong. Oh my God, I was so depressed. I couldn't even get out of bed. I was so alone and confused and not knowing why everything I was doing I was fucking up." All her pent-up hurt from childhood led to the equivalent of a psychological explosion once she reached adulthood, and for the first time ever, Theresa started to talk about her parents' divorce.

Mourning the loss of our families doesn't invalidate our parents' decision to divorce or necessarily mean that we wish our parents were reunited. It is about recognizing that we have been shaped by our parents' breakup, that their history has informed our own. It took thirty-two-year-old Joseph almost two decades to discover how his parents' divorce affected him. "For a long, long time, my official story—to myself as well as others—was that I was only affected positively by the divorce. The fighting stopped. My parents hated each other before, and after, they were both in better moods. It was wonderful. No problems." As he got older, however, he started to realize that there were other side effects to his parents' splitting up: Their economic status had dropped significantly, and his mother bitterly resented any affection Joseph displayed toward his father, always encouraging him to take her side.

With this revelation, Joseph started to question some of his other "official" stories. "All through my teenage years, I had almost no memory of being a little kid," he explains. "Then one night, after I left home, I was lying in bed, and it was like, boom, it all came back: The little town I lived in when I was five. The creek we used to play at. I realized that I was actually a happy little guy, and that I had stopped being happy when my parents divorced. So all through high school, along with my official story that none of this bothered me, was the story that I was born depressed and there was nothing I could do about it. When I left home and stopped being depressed, I think my memory was somehow unlocked."

I didn't unlock my own memories from my parents' divorce for thirteen years. The first time I travel back to childhood to give words to my experience of divorce, I start to recall the images, so sharp in my mind I can hardly breathe. Then the words start to come out fast, punctuated by tears. Facing these emotions is not easy. When we allow ourselves to finally feel, we make way for a powerful tidal wave of emotion: abandonment, anger, guilt. But working through these intense emotions, rather than cocooning ourselves from them, is ultimately, I think, what helps us to move forward in our own lives.

2

The End of the World

WHEN I WAS FIVE YEARS OLD, my parents and I moved into a beige split-level home with shuttered windows and a towering maple tree in the front yard. Every fall, the leaves would scatter to the grass, turning into crisp markers of time. Every spring brought the pink bloom of the cherry blossom tree in the backyard, its petals fluttering like snowflakes past the living room window.

My room was painted blue and was right next door to my parents' bedroom. My mother picked out the bed, a starter bed that hovered close to the floor and was shaped like a rectangular box, each side barricaded to prevent accidental falls. My father installed dark blue painted shelves that spanned the height of one wall, from ceiling to floor, to organize my stuffed animals, Lego sets, and Beatrix Potter books. I measured my growth in inches every week, standing tall against a measuring tape with a stuffed Snoopy at the top, chest puffed out and stomach sucked in for added height. I slept with a night-light on to chase away the darkness, but sometimes, after a bad dream or when the shadows contorted and flickered, I would wander the ten steps into my parents' bedroom and creep under the covers between them.

Our house was conveniently located within the constellation of the local elementary, junior high, and high schools, and so, this was a neighborhood of families—a neighborhood where fathers mowed the lawn on the weekends, mothers carpooled to soccer games, and during the summer, against a humming backdrop of crickets, children roamed the tree-lined streets until dusk. Life was tidy, calm, and predictable, at least on the outside.

I remember seemingly insignificant events with a weird clarity: My mother bringing a birthday cake decorated with a candy clown to my nursery school; my father and I spending an afternoon picking out a dress for my mom for Mother's Day; the three of us stopping at a gas station, where I bought a box of pastel-colored Jordan almonds on the way to a weekend in New York City. In broader strokes, I remember that I adored my parents, who were at that point struggling to get a foothold in their respective careers, spending much of their time at work, and I became defined by another popular label coined during my lifetime—the latchkey kid. My childhood seemed filled with pangs of anticipation for when we could all be together, but the thing is, looking back, my parents never really seemed like a unit apart from me—they never held hands or went out to dinner alone. Yes, the house was filled with laughter, camaraderie, and a sense of being complete, but it needed the three of us to work. Us against everyone else.

Somewhere along the way, I started to become aware of a malaise between my parents, a certain chill that came and went. I'm not sure when or why, but gradually the moments of togetherness spread further and further apart until I found myself torn. The configuration of my family had shifted. Instead of being three equal sides of a triangle, we had turned into a straight line, with my parents at either end and me in the middle. On the nights my father worked late, my mother became more animated, as if she had just stumbled in on an unexpected party. We would carry our dinner into the bedroom and lounge on the bed, watching television. On Saturdays, my father and I would go off by ourselves, spending a couple of hours at the library and then eating at a small hole-in-the-wall nearby. At the time, I didn't dwell on this subtle separation. These were my parents, this was my family, and the possibility of divorce only skirted the fringes of my consciousness, a Judy Blume plot twist. I knew something was wrong, but in the absence of any overt hostility, I truly believed everything would be fine. Sort of.

I am nine years old, squeezed in the backseat of my aunt's station wagon with my three cousins. We have been cooped up for a couple of hours and the appeal of a road trip has started to lose its luster. There isn't enough room to pull out a board game, and we are all bored, cranky, and getting on each other's nerves. Too hot— desert-dry heat—and too many bodies. The air conditioner sputters, blows lukewarm air. My cousin leans over and whispers that he knows a secret. I punch him lightly on the arm, demanding he tell. He holds out for as long as he can, which is not very long, and then, with a quick look at the front seat to make sure the adults aren't listening, he gives.

"Your mother was pregnant with you," he smirks, "*before* your parents got married."

Stunned, I need a moment to recover.

"I knew that," I cover up, voice casual. "It's no big deal."

I stare out the window, squinting in the glare as the sun bounces off the glass. With this revelation, the simple fairy tale has turned into a much more complicated maze of emotions. For the very first time—despite the frosty air between my parents—it enters my consciousness that perhaps love has nothing to do with their marriage. Sure enough, I do the math in my head, and my cousin is right. I berate myself for not having figured this out before. "Stupid," I think, "stupid, stupid me."

"You promise you can't tell I told you," my cousin whispers fiercely. "Promise?"

I nod, wishing he would just shut up.

As I try to digest this new information, I feel an unrecognizable flutter in my stomach, which in retrospect I recognize as fear. Such a calculated motivation for marriage, even to my young mind, does not have the diamondlike strength of love. This sudden snag in the fabric of my beliefs makes me realize how easily things can fall apart. Maybe nothing is holding us together. But I had made a promise not to tell, and so I keep this secret to myself, filed away.

By the time I am finishing up elementary school, my parents hardly see each other, and on those occasional nights when the three of us are together, they retreat into silence. My father snaps the newspaper open in front of his face, an insta-wall. My mother immerses herself in a magazine, mechanically eating as her eyes rove across the page. I turn my head back and forth, humming with nervous chatter, until one of them gives me a sharp look. Calm down. Relax. We need quiet. The newspaper goes back up, a page of the magazine turns, and I sit there, with my hands underneath my legs, nearly bursting from confusion and the need to do *something* to fill the air, to get us back to where we were.

The distance that shudders between my parents grows larger and larger, so large it takes a noticeable shape. My father begins to spend more time puttering around the basement. First, he moves his desk into an empty room down there. Then, he starts to decorate, putting up a couple of posters he picked up at the National Gallery of Art as if he is moving into a college dormitory. It doesn't stop there. He buys a dresser, followed by his own refrigerator, and finally a bed. Soon, after dinner he is disappearing behind the closed door of his "study"; the acrid scent of cigar smoke sneaks out from beneath the door, but my father does not emerge until the next morning. The house is now divided, and I travel between my two parents—upstairs, downstairs, upstairs—like a desperate emissary of goodwill.

Then, suddenly, or so it seems, everything is fine. When I am eleven years old, I return from spending the summer with my grandparents, and my parents arrive at the airport to pick me up. At the baggage carousel, as my father heaves my suitcase off the conveyor belt, my mother leans toward me and with a wide grin announces she is pregnant. The comforting thought that, finally, I have an ally overpowers any primal wave of sibling rivalry. The three of us are once again linked, by the excitement over my mother's pregnancy. In the following months, as her belly begins to swell and grow, I step in with a frightening officiousness. I demand the exclusive right to choose the baby's name, and after poring over books, come up with such exotic appellations as "Flora" and "Dominique." I flip through pregnancy manuals, brow furrowed in concentration, learning all I can about such things as amniocentesis, epidurals, and spina bifida. I worry about chromosomal deficiencies and limb growth. I choose the wallpaper for the baby's room, and on a weekend afternoon, I help my father paste it up. And when my sister Caroline is born, a little blue but perfectly healthy, I feel such relief that now, thank God, I am not alone with the burden of keeping this family together. The moment I see her, small and wrinkled with a thick cap of dark hair, I fall in love. With the four of us, it looks like the clamp will hold.

Nowadays, images of my early childhood come through like bad videotape—the sound and picture, fuzzy with static, keep dropping out, leaving me unable to get inside that little girl's head. What does seem clear is that the quality of my memory was forever changed in the span of one night when I was twelve years old. I often wish the situation were reversed, that I could remember clearly what life was like before the divorce, and lose what happened after in a vague haze. But unfortunately, that's not the case. Memories from my parents' breakup spring from dark corners of my mind with a brilliant clarity, every detail permanently etched with a sharpness that still brings tears to my eyes, even today.

It's late autumn, and the leaves have transformed into cool fire, all burnt reds and oranges. My mother has gone out of the country on a business trip, something she has started to do more often of late. My father tells me he has to do some research at the library, and shortly after dinner, he puts on the blue leather jacket my mother gave him for Christmas and walks out the door. It is a typical school night, I suppose: I chat on the phone with a friend about teachers, boys, the scary wonders of starting junior high. I am almost bubbling with good mood, and before I put my sister to bed, I dance across the living room with her bunched up in my arms while the radio belts out some Top Forty tune, Madonna's "Lucky Star," I think. Afterward, I go downstairs and splay out on my stomach in front of the television to do homework. The front door opens, and I see my father's shoes peeking through the staircase railing. He walks down the stairs, with such slow, heavy steps that I twist around and sit up, and as soon as I see him, I know something is wrong. His face is flat, ashen.

He looks at me, spurts out, "Your mother," then chokes back the rest.

I turn to ice, skin tingly. "She's dead," I think. The room is spinning and I feel this overwhelming desire to stop time right then and there, to not know what I'm about to know. Nevertheless, a voice, my voice, asks, "What is it?"

He crosses the room and crumples into a tan easy chair. "She's been having an affair," he says, and as if the act of uttering the words has stolen his last bit of strength, he collapses with his head in his hands, sobbing.

Back then, I had never seen my father cry before. He was always the rational one, the responsible one, solid and stoic, and the sight of him, of the red bruises forming around his eyes from his tears, paralyzes me. I can't move. I can't speak. Finally, I pull myself up off the floor and walk over to him, then pat his shoulder awkwardly as he spits out, "You love someone and this is what they do to you," over and over again, a hoarse, bitter mantra that makes me want to run away.

The television is still on, canned laughter hanging in the air. I sit

on the arm of the chair. With his every jagged heave, I pat, and after
what seems like forever, my father gets up and goes to his room in
the basement. I go to my bedroom and crawl under the covers, but
I'm too dizzy and numb to sleep. I have no one to talk to. I stare at
the ceiling wide-eyed and then get up and quietly walk into my
mom's bedroom to use the phone. With the number pad lighting up
the darkness, I sit on the edge of the bed and call my grandparents.
When I hear their voices, sounding so close even though they are
thousands of miles away, the cold knot I've been feeling begins to
loosen and unravel. Only then do I start to cry, barely getting out
what I believe my father has told me.

"I think my parents are getting a divorce."

My parents didn't get a divorce, at least not right away. A couple
of days later, my father, sister, and I go to pick up my mother at
the airport. Her face, pale and drawn, emerges from the crowd
surging off the plane. She doesn't look at my father, but comes forward to give my sister and me a hug. I stay rigid in her embrace,
but something cracks inside, because this is my mother, not some
cardboard villain intent on destroying the family. She tucks a
strand of hair behind my ear, and looks away. We drive home. I sit
in the front seat. My father turns on the radio. Everyone is quiet,
and I stare out the window. Highway. Trees. Night. Back at the
house, we sit in the living room, backs straight and hands folded,
each of us inhabiting our own private section of the couch, until
my parents finally tell me things are up in the air. "We just don't
know what is going to happen," says my mother. "Your father and
I have to figure this out." The tension wraps around the room.
"Well, nothing is going to be decided tonight," says my father, jaw
set. "We might as well go to bed." We all go to our separate rooms
and shut our doors.

Actually, nothing is decided for a year—probably the most ex-
cruciating year of my life. The possibility of divorce hangs over

each day, and I wake up in the morning not knowing what to expect. I wander nervously through the house, constantly monitoring the conflict meter: My mother moves out, moves back in. My father wants a divorce, then wants to try and work things out. I mediate, the twelve-year-old marriage counselor, and when my mother is swinging toward leaving, I take her aside and plead with her to "focus on what's important." When my father's mood darkens, I insist, "She feels like you don't love her." I am passing along impressions, advice, messages, encouraging them to go out to dinner, maybe spend some time alone to rekindle the romance. But this is a different kind of combustible environment, one of resentment unbound, and sometimes they clash with such fury that I want to duck for cover.

Yet just as bad as the eruptions of fighting between my parents—those fiery rounds of accusations fueled by the slightest comment—are the periods of forced family cheer, those times when we sit and smile around the dinner table, engaging in stilted conversation, all the while gritting our teeth from the strain of trying too hard. I start to spend less time at home, to stay away from my parents as much as possible. We are all wilting under the pressure. I remember one evening, after I've attempted to wheedle my mother to let me go see a movie with a friend rather than eat dinner at home, she pulls me close and hisses, "Don't you want this to work?" And I do, so I stay without complaint. I desperately want to keep my family whole, want my parents to stay together. But not like this. Not like this.

One night, I creep out of my bedroom, awakened by my parents' fighting. Suddenly my father rushes down the hallway carrying armfuls of my mother's clothing. He kicks open the front door and tosses her dresses into the front yard. They sail into the darkness for a moment, then drift down like colorful parachutes to fall limp on the grass. My mother follows him out the door and stands with her arms crossed under the yellow streetlamp, watching as he brings out more clothes, time and again, until there are no clothes left inside the house. Outside, amidst a lawn sprayed with clothing, their renewed screaming rises up in the darkness. From the kitchen window, I see my mother open the door of her Volvo and start the engine, drowning out my father's curses. She sits in her car, thinking, waiting, before finally pulling out of the driveway. My stomach drops, as if her departure has pushed me over and I am tumbling fast down an endless tunnel. I want them both to stop, to go away. My bare feet move silently across the tile and, holding my breath, I lock the front door. I sit in the hallway, my knees tight against my chest, shaking. My father pounds on the door with his fist a minute later. He jiggles the knob, threatens and cajoles, then finally retrieves the spare key from the backyard. When he comes in, anger and frustration etched on his face, he says to me, "Don't you ever do that again," and walks away. A couple of days later, my mother moves back in, and we start all over again.

Winter. Spring. Summer. I turn thirteen, and as soon as school is out, I escape to my grandparents' house across the country for three months. Almost the day I step off the plane, I become a different person. My chronic stomachaches subside. I feel light and, for the first time in almost a year, happy. My grandparents and I have always been close, but this particular summer, they are my saviors. We spend lazy days on the beach, watching the sunset, camping, and, best of all, having long conversations—real discussions, not the exchanges encased in a hard shell of defensiveness I have grown used to. I even successfully block out the life waiting for me back at home, until a couple of weeks before I am about to leave, my grandfather asks me to take a walk with him on the beach. We crawl over the rocky sand, then rest on a gnarled piece of driftwood as the sun lowers in the sky. I can sense that this walk has a purpose.

And I'm right. I've become skillful at recognizing the facial expressions, the tone of voice, all the telltale signs that mark the preface of painful words. I steel myself. My grandfather looks at me, and speaks. *Your parents have finally decided to get a divorce. Your mother is moving out.* I listen, feeling nothing, absolutely nothing, least of all surprised. "I wasn't supposed to tell you, they didn't want me to," he says, squeezing my hand. "But I didn't think that was right. I thought you should know." I latch on to this last bit— not tell me?—astonished that my parents can treat this as a private matter that doesn't include anyone else. For the remainder of my visit, anger and dread intertwine. When my grandparents drop me off at the airport, I clutch on to them until the final boarding call, not wanting to get on that plane. I cry for the entire six-hour flight, sobbing so hard that my eyes swell to slits, so hard that the woman in the seat next to me leans over and tries to comfort me. She thinks someone has died.

When I get home, my mother informs me she is leaving in a week and taking my sister with her, that it's easier that way. My father stands by the window holding Caroline, who sleeps peacefully against his shoulder, their faces iced by the early morning sunlight. I can't even contemplate the absence of not only my mother but my sister. The days of family are now numbered. The word "divorce" is never mentioned, but implicit is the understanding that this time, she is not coming back. I accept the news with a simple nod of the head. No protests, no angry words, no attempts at convincing them to change their minds. It is as if some tap has been tightened shut.

There is nothing worse, I think, than when your parents break your heart.

A friend of mine once said the memories of her parents' divorce are so vivid, she often feels as if she's living parallel lives, one in the present and one in the past. I nodded when she said this, because over a decade later, my memories of my parents' extended breakup are still led by a twelve-year-old's anguish. Japanese novelist Yukio Mishima once wrote "The period of childhood is a stage on which time and space become entangled"; compressed within this chamber of youth, any disturbance can take on cataclysmic proportions. Divorce is one of the ultimate disruptions of order in a child's world: A parent leaves, the family breaks apart, our lives are altered.

When children of divorce say "I felt like my world was coming to an end," they are usually not exaggerating. The announcement of divorce and a parent's departure can remain forever imprinted in our minds, with certain moments circling us back to the point of change and loss as we grow older. Duane, twenty-seven, remembers following his father out to the driveway as he got in his car to leave the family for good. Before his father could close the car door, Duane and his sister stepped in the way, begging him to stay. "He got pissed off after five minutes of this and raised his hand as if to swat us free," he recalls. "So we backed away and he left. I was eight years old. That night I couldn't sleep because my father wasn't home. I finally cried myself to sleep, thinking and saying all the things in my life I was going to miss with him gone, both the things we had done before and the things we would have done in the future. That was the last time I cried until I was twenty-three." It wasn't until Duane found himself in an unhappy marriage, and as he puts it, "was so depressed and sad like I had been the day my dad left," that he finally broke down and cried for the first time in fifteen years.

On the other hand, those who were very young when their parents split up, with the divorce papers already filed before they even understood what the word "divorce" meant, often say as adults that having two parents with separate lives was simply all they had ever known. As one twenty-nine-year-old woman, whose parents divorced when she was three, recalls, "When I was in the first grade, I even remember being on the bus on the way to school and telling everybody 'My parents are diversed.' " Because younger children have a limited capacity to conceive of the events unfolding around them, later recollections from the breakup period can resemble an uneven collage. Thirty-one-year-old Erica, whose parents divorced when she was three, has only vague recollections from when her parents split up. "My mother went off to the hospital to give birth to my sister around the same time my dad left and my nanny, who I adored, also left," she remembers. "I do have a clear memory of my new nanny telling me what was going on. And my dad tells me that the day he left, he came to tuck me into bed and told me he wouldn't be coming back. I asked him who would read me bedtime stories. But that's it, really."

With younger children, some parents will employ elaborate subterfuges rather than discuss their marital breakdown: Dad is always "working late," Mom is staying over at a "friend's house." According to one study, *80 percent* of preschoolers weren't given any explanation of their parents' divorce at all. Marcia, whose parents divorced when she was two, accidentally discovered her parents were divorced when she was ten years old. "I found the papers in the basement," she explains. "Before that, I was just told that my dad had been transferred with his job and we couldn't go with him. The actual divorce part didn't faze me, because by that time I was used to my dad being gone. I think I was just sad that they never told me the truth. I'm twenty-two now, and it *still* hasn't been addressed!"

Those who were too young when their parents divorced to depend on their own memories must rely almost entirely on information from others, not only to shed light on the chain of events leading to the breakup but to also offer clues as to how they were affected. "My parents kept me in the dark about a lot of things when they split up, which was good, because I was too young to really understand what was happening," explains twenty-three-year-old Lydia, whose parents separated when she was seven. "But now I feel like there's so much about myself and my family that hides in that time and because I don't remember much, there's a lot for me to learn." Lydia, who has seen her father only once since her parents separated, recently discovered from her older brother what happened right before her father moved out of the house:

My dad had been cheating on my mom with the same woman for a long time. He had set up an apartment by his office, and my mom knew about it, but I guess she didn't fully get it. One afternoon, one of my mom's coworkers told her that my dad's car was parked outside the apartment, and she drove her there. My mom knocked on the door, but my dad refused to open it, and she knew then what was going on. The coworker called my brother, who was in high school, and he came to get my mom, who was frozen outside the door. My brother yelled for my dad to come out, and when he finally did, my brother put him in a headlock. A lot of my dad's things were in the apartment, in suitcases. I don't know what happened after that. I think they all waited for the police to come.

It's funny, but what I remember from that period is my mom coming home with a puppy. I had always wanted one, and my dad had promised he'd get me one, then he was gone. Turns out my mom went to live with relatives for a month because she was depressed. I imagine she was depressed for a long time, but I don't have many memories of her; they start to trickle in around junior high and high school. My aunt, who lived with us after my parents separated, tells me that I missed forty-eight days of school in the third grade because I just didn't want to go. I kept asking when my dad would come home. I don't remember that at all now. Similar to how I don't remember my mom until later in life, memories of my own life are quite spotty until high school.

Our age when our parents separated played an important part in determining our ability to comprehend the news of their divorce and how we handled the accompanying stresses of their breakup. During each phase of childhood we work on specific developmental tasks in our psychological growth. Therefore, the age when our parents divorced is a telling indication of what emotional tools we had at our disposal to deal with the immediate crisis of divorce and guide us into the next stage of development. In general, preschoolers and children in elementary school tend to feel a great deal of confusion, guilt, and fear when their parents split up. Preteens and adolescents, who are better able to make the cognitive leap from "my parents are getting divorced" to "my life is never going to be the same again," are more likely to feel anger toward their parents and a sense of alienation from their families.

Nevertheless, these remain the most sweeping of guidelines. I found that in conversations with others, the influence of age was usually tempered by the individual context in which the parents' breakup occurred. While parents who divorce have obviously reached a breaking point in their love and commitment to each other, children's awareness of the strife in their marriage varies greatly, depending not only on their capacity for understanding but the ways in which their parents chose to express their unhappiness. We often responded to their decision to divorce according to how our parents' marriages fell apart: shock and disbelief for those of us hit with the news with the lightning speed of a car crash; sadness and perhaps even relief for those of us who watched our parents' marriages go through a protracted period of collapse before they divorced.

When we speak of divorce in terms of emotion, it becomes clear how so many of our parents' marriages came apart along crooked lines, with some more visible to us than others. Children experience the immediate impact of divorce in a variety of ways, but in the end, there's no easy way to lose your home, just—according to one woman—"different kinds of pain."

Waiting to Exhale

Divorce may act as the official end of the marriage, but a child whose parents are openly antagonistic toward each other has usually sustained other major losses by the time they reach the point of permanent separation: Constant fighting may dominate one or both parents' attention, leaving the child's emotional needs unmet. A parent may start spending less time at home, or be cranky and irritable when present. Sometimes a child is forced to play referee or confidant within the warring family. As one twenty-eight-year-old woman remembers, "My parents had a big, loud argument one time just before they announced the divorce. I don't know what it was about, but I thought my dad was going to hurt my mom, and I screamed at him. I actually got him to leave the house. I was only eleven."

Some parents can discuss the possibility of divorcing, even separate and move back in together several times before taking the final step. In the process, they send their children on a merry-go-round of uncertainty. "I remember sitting in class one day and seeing my dad drive by the window with all his stuff packed up in the trunk, and I thought, 'Here it goes again,' " says twenty-two-year-old Laura. "They probably split up two or three times before the divorce, and it was always my mom kicking my dad out of the house. Each time, it got a little bit longer. I wouldn't really know where my dad was or when he was coming back, and they always seemed to be able to work things out. Once my father mentioned the possibility of divorce, but then things were fine for a while. When he moved out for the last time, no one told me 'Hey, we're getting a divorce!' I just kind of assumed."

For children trapped in a tense home, watching the unhappiness eat away at their parents' marriage can, in some ways, be more painful than going through a divorce. The anguish of being caught in the middle, listening to parents' venom fly over the dinner table, or seeing them eye each other with distaste, has already taken its toll. Many children emerge battered and wary. As twenty-five-year-old Brent, whose parents divorced when he was sixteen, recalls:

There was very little physical contact between my parents. Dad drank, as he always did, to numb the mundaneness of an unphysical marriage. Mom drank to pass time and numb the pain of an uncommunicative marriage. When they told me they were getting a divorce, I kind of expected it.

I was able to handle everything but Mom's spitefulness, but after she started dating and was no longer as vocally spiteful, it was easy to continue on with my life. I knew enough of the family secrets to understand why they divorced. Heck, I knew more than they did since they talked to me and not each other. I also came to the conclusion that they probably should have divorced sooner and saved me a lot of the annoyance of living in a dysfunctional household— like maybe when I was twelve or so.

"Staying together for the sake of the children" just messes with their heads. Better a healthy divorce with closure so people can get on with their lives than a hostile household filled with bitterness and resentment. If both parties consent to a divorce, why not?

Children forced to travel between two enemy camps created by their parents in the same house often draw another emotional boundary for their parents' divorce other than the moment when they physically separated. These children recognized that their parents had left each other long before, and their homes were already torn apart. "It was obvious to me that my parents would probably be getting divorced soon, since all they did was fight," recalls twenty-nine-year-old Scott, whose parents divorced when he was thirteen. "My father would spend hours on end in the garage, working on anything from building an ultralight airplane to building a television from scratch. My mother was visibly unhappy, although she tried to hide it, and while my father became consumed with his hobbies, she became consumed by work. I would find any excuse necessary to be at the park, or at school, or at a friend's house to avoid the tension at home." Like Brent, when Scott learned his parents were getting a divorce, the announcement only confirmed what he had been expecting for a while.

It's impossible to evaluate the impact of parental divorce on children without taking into account what the family life consisted of beforehand. Sociologists Paul Amato and Alan Booth, after following over two thousand married individuals and their children during the eighties and nineties, found that the key factor in predicting a child's adjustment following divorce was the level of conflict *before* the divorce. They suggest that children from high-conflict homes fare better after their parents split up than did those coming from relatively low-conflict homes, because divorce generally improves their everyday life by removing the source of tension. Many of those I spoke with, who recognized the hostility within their parents' marriage, agreed with this finding, viewing the divorce as a difficult but necessary event in their lives. "Those who haven't lived through life with unhappily married parents—the tension, the arguing, the slaps, and, most lasting, the tears—don't understand what it's like," explains one thirty-six-year-old woman, whose parents separated when she was nine. "My parents' divorce freed us from that. And while my mother struggled financially, she had emotional and physical peace of mind."

Divorce can open the sole and vital exit out of a union that is clearly damaging to both parent and child, especially when severe emotional or physical abuse, drug addiction, or mental illness darkens the home. For twenty-two-year-old Heidi, whose parents divorced when she was eight, the world created by her parents' marriage was one she was glad to leave behind. "My parents' divorce was the start of a whole new life for me," Heidi explains. "Unfortunately, their poor marriage still affected me. I am too insecure and lack confidence in some situations, and I think that's because during the years when my personality was forming, I was always so scared and worried."

Heidi's father was an alcoholic, and was unemployed by the end of her parents' marriage. "He stayed home during the day, until my mom came home from work," she explains. "Then he went to a local bar to get drunk. Every night. When he was home, he was always yelling at my mom, saying things like 'Get the hell out of here.' I was always scared when I heard him come in at night." Heidi's relationship with her father was strained by his behavior, and she admits they weren't very close. "He never showed an interest in me. When he was home, he was watching football. Sometimes when he would come home from drinking, he would bring me a candy bar and act like he was a hero. I felt like I didn't know him." After her father stumbled home late one night, drunk, his shirt smudged with makeup and reeking of another woman's perfume, Heidi's mother finally decided she had withstood enough. On Heidi's last day of second grade, her mother packed up their belongings and moved them both in with her parents in another town.

Heidi remembers having been unruffled by the move. "I was old enough to recognize how terribly my dad treated us, so I understood why my mom left him. I was happy about it," she recalls. Away from her father, and nestled in the loving home of her grandparents, both Heidi and her mother started to gain more confidence. "Before the divorce, I was incredibly shy, withdrawn, and scared," Heidi remembers. "But after the divorce, I blossomed, like a huge weight had been lifted off my shoulders. I became more relaxed and happy, the way a child should be. I didn't have to worry anymore." She hasn't seen her father in the past six years. "I don't think about him very much, although I guess I always wondered how he could have such little interest in his daughter."

Living in a conflict-ridden home is similar to sustaining a long-term trauma. Feelings of disappointment, helplessness, and fear are renewed with each clash between our parents, and by the time they choose to divorce, we have already been affected by their misery. We have learned just how cruel or indifferent two people, who were once purportedly in love, can be to each other. Yet, while children who apprehend how miserable their parents are together may be better prepared to accept their decision to divorce, this increased awareness does not necessarily make the transition any less distressing.

"By the time I hit adolescence, my parents were fighting all the time," says thirty-two-year-old Molly, whose parents divorced when she was fourteen. "The funny thing about the fights—and this is symbolic of when a relationship goes awry, I think—was that they were about the stupidest stuff you can imagine. At one point, Mom decided she would stop sleeping with Dad, and he used to yell at her about that. Then they went through this whole yearlong 'reconciliation exercise,' I'll call it, where they would go away for weekends together, but it seemed sort of futile. When they told us they were getting a divorce, it wasn't a surprise in the least—but that doesn't mean it didn't have an impact. I remember they were fighting about something stupid, and I think my sister said, 'Dad, why are you having such a spaz?'—we were teenagers, so we talked like that—and he said, 'Because your mother filed for divorce.' And that was the big bombshell. We were crying, and it was really sad. We weren't crying out of shock, but it was still a big emotional thing."

Losing the ideal of a two-parent home is always difficult, but we measure the loss in comparison to the reality of our families. By the time my parents finally decided to divorce, I had lived with the possibility for a year and had resigned myself to what seemed like the inevitable. Unlike the night when I learned of my mother's affair, the final denouement of my parents' marriage did not come as a shock; in my mind, it is that night of revelation when my family abruptly came undone, even though my mother didn't actually move out for another year. That night, in the span of minutes, my entire belief system was shattered. And sometimes when the phone rings late at night or someone walks into the room with a stricken look, I feel the same icy tingle I felt so many years ago, as if my body has programmed itself to receive the unexpected jolt. That's how deep the memory lies for me.

Paradise Lost

When thirty-year-old Theresa talks about how she found out her parents were getting a divorce, she recalls the details with a terrible clarity. She remembers the hot, blue Saturday morning in August, only two weeks before she started the first grade, when her father took her to a local diner for breakfast. She describes how his eyes nervously flicked around the restaurant, never resting on hers, and she just knew something bad was about to happen. "I felt awful," she says, lost in memory. "I had never felt like that before." She remembers how her stomach cramped, her throat tightened, and a flush fanned out across her face. She remembers how she pushed away her plate of scrambled eggs, hardly eaten. Around her, the world was suddenly amplified—the sunlight too bright, the chatter at other tables too loud.

It wasn't until they were outside the restaurant that her father finally crouched down, looked her in the eye, and told her he wasn't going to come home anymore. "I was in shock after that," Theresa says, and her voice still shakes almost twenty-five years later. "I remember having this sick feeling that my life was over. The rug was just yanked from under me and then it was never the same again. No safety zone replaced it. I was shell-shocked for years." She takes a breath, and adds evenly, "Everything I do in my life is to never let that happen to me again."

Time and distance may later uncover the unhappiness that simmered beneath the surface of our parents' marriages, but since children don't usually assess the state of their parents' relationships, many were caught unaware by the announcement of their divorce. Some even described happy memories from their family life before the breakup: birthday parties, family vacations, and a daily life devoid of serious arguments. Of course, truly happy parents don't separate, but these remembrances indicate a child's impression of what came before; within this context, the news that two parents are splitting apart acts as a shock to the system. When a home is suddenly torn apart with one explosive bang, children don't have time to prepare themselves but are left to absorb the impact, whether they are ready or not. We learn how quickly both situations and people can change, hard and fast lessons that can dramatically shape our emerging identities, instilling us with the belief that nothing is stable and no one is beyond doubt.

In describing his life before the divorce, twenty-eight-year-old Ethan remembers his parents scooping him up at the children's center across the street from his house at the end of the day. His family lived in an urban neighborhood, the kind where children play on the streets until dark and all the parents have at least a nodding acquaintance with one another. His mother and father owned a business together, sharing an office at home, and they arranged their schedules so as to spend more time with the family. "I always believed they were a real unit," he recalls. "And as the parents of my classmates began to divorce, I convinced myself, and my friends as well, that my parents had the strongest marriage imaginable. I think I was terrified that my parents would be next."

When he was in the fifth grade, Ethan and his family took a trip to Europe, and he started to detect signs of trouble between his parents:

When we got there, I realized there was a hidden agenda: My parents were testing their marriage, and it wasn't going well. They fought after my sister and I went to sleep; the apartment we were staying in was smaller than our house, and it was clear they weren't getting along. I woke up one morning and found my mother sleeping on the couch alone. It was the first time I had ever seen this, and I knew then that their marriage was in trouble. I was horrified.

On a Sunday afternoon, a few weeks after we returned home, I was sitting in my room, alone and withdrawn, doing whatever eleven-year-old boys do. There was a knock on my door, or maybe it was a shout from downstairs, and my parents were asking my sister and me to come down for a family talk. My parents sat on a little couch in the back of the dining room, and my sister and I crouched on the floor, waiting. I remember looking up at them, hearing the words, and then letting the news that they were getting divorced flood over me, like a tidal wave drowning out the idyllic life I had dreamed of for all of us. I remember protesting, struggling to fight it all back, imagining that I could change their minds and convince them they could try again and make it work. I remember my sister crying. I remember asking my parents to stay together, and being crushed at how stubborn they were, how determined to ruin our lives they seemed.

Confusion, fear, anger—these are common responses when the announcement of divorce violates our expectations of family. Unless parents openly discuss the reasons why they have chosen to divorce, without bad-mouthing or leveling accusations at each other, the event takes on powerful weight. Ethan points out that initially he blamed his mother for the divorce. "My father made it clear to me that my mother was the one who wanted the divorce," he explains. "And I told her how upset I was about her decision, even charged her with ruining the family, and I think, my life." But through several long, honest conversations with his mother about his parents' marriage, he was able to let go of his resentment and grasp a better understanding of why his parents divorced, which helped him adjust to the changes happening around him. If, however, children are left alone with their confusion, their parents' decision to divorce can continue to trouble them for years afterward. The notion of happiness can become an increasingly elusive one: If we thought things were fine—and they weren't—what is real and what is illusion? As adults, some of us must constantly search for clues to anchor our reality.

Up until the day her mother kicked her father out of the house when she was eight years old, Nicole thought they were the typical "all-American" family. Her mother was what she calls a "Doris Day type," who stayed at home to care for the children, while her father was more outgoing and social. Her parents feigned harmony, taking careful measures to never fight in front of the children. Now thirty-three, Nicole still remembers the day when all her parents' hidden conflicts erupted with startling force. "My father was sitting at the typewriter, and my mother yelled something and ripped the paper out, telling him to leave," she recalls. "That afternoon, after he left, she sat us down on the couch and said he wasn't coming back. I can't even remember my reaction. I know I couldn't understand what was happening. But I know exactly how I felt. Lost. Now everything I see I have to know the cause, so I can explain the effect. Since I can't really understand why the divorce came about, I constantly struggle to make sense of my family. I don't know if my father knew what hit him when my mother told him to leave. I think of how easily he left the house that day, without putting up a fight or pleading. Maybe he knew it was coming, but I didn't."

Only recently, Nicole discovered there were incidents of physical violence between her parents before she was born, offering her some insight into the quality of their marriage. Still, she wishes her parents had given her some warning beforehand, so she could have been better prepared for their divorce. "I guess it would have been easier if they had eliminated the surprise of it all, or had been more honest about their attitudes and feelings about each other. As a kid, I thought it was my fault they had divorced; there is a seven-year age difference between me and my sister, and I often felt like I was the beginning of a second phase in their marriage that led to its failure."

Others told similar stories of a parent's leaving immediately, either before or after announcing the divorce; some children came home to half-empty houses, a parent already gone without saying good-bye. When divorce seems to suddenly appear out of nowhere, the news can strike a dangerous blow to a child's self-esteem. Without the preamble of severe conflict between their parents to pave the way for their separation, some turn the blame on themselves in one way or another. Says twenty-eight-year-old Janet, whose parents divorced when she was eight, "We had just come back from summer camp, and they sat us down at the kitchen table and told us. I remember thinking, 'Let's talk about this. Let's negotiate this.'

I remember promising that I would be good, and I wouldn't fight with my brother anymore, if they stayed together. It turns out my dad had actually moved out during the summer while we were gone, so his stuff wasn't there, and I think that was really wrong because it was too quick. It was too much to handle all at once."

Janet immediately started to see her father every other weekend. The quick transformation in their relationship—from seeing each other daily to going out for pizza on the weekends—proved to be difficult. "In retrospect, I should have had time to get used to my parents getting divorced, instead of this radical change with my father not in our daily lives anymore," Janet says. "There's a chunk of time I totally blocked out after my father left, and it blows my mind that, at twenty-eight, I can't really tell you what happened. I think I protected myself by forgetting, but I *want* to remember. It's a part of who I am and it informs me, but because there are certain pieces that don't connect in my own mind, I feel like it's something I still need to unravel."

Many children, faced with such a drastic shift in their families, initially react by shutting down. We become frozen and numb, too overwhelmed to wrap our minds around what is happening. Few of us are willing or able to sift through the sudden pile of our emotions, especially if our parents are also upset by their impending divorce. As twenty-three-year-old Lance, whose parents divorced when he was fourteen, remembers:

My mom came into my room, sat down on the bed, and told me they were getting a divorce. I guess I was pretty unemotional. She broke down crying and hugged me, but I just kind of stood there, frozen. And I don't think I told my friends for a while, because they always thought I had the coolest parents. After my mom left me alone, I just lay on my bed and started to cry, thinking about it. I couldn't believe it, really. I thought it was too late for them to get a divorce.

They had been together for twenty years. Looking back, I should have talked to someone about it, instead of dealing with it all alone.

Unless addressed, this emotional numbness can last into adulthood. Just recently, twenty-eight-year-old Danielle has started to think back on her parents' divorce and how she responded to it. When she was ten years old, her mother discovered her father was having an affair and confronted him that night. As Danielle listened at one end of the hallway, her parents fought at the other end; finally, her mother demanded that her father leave, and he did. "I was just sitting there while my brother and sister cried," she says. "It was so unexpected that I didn't really know how to take it all in, I guess." That night after her father left and her two younger siblings had gone to bed, Danielle's mother came into her bedroom. "She kept asking me, 'Do you need to cry? Do you want to talk about this?' And I would say no. Then she would hug me. I think she needed to cry with me. I didn't cry, though. It was so shocking that the only way to deal with it was to not pay attention. I just saw everyone around me falling apart, and I think I very consciously told myself, 'I'm not going to cry,' that I had to be strong, because if you let yourself feel something, this is what it turns into."

The sudden drama surrounding her parents' divorce left a deep impression. "I'm starting to see how this feeling now negatively affects every relationship I've had, in a way," Danielle explains. "I put all these walls up, and I won't let myself go there. I'm a happy person, but it's all been even keel. I don't have huge highs and lows. I don't let myself really miss people. Even today, I can't stand discord. I avoid it to the point where I can't say 'no' to someone, because I don't want to deal with the repercussions. I think that has to do with feeling like you had to make things right or you didn't want to get involved with the whole breaking up of the family."

In the past, Danielle was drawn to difficult relationships

precisely because of the heightened emotions they produced. She tells me about a relationship with one boyfriend, who always made her feel insecure, and in the end, her worst fear came true—he cheated on her. "This is what worries me though: I found that it was sort of exciting to feel like I couldn't get my hands around him and feel secure. I couldn't eat. I couldn't sleep. I thought, this is what love is—that sick, panicky feeling in your stomach. I'm still drawn to it. I have to remind myself that it doesn't last, the danger and the insecurity are not what's healthy. But I think I'm so used to not feeling things that it actually feels good when I do," she says. "In good, steady relationships, I don't necessarily feel things, which is why I'm working to move beyond this middle ground I'm in, to feel more. Being solid and happy all the time, it makes people like you, but in the end, it's not as rewarding. I know my friends have gotten annoyed in the past year. They say, 'You're depressed sometimes. What happened to the old you?'" She pauses, and adds, "They don't understand that I don't want to be that person anymore."

Divorce effectively sends a reverberation through our childhood, at a time when our identities and personalities are still forming. When parents separate, and the structure of our homes crumbles around us, we are no longer fluent in the accepted language of family; even in homes where these emotional comforts were in short supply, family still provided an important framework. As children, we have certain expectations that our parents will take care of us and provide us with a place where we feel safe, and losing our families at an early age breaches our assumptions.

As adults, our perceptions continue to flex and fumble as we try to make sense of our parents' divorces and the effect it had on our lives. "I think my parents did what they had to do," says a thirty-year-old woman. "Ultimately, it was their decision and not really my business—except it is, and I guess a part of me will always be angry at them for getting divorced, no matter what the reasons. But that's one side. The other side is that I love my half sisters, and my dad now has a great relationship with my stepmother, and I'm happy for all that. At the same time, my mom is pretty happy with her life too. My guess is that if they had stayed together, neither one would be so happy now. It was just a long and difficult struggle to get to this place, and this 'happiness' has only come in the past few years."

For a long time, I blamed my parents' divorce entirely on the fact that my mother had an affair. It was easy to embrace her infidelity as the root of all their problems, the one act that broke my family apart, and while I still occasionally rankle with resentment over it, I now understand that the reasons my parents finally divorced were far more involved. My mother's affair was merely a symptom of a sickness that ran underneath the skin of my parents' marriage, one I couldn't quite make out as a child. In all likelihood, their union would have come to an end one way or another. Still, this ability to see beyond blame enters on a purely intellectual plane; on an emotional level, the passage of time has little effect. Somewhere in the back of my mind echo a child's questions: How could my mother do this to me? How could she hug and kiss me while carrying on a double life, one that did not include me at all? I was still young enough when my parents divorced to believe that if she was the center of my world, I should be the center of hers.

It is a cool, breezy afternoon, on the cusp of winter, when my mother leaves. I stand at the screen door, looking out at the field across from my house. The scent of dying leaves and burnt wood hangs in the air, a signal of the approaching cold. Behind me, I hear the clang of keys, and then my father muttering, "I don't have to stay around for this." My mother follows close behind him, yelling, "Don't you dare leave her alone. Don't you dare." My father ignores her, avoids me, and storms outside. I see a blur of arm as he slams the kitchen door shut; his figure cuts across the hay-colored grass, ducks into his car, and drives off. My mother comes up next to me and says, "Damn him," but I don't respond. In fact, I don't say a word the entire day.

I stand in the front hall as my mother fusses over her suitcases, then fusses over my sister, zipping and unzipping her jacket, afraid she will be too warm, then too cold. We wait. When the taxi finally pulls into the driveway, I help my mother carry her bags out and put them in the trunk. I pick up my sister and settle her in the backseat. My mother hugs me, and I hug her back. There are no more tears left. I wave good-bye as the taxi putters up the street, gaining speed, and, after it disappears, I go back inside to an empty house.

And so it ends, this marriage between my parents, but for me it is only the beginning.

3

Family Business: When Money Equals Love

ON A HOT SUMMER MORNING, the streets quiet after the early morning commuter rush, I push my way through the double glass doors of the County Circuit Courthouse, where my parents filed for their divorce. The entrance is air-conditioned, cool and cavelike, untouched by the lights farther down the hall. I wait in a line that snakes slowly through the metal detectors, rubbing my shoulders to stay warm. When I reach the front of the line, I keep up the rhythm, placing my purse on the conveyor belt to be X-rayed, stripping off my watch, and emptying my pockets of loose change. I walk through the metal detector and am greeted by a loud beep. Before I know it a security officer is upon me, waving a thick wand around the outline of my body. Once satisfied that I'm not packing any weapons, she ushers me through with a wave of her hand. She turns her attention to the next visitor in line, and I step out of the way.

After a quick scan of the main directory, I head over to the Office of Central Files; it seems like as good a place as any to start in locating a record of my parents' divorce.

As it turns out, Central Files is the heart of the county court system, the final resting place where every case from the past twenty-five years lies color-coded, alphabetized, and catalogued away on metal shelves visible in never-ending rows behind the clerk's counter. In this small room, devoid of windows and filled with musty air, I run my finger over a dusty register printed rather primitively on green-striped computer paper until I find my parents' names: *Staal vs. Staal.* It's surprisingly easy. I scribble the case number down on a scrap of paper and hand it to the round man who sits behind the counter.

"What's your name, dear?" he asks, pen poised to mark it in his records.

"Staal," I reply, waiting for a spark of curiosity; waiting for him to ask why I'm here. My explanation runs through my head, already rehearsed—a gentle but firm plea convincing him that my interest is strictly personal. Family business, I would say, but he doesn't ask. Apparently, my request is nothing out of the ordinary, and he just nods, pushes his glasses up on his nose, and disappears into the back. Less than a minute later, he returns carrying a manila folder. He points to a numbered box on a clipboard.

"Sign here. When you're done, you can just drop it off," he instructs, then adds, "Have a good day." I grab the folder, mumble my thanks, and sit down underneath the bright wash of fluorescent lights.

The folder is thin and sleek. So this is it, I think. Fourteen years of marriage reduced to less than half an inch of paperwork.

I have never seen my parents' divorce settlement before, and I pause before delving in. My parents never discussed the details of their divorce with me; everything was decided quietly, outside the courtroom and beyond my ears. So with a shiver of apprehension, I wonder if I will discover something horrible, some secret that I've been shielded from until now. I take a deep breath, then flip the folder open to the first page. It reads "Judgment of Absolute Divorce" in bold letters. As I quickly rove over the pages, I realize that I have nothing to worry about: The prose is pared down to the most basic legal lingo. Maryland, like most states, has no-fault divorce laws on the books, so the document doesn't attempt to prove guilt by dissecting my parents' marriage. Instead it deals solely with the flotsam and jetsam of their broken union: personal property and children.

My parents never entered a courtroom, and as far as I know, they didn't have a particularly contentious divorce, at least in the legal sense. There were no court battles over custody or child support. So within these pages, I get the brief, official breakdown of the practical aspects of our postdivorce lives, choppy and impersonal in its vagueness. An entire four pages are devoted specifically to me, the minor child Stephanie—"hereinafter referred to as 'the child.' " My father is granted custody in paragraph one. Paragraph two stipulates that my parents will equally split the child's college expenses, if the child is inclined to attend such an institution of higher learning. Paragraph three ensures an equal split of all health insurance fees; my mother is ordered to open a life insurance policy with me as the sole beneficiary—standard operating procedure, I've learned, to safeguard the flow of child support in case the noncustodial parent dies. Paragraph four outlines that my parents must consult with each other in matters regarding my health, welfare, education, and upbringing, always keeping my "best interests" in mind.

The section closes by stating that my parents "shall make every effort to foster the respect and affection of the child for each other and shall do nothing which would injure the child's opinion of the other parent, or which would hamper the free and natural development of the love and affection of the child for the other." Doesn't exactly slide over the tongue, does it? Although my father retains custody, my mother reserves her right to see me at "reasonable" times and places and for "reasonable" durations. And with the flourish of their signatures at the bottom of the page, Mom and Dad agree that they "shall continue to live separate and apart, free from interference, authority, or control, direct or indirect, from the other, as if each were single and unmarried." It's all very neat, efficient, and to the point, and when I've read the very last page, I feel strangely detached. This document is all smooth surfaces, with no emotional handles.

While the words offer nothing, I read volumes in between the lines. Did my father really want me, or did he just want to get back at my mother? Or maybe my mother didn't really want me, and my father had no choice but to take me in? I try to imagine how my parents felt as they signed away their marriage, studying their signatures for any slight trembles of the hand, but to no avail. Even though it happened over a decade ago, the suspicions still stick like pins.

If I try, I can explain away the hurt with logic. I can see how the choices they made conformed to a certain rationale: My father was keeping the house where we had lived together as a family for the past seven years, so by remaining with him, I wouldn't have to switch schools. If the decision had been up to me, I no doubt would have fought to remain close to the friends I had grown up with; still, every now and then, I can't help but feel the old sting of rejection. But then, love isn't supposed to conform to rationale, is it? No matter how much my mother wanted to remain a part of my life after the divorce, I always come back to this: When she moved out, she didn't just leave my father, she left me too. I know this sentiment has become almost a cliché, but underneath all the rules and sensible measures lies a strong core of grief: Maybe my mother didn't love me quite enough.

There is something deeply chilling about picking apart and translating into legal jargon the one love that is supposed to be unconditional. It leaves a hollow space inside. Despite the court's best intentions to keep our love "free and natural," I am surrounded by conditions, and so are my parents. The proof lies in this document that, more than thirteen years later, is still available for public viewing.

"Love implies not only the morality of the family as against the immorality of the business world," writes Robert Bellah in

Habits of the Heart. "Love implies feeling against calculation." With the legal wrestling of divorce, many of us lose this distinction between business and family. After witnessing how easily love can turn into a battle of "yours" and "mine," we become all too aware of how relationships can carry a brutal epilogue, and this knowledge propels us to protect ourselves emotionally and financially as adults. "In the back of my head, I'm always preparing myself for what I will do if my relationship ends, even though I don't see it ending in the near or long-term future," says a twenty-six-year-old woman who has been living with her boyfriend for three years. "I think about whose house I can stay at if I have to move out, where I'll get my first and last months' rent for an apartment, what would happen to all the joint friends we have now, how we will divide up the furniture . . . and the list goes on and on."

When parents split up, we learn that relationships are fragile and that certain situations are beyond our control, but it is the level of animosity that exists between them that determines the extent to which these lessons instruct us in our own relationships. "If my dad died, my mom would do a jig on his grave," says one thirty-two-year-old woman. "They hate each other, and I am the product of that hatred. Sometimes my mom will say things like 'God, you look like your father' or 'You do that just like your father. How are you supposed to live like that?'"

Let's imagine the ideal postdivorce world: Two parents don't get along—enough so their children know the depth of their misery, but not so badly that the kids are traumatized by their fighting. Mom and Dad decide to part, both of them sit down with their children to discuss calmly and rationally the reasons why they are getting a divorce. After one parent moves out, they continue to be cordial, constantly reassuring their children that they will always be loved. Property division, child support, and visitation rights are decided fairly, amicably, and without court intervention. Meanwhile, the noncustodial parent remains a central figure in the lives of the children, maintaining a close, supportive relationship with them. Mom and Dad still provide a united front, engaging in what sociologists call "coparenting." Perhaps both parents remarry loving partners, widening the circle of family. At graduations and weddings, Mom and Dad, Stepmom and Stepdad can sit alongside one another, in the same row, and celebrate as parents, not adversaries. In this scenario, love wins.

Although hard to achieve, requiring cooperation and civility from parents who are splitting apart, such divorces do happen. Thirty-four-year-old Stacey, whose parents divorced when she was six, says her parents made it a priority to protect her as best they could from the painful repercussions of their divorce. "I think it may have been a little hard on me at first, but both my parents were really careful to let me know that they loved me and that it was okay for me to love both of them. They made sure I knew that neither one of them had hurt the other or done something bad."

After they separated, her parents remained on friendly terms, and as Stacey puts it, her mother "flourished," eventually marrying a man whom Stacey adored. After the wedding, her father wrote her a poem, telling her it was okay to love both him and her stepfather; when Stacey was a teenager, her two dads even took her to a baseball game together. "I feel lucky, lucky to live with and be related to such cool people," she explains. "I really liked all my parents growing up—all three of them!—and I like them even more as time goes on. I guess I mostly felt privileged to be a part of my family, because of their maturity and honesty." Not only were her mother and father happier after their divorce than during their marriage, but they continued to provide her with a stable, affectionate environment. As a result, Stacey feels she developed a healthy source of strength and self-esteem during childhood that she carries with her as an adult. "I think the way they explained things to me and the example they set—unlike some of the horrible, petty battles I've seen—really helped me understand early on that good people can still make bad couples," she explains. "And that I need to be true to myself in my own relationships."

It may be an emotional act, but divorce, when we strip it down to its barest definition, is a cold, hard thing. We all know what the legal process entails: Parents must disentangle their joined lives, and the transaction can grind along slowly, the cogs stiff and intractable as Mom and Dad haggle over all their shared possessions, including us. They must settle the new ground rules of their relationship in terms of financial support, visitation, and custody, translating their years of marriage into what each person "owes" and "deserves." Every claim demands negotiation between two adversaries who, more likely than not, cannot stand the sight of each other.

The assumed realm of judicial procedure often acts as a ruse, with the fierce emotions unleashed by divorce simply channeled from the bedroom into the courtroom, but this time with lawyers and judges occupying the powerful position of legislating the emotional content of family life. Affairs, sexual habits, the time Dad worked late instead of attending your birthday party or Mom left you in the care of an incompetent baby-sitter—all these personal exploits and failings can now be aired for public scrutiny, interpretation, and judgment with the full brunt of the hurt and anger that lies behind them. "What's the moral of this story?" asks a divorce lawyer played by Danny DeVito toward the end of the 1989 film *War of the Roses,* a black comedy illustrating how quickly divorce can escalate into a cruel battle of wills. He leans forward and says, "A civilized divorce is a contradiction in terms."

Nothing gives more insight into the gritty dealings of divorce than reading through some of the volumes for men and women that line the bookshelves. *Winning Your Divorce: A Man's Survival Guide; Divorce: A Woman's Guide to Getting a Fair Share; Screw the Bitch: Divorce Tactics for Men.* The titles are no less harsh than the advice found within their pages.

Here's the game plan: If you're considering a divorce, clean out your joint bank accounts, change your will, and cancel your credit cards before even discussing the possibility with your soon-to-be ex. If you want custody of the children, start shutting your spouse out of their lives. Men, learn how to cook (judges love a father who serves his child a hot meal). Women, keep track of and document all your husband's defects as a father. Stay put in the family house, no matter how unpleasant, and be prepared to barter custody terms for reduced child support payments, if that's an option. If you suspect your spouse is having an affair, hire a private detective; if you're the one having an affair, put it on hold for the time being, or if you are too much under passion's knuckle, watch your rearview mirror for any suspicious-looking vehicles. Don't let guilt affect your ability to play hardball. "Your wife and others may attempt to work on your emotions. They will argue that your tough tactics are indeed hurting your children," warns a divorce guide for men. "This is nonsense: Your children do not leave you voluntarily; the system takes them away. Your children do not destroy your standard of living. But the system will destroy you economically if you let it."

Besides, all is fair in love and war, and make no mistake: This is war.

Whether our parents followed such counsel or not, the mere existence of these show-no-mercy advice books reveals just how far the best interests of the parent can acceptably diverge from the best interests of the child. On some level, almost all children of divorcing parents must, at one time or another, make the difficult traverse across the middle ground between the two of them; but when parents continue to engage in open conflict rather than compromise, their children are sentenced to remain there in virtual isolation.

"I was always trying to keep peace between my feuding parents, worried all the time about one of them getting angry at me for something I did or said about the other, like innocent comments that weren't meant for repeating. I felt like I had the weight of the world on my shoulders," explains thirty-one-year-old Amanda, whose parents divorced when she was six. "It was one big, ongoing, twelve-year conflict over everything: custody, who was sleeping with whom, schools, tuition . . . you name it, they fought about it." She describes waiting in her father's driveway one night while her mother broke into his house to repossess some of her belongings, including the family cat. "My father came home during the 'robbery' and locked her out of the house. My mother started throwing rocks at the window, and he came out and threw a rock through her car window, with my brother and me in the back. The window broke and the shattered glass cut my brother's arm. My mom saved the bloody rock for years as 'evidence.' "

For Amanda, the animosity between her parents continues to mark the zones of her past, present, and future. "My parents are enemies still," she explains. "They ruined my wedding by fighting—through me, since they don't talk—over every little thing: My stepfather not participating in the wedding. My mother wanting a front-row seat far away from my father. My parents even had a huge blowout at the rehearsal dinner, with my father threatening not to come to the wedding because my mother came over to 'his side' of the room and spoke to his sister. I regretted attempting the traditional wedding. It was as if the divorce happened yesterday." Amanda has now been married for two years, and recently gave birth. "My biggest fear is putting my kids through what I went through. I will never divorce my husband, because I don't want to hurt my children," she admits. "But I also think I'm very defensive with him. When we fight, I will say, 'If you want a divorce, fine, but I'm keeping the house and the kids.' It's like I don't want to get hurt by him, so I'm mentally putting up my guard in case he leaves." It's not that far a stretch, once we've witnessed divorce as a child, to believe that a disagreement puts us one step away from the court-room.

When parents become so involved in their campaigns against each other that they lose sight of how their behavior is affecting us, they offer up an especially damaging model of love in reverse; their unions have not ended with a divorce decree, but mutated into another type of marriage altogether, one bound by bitterness and animus. After treading through the wreckage of our parents' battles—from alimony payments to custody suits—we come away with a deep, lasting impression of how high the stakes are in marriages gone wrong. As one thirty-year-old woman whose parents divorced when she was seven puts it, "I have ended virtually every relationship I've been in because sharing my fears, my needs, my expectations feels more risky than just leaving. People can get married, then divorced, and the person you thought was your lifelong partner becomes a complete stranger—or even worse: someone who turns on you, hates you, and knows your weaknesses." This is not simply paranoia. We've seen it happen before.

Courtroom Dramas

When twenty-two-year-old Dana describes the day she had to testify in court during her parents' custody battle over a decade ago, her voice still catches. "That was the hardest thing I ever had to do. My sister and I were sitting with my dad and his new wife on one side of the room, and my mom was sitting by herself on the other side. I felt so bad for her." At the time of the divorce, when she was in the second grade, Dana and her sister began living with their father and stepmother during the school year and spending summers across the country with their mother. Four years later, however, her mother remarried and, feeling financially secure enough to support her two children, sued for custody. Although Dana was eager to live with her mother full-time, she was also torn about leaving her father. "I was in the sixth grade, too young to form my own opinions about what was going on," she explains. "Meanwhile, I was getting secondhand information from my parents, who wanted me to like them for some custody battle. I couldn't be who I was; I was whoever my parents wanted me to be. It was *awful*."

Back in the courthouse, Dana and her sister were separated from their parents and led into a separate conference room to speak with a mediator, who asked them questions and scribbled down notes when they answered. Then he asked them point-blank where they wanted to live. "My sister said she wanted to live with my mother. As for me, well, my father had been giving me such special treatment, and I thought he loved me and wanted me to stay with him, so I said I was having second thoughts, but I still wanted to live with my mother," Dana recalls. "After that, he brought my parents in. My mother was crying, and the judge told her to stop, that her crying would influence us. That made me angry. What right did he have to tell my mother what to do? Then we all went into the courtroom, and the judge said, 'Since both children want to live with their father, I see no reason for this case. Case closed.' I remember his exact words." Dana pauses. "I turned to my mom and she just started crying, then I turned to my dad, and he had this big smile on his face, like he had *won*. All I could think was 'That's not true. That's not the way it happened.' For a while, I wanted to become a lawyer, because I felt like that should never happen to someone else."

Like Dana, many children exposed to the legal workings of custody gain an alarming sense of their own powerlessness against a larger system. With divorce, essential strangers—namely lawyers and judges—are given the right to intrude into our lives. Even the most basic matters of family interaction, the kind usually taken for granted, are now potentially subject to legal mediation and final rulings: Family court can conceivably dictate the terms of a child's participation in religious holidays, summer vacations, birthdays, weddings, and reunions. Lawyers can be hired to resolve conflicts over anything from paying school tuition to contesting the other parent's choice of a child's dentist, doctor, or therapist. In short, the family opens up into a fully regulated, glaringly public, institutional arrangement.

The law is supposed to protect children in divorcing families, placing them in the care of the most capable parent; unfortunately, this is not always the case. Sometimes the whims of judges preside over fact, or the genuine interests of the child become muddled in wildly divergent testimonies and twisted truths. Says a thirty-six-year-old woman whose father was awarded custody in her parents' divorce when she was eleven, "In the eyes of an old-fashioned small-town judge, my mother was not a 'fit' mother—she was running around with 'unacceptable' men—but she was definitely the better parent." As each parent jockeys for position, a child's wishes may not be adequately represented or understood during custody suits. In *The Custody Wars,* attorney and law professor Mary Ann Mason points out that juvenile delinquents receive their own counsel in the courtroom, as do children who are allegedly the victims of abuse, but children of divorcing parents are often deprived of a voice. Rather, Mason concludes, in the current legal system, these children are reduced to an "emotional property right," with courts focusing more on a parent's access to a child than what would be the healthiest situation for that child.

Thirty-eight-year-old Malcolm, whose parents divorced when he was fifteen, was horrified to discover that his mother had been granted custody. His mother was both emotionally and physically abusive, and Malcolm had assumed it would be a clear-cut case in determining custody: He should go and live with his father. "I thought I would die," he says, remembering his reaction to the news. "I knew the only thing worse than living with both of them would be living with my mother alone, and I was right." As Malcolm later learned, the question was never even raised at the custody hearing; his father had been informed earlier by his lawyer that he had "no hope in hell" of winning custody and should drop the issue. "I saw how divorce law can penalize men and children. My father, who is almost seventy now, and makes less than ten dollars an hour, is still required to pay alimony to my mother, who got ownership of the house, made more money than he did until her recent retirement, and has approximately a quarter-million dollars in the bank," Malcolm says. "I know firsthand how lawyers may use a couple's unhappiness as a vehicle for degrading both parties and how judges can use the law as an alibi against human responsibility."

Parents can also use the dog-eat-dog mentality of the legal system as justification for abdicating parental responsibility. For twenty-two-year-old Laura, watching her mother descend into battle blindness during the divorce settlement was perhaps even more disturbing than the prospect of relinquishing her fate to judges and lawyers. Without an advocate of her own, Laura found herself at the mercy of her mother's angry determination to triumph over her father; she regularly disparaged him in front of Laura and actively sought to influence her child's testimony. "She fed me a ton of lies about my father, even tried to convince me he was gay," Laura explains. "She was able to turn me against him, and for a few months I wouldn't even speak to him. I was afraid of him. The worst thing I had to do was actually get on the stand and answer pointed attorney questions that tried to imply every horrible thing imaginable about my father. They were loaded questions, and I had been coached on how to answer them. I did what my mom wanted because I didn't want her mad at me—it would only make my life a living hell. In the end, she got everything—two cars, the house, half the escrow, me, almost all the furniture, plus child support."

During the divorce proceedings, her mother started dating a man whom she would later marry, and for Laura, this new relationship provided added tension to the drama unwinding in the courtroom. "My stepfather was always concerned with how much money my mother was getting," Laura says. "One of the few things my father did get in the divorce was the kitchen table. So my stepfather took a knife and carved his name and my mom's name on the surface. Later, he tried to say I did it. I didn't even like him—why would I do that?" She sighs. "It was a really bad situation."

A few months after the divorce settlement went through, Laura was so miserable living with her mother and stepfather that she decided to move in with her father. "My mother had changed, and she and my stepfather would drink excessively when they were together, and I mean a lot," Laura says. "I would go to my room, shut the door, and listen to music. I also read a lot. The two of them didn't really care what I did." So without warning her mother beforehand, Laura and her father arranged for a policeman to escort her to his house the day she moved out. "That way I could pack my bags and leave," she explains. "It wasn't to hurt my mom, it was just what we thought was best; I could leave with all my stuff. Because to this day, my stepfather still has a lot of my father's things—tools and fishing poles—that my father will never see again."

In the context of a contentious divorce, Laura and her father saw no other option but to orchestrate her escape from her mother's home, with a policeman running interference. Laura's mother never challenged her decision to leave, but she also never paid any child support to Laura's father. Today, resentment still lingers between mother and daughter. "My mom makes little comments that she's mad at me for choosing my dad over her," Laura says. "I don't think she understands that I wasn't choosing one parent over the other. I was choosing a better environment for me to grow up in."

Thirty-one-year-old Alice faced a similar choice during her childhood. When Alice's parents divorced, she was only four years old—too young to make a decision about where she wanted to live—and her mother was granted custody. By the time she entered first grade, however, she was well aware that her father found the situation unacceptable. "My mom was living in an apartment with this guy who was in the entertainment business," Alice explains, "so my father thought she was leading this wild life." Her father had remarried and moved into a house in the suburbs—a more suitable environment, he believed, in which to raise his daughter. "Every weekend when I would go to visit him, he would say, 'Don't you want to live with me?' Of course, when you're a kid, you're like, 'Sure!' " One Sunday afternoon, while she and her father sat parked in his car outside her mother's apartment building, they rehearsed the speech she would give her mother when she went inside. "My father said, 'Now when you go upstairs, what are you going to say?' And just like he had told me, I said, 'I'm putting my foot down. I want to move out of the city.' And I did it. I walked upstairs and put my foot down. My mom just looked at me and said, 'Okay. I'm not going to stop you.' "

But after three years of living with her father, Alice wanted to move back in with her mother. "I was kind of a pariah in the suburbs," she admits with a wry smile. "It was the mid-seventies, and not too many parents were divorced yet. So there I was, this girl from the city with divorced parents who spent every weekend visiting her mom. And my mom would dress me up in these Laura Ashley–type dresses and cowboy boots, and I had really long hair. I looked different. I felt it," she explains. "But I was too afraid to say to my dad 'I don't want to live with you anymore.' How could I say that? And the truth is, my father would never have let me go without a fight."

So Alice's parents hired lawyers to solve the question of where she would live. At one point, tempers raged out of control—with her parents each taking a turn "kidnapping" Alice outside of their prescribed visitations—causing the judge to appoint Alice's grandparents as her legal custodians until the end of the hearing. "It finally came down to the judge calling me into his quarters and saying, 'Look, I need you to make a decision. You seem relatively mature, so what's it going to be?' " Alice frowns at the memory. "So, in front of both of my parents, I had to say what it was going to be." Even years later, her discomfort at saying aloud that she wanted to live with her mother is apparent. "I can remember getting into my dad's car after the ruling. My parents had agreed that I would finish up the school semester with him. He slammed the door shut after I got in and wouldn't talk to me the entire ride home. Later, he said to me, 'If you don't want to be a part of this family or this community, then I'm pulling you out of band and Girl Scouts and the school play.' And he did."

When our parents have unalterable and opposing aims some of us can find ourselves weaving in and out of the courtroom to settle family matters throughout our childhood. Arguments over child support in particular can last for years. Thirty-year-old Megan recently testified at her father's third divorce hearing, as a witness for his soon-to-be ex-wife, offering up information about her father's finances. After her parents divorced when she was thirteen, her father rarely paid child support and refused to contribute to her college education. "I showed up in court with bags—all my financial information from college and graduate school. I had the paper trail," she says. "I am still furious. I pay the bills for my education simply because he didn't want to accept his responsibilities. My choices are limited." She adds, "I never expected that more than fifteen years later, I'd still be feeling and living the repercussions of my parents' divorce."

Money Equals Love

Most of us have at least one story involving an argument about money following our parents' divorce, and here's mine: I am seventeen years old and have just traveled across the country in preparation for my first day of college—a college that happens to be only a few minutes' drive away from my mother's new house. I'm in my dorm room, and have already unpacked my bag, hung my clothes in the closet, and put my books on the shelves. Sitting in my room, which overlooks a grassy quad, I watch as the other students arrive lugging their suitcases, with parents by their side. A rap song blares out of someone's open window, and as I take in a breath of warm air, a wisp of excitement rises in my stomach.

A couple of hours later, I stop by my mother's house to pick up a check for the first semester's tuition so I can register for my classes the next day. "*Your father* has still not paid his half," she complains when I show her the bill. Of course, it is my duty to smooth out the wrinkle. I call up my father and am stunned when he tells me that after thinking about it, he has decided not to pay. His voice is tight. "I don't want you in *that woman's* sphere of influence," he says to me. "If she wants you nearby, let *her* pay for it." We argue, but he refuses to budge. My mother, who has been hovering by the phone, finally grabs the receiver away from me.

Then all hell breaks loose. As they scream at each other, I run upstairs to my sister's room and close the door. The tears come, and I desperately try to swallow them away. My sister joins me, alarmed by the sight of my crying, and we huddle together on her bed. In the distance, I hear the phone slam down, then my mother climbing the stairs. She swings open the door in a rage. I gather from her ranting that my father said some version of "Fuck you" before hanging up on her.

"I could slit his throat," my mother yells. "I will not be taken advantage of like this. He has to pay his half."

I suppose I could have convinced one or both of them to give in, but suddenly I am too exhausted to even try. The next day, I pull down my one poster, throw my clothes back into my bag, and load up the car. All I know is that I have to get out. I spend the next few days scrambling to find another college that will accept me on such short notice, and eventually, through some quick talking and downright lies, I finagle my way onto a campus that is suitably distant from both my parents. Not quite the auspicious beginning I had imagined, but at least my tuition was paid.

In my junior year of college, I am talking to my father on the phone when I decide to bring up the whole incident for discussion for the first time.

"I was really hurt by that," I say, twisting the phone cord around my wrist.

He is immediately defensive. "No, no, I wasn't trying to hurt you," he insists.

And while I may not agree with his actions, I believe him. When it comes down to it, my father was there for me every single day I was growing up; he paid for my food, my clothes, my shelter, my vacations and summer camps. Part of me can sympathize with how he might have felt betrayed when, as soon as I was old enough, I ended up moving a six-hour flight away from him and a few-minutes drive away from my mother. Besides, my mother hadn't exactly jumped in and offered to shoulder the full tuition bill, even though she could certainly have afforded it.

I know I was fortunate after my parents' divorce; both had well-paying jobs, and I escaped the fear, shame, and confusion experienced by those who found themselves plummeting on the economic scale after their parents split up. I remained in the same house and was never left wanting for material goods. Rather, except for the occasions when my parents haggled over his and her payments, money became a substitute for love. I admit I often took advantage of this new equation; I used to shamelessly extract money out of my mother, playing on her guilt to win financial compensation—she owed me. We both acted as if a check or a new outfit could make up for her absence from my daily life.

From something trivial like buying a new pair of shoes to footing the cost of an education, the financial responsibilities once implicit in the vague calculus of our parents' obligations must be reestablished in painfully explicit terms after they divorce. In the process, almost every child comes to recognize that love *can* be measured in dollars—from lavish gifts aimed at securing a child's affection to blank refusals to pay child support. Our relationship with a parent now contains a clear system of measurement: How much money am I worth? Twenty-five-year-old Cheryl, whose parents divorced when she was two, remembers looking through her father's chest of drawers once and finding a pad of paper on which he itemized everything he had bought for her in the past year. "It really hurt my feelings to see that," she says. "I thought, 'Why can't it just be normal? What can't he just buy things for me?' I knew it was something he had to do because my mom was taking him to court, but it still hurt." No child wants to convert a parent's love into dollars, but when the daily expenses of our lives are split between two parents, we often must.

With money acting as proof of a parent's love, any failure to provide support can easily be construed as a personal rejection.

"My mother would always say things like 'Tell your father to go to hell' and 'Don't you see what your father is doing to you?' On the other hand, whenever I brought up the child support issue to my father, he would say, 'All you ever want from me is money,' " says a twenty-five-year-old woman, whose parents divorced when she was thirteen. "You don't want to think that your father doesn't care about you. How do you deal with that? It slants everything." As many of us quickly discover, it is not only money, but also what it represents. We learn in no uncertain terms that money is power, and usually the most tangible link connecting mother, father, and child after divorce. Parents can wield it as a weapon with a bitterness that cuts deep.

Twenty-eight-year-old Denise grows visibly upset when she recalls a fight between her parents during her graduation from college. "My uncle threw me a brunch, and my mom said I could invite my dad," she says. "But as soon as my dad shows up, my mother makes some comment like 'You better thank my brother for paying for this.' It's always all about money with my mom. My dad started to raise his voice a little bit, and things escalated until I was ready to just walk out. My brother finally stood up and told my mother to shut up. This was my day, and she had no right to spoil it. I couldn't take it anymore. I stormed out then, and my mother yelled at me later for behaving like a baby." She stops to brush the back of her hand across her eyes. "To this day, I have major, major money issues. I'm not a cheap person, but I budget things well. My boyfriend thinks I'm nuts when I sit and balance my checkbook to the penny every month; he hasn't balanced his checkbook in years. But I always feel like, financially, I want to take care of myself," she explains. "I never want to have to worry about where the money is coming from again."

Underneath the nasty comments and subtle jabs, these arguments over money are often critical. Not only do married parents generally agree on how to spend their money when it comes to their children, but two parents together usually have more money than they do apart, and for many children, divorce brings on a significant drop in economic status; and this drop was exacerbated by the economic recessions that periodically occurred during our childhood. As the rising divorce rate was causing ruptures in more and more homes over the past three decades, the world at large was also going through what historian Eric Hobsbawn calls the "crisis decades," a period marked by rampant unemployment and raging inflation. By 1988, 45 percent of single-mother homes with children under eighteen were poor, compared with only 7 percent of families headed by a married couple. For many single parents laboring to support a family on essentially one salary, economic insecurity became a way of life, and in a cruel twist, some ex-wives found themselves financially dependent on their ex-husbands after all other ties had been severed.

How many children of divorce told stories of not receiving enough child support from their fathers? Far too many, I'm afraid. Although these testimonials were one-sided, I heard about constant pleas for money, the sense of being purposely deprived of basic comforts, and parents' stubborn refusals to pay out of spite. Some fathers had remarried and were more concerned with supporting their new families. Many remember waiting for a check that never came, or came too late, or was for the wrong amount. Several told of lying about a father's salary on financial aid forms for college when he refused to pay for tuition, because they wouldn't qualify otherwise. Some were even put in the position of having to read through a father's tax returns to try and figure out whether his inability to pay was valid or not.

Thirty-year-old Theresa describes how her father, who earned a six-figure salary, refused to pay child support to her mother. Ten years after their divorce, he had racked up $60,000 in back payments. "This is when the laws were changing about being a deadbeat dad," she says. "And the judge said he was going to have to put my father in jail unless he gave us some money. The judge told him, 'You can give me a hundred dollars, give me anything.' And my dad said no, like he was in some sort of pissing contest." Rather than pay, her father spent a month in jail. "The day he got out, he picked me up from school and took me hiking, of all things. I'm sixteen, and I don't want to go hiking, but we go because apparently when I was three we would hike in this place. The entire time I'm thinking, 'You're having some kind of moment and it's lost on me.' We're sitting on this rock, and he asks, 'Do you know what your mother did to me?' I say, 'I know you were in jail,' and he says, 'I was in jail because of you.' He actually tried to blame it on me, saying I was selfish, that he didn't owe me, that just because I was his daughter didn't mean that I was entitled to anything." She shakes her head. "After that I pretty much stopped talking to him."

After a childhood of watching her mother struggle financially and her father manipulate money at her expense, Theresa is grappling with money issues in her own relationship. "My mom is always telling me to keep my money separate. 'Don't trust anyone.' So I'm very leery of talking about money with my boyfriend. But at the same time, I think, 'If he really loved me, he would put everything in my name.' It's so frightening for me, because money's a big one. I see it as freedom."

In divorces that bring about a drastic change in economic status, the fallout can be far-reaching. During her first seventeen years, twenty-nine-year-old Caitlin lived in several different towns across the country and in Europe, while her mother tried to move forward financially; when a new location promised easier circumstances, such as the help of a relative or the prospect of a better job, they picked up and left. "I was a year old when they separated, so the divorce itself was minimally traumatic," Caitlin explains. "We slipped into poverty, and I blame the financial impact for most of the unhappiness in my childhood. We moved a ridiculous amount, so I never got to establish long-term friendships where I felt like people knew me well enough to be like, 'Hey, let's hang out.' I was always the new kid in class, and I felt like I had to very quickly impress people and make friends, because we would probably be leaving in a few months. I started to think that if they got to know me, maybe they would find out I'm lacking in some way."

The strain was hard not only on Caitlin but on her mother too. "When my mother was relaxed and happy, she was so loving, really affectionate," Caitlin recalls, talking fast. "But most of the time, we were worrying about bills. Or you would ask for something you shouldn't have asked for. Or you accidentally left dishes in the sink, and Mom has just come home tired from working so many hours so she can support you and it turns into this terrible thing. There was a lot of shame around our household; we did not have visitors, and part of that was due to money. We were not going to live up to the expectations of a household. We didn't sit down together as a family. We felt sort of unofficial."

Compared with her mother, Caitlin says, her father was "living the high life," with an array of new cars, gourmet groceries, and travel to exotic locales. On the rare occasions when Caitlin saw him, her father treated her like a princess. When the difference between two homes is one of grittiness versus glitter, we become caught in a web of stinging resentment and guilty pleasure.

"There was sort of a Dr. Jekyll/Mr. Hyde thing going on," she explains. "When I was with my dad, it was great. He was bestowing all this fun stuff on me—fancy restaurants, hot-air ballooning, and amusement parks—but when I was with Mom, away from it all, there was a general understanding that Dad was a bad guy and not sharing all he has. My mom would tell me I had a separate relationship with my dad from her, but then I would come back from seeing him, wearing some new satin outfit, and she would freak out." She pauses. "So that was a total lie. I tried to divide my father in my mind between the stories I heard and the person I knew, but you can't really. And he can't be let off the hook just because he called once in a while and asked us how we were doing. He never asked anything deeper than that, like, 'Are you embarrassed by the clothes your mom is getting you from garage sales, the 1960s grandma dresses you have to wear when everyone else is wearing Guess? jeans?' "

Children must devise narratives complex enough to encompass both their love for each of their parents and an unreliable flow of child support that affects their everyday lives. This is not an easy task, especially when they become involved in the battle over money. As Larry, twenty-eight, remembers, "My mom held herself together as best she could, but the money coming from my dad was sometimes late and she had to fight him for it. People thought she was nuts for keeping us in private school and preserving the Harvard/Yale–type college dreams for us, but she stuck to it, and that in itself created more pressure." Although Larry realizes how hard his mother had to work to support her children after the divorce, and knows her efforts were rooted in love, he disagrees with how she handled the issue of child support. He explains:

> Her reaction was to basically shove all of it down our throats. The bad-mouthing of our father was constant. When she couldn't get money from him, she made us essentially go beg for it for her. I ended up playing judge and jury much more than I wanted to, going back and forth between them trying to determine the truth, as if I was putting both of them on trial for lying and hiding money and slander. It was not fun. It was difficult to acknowledge her sacrifices when she shoved it down our throats constantly. Which made her disappointed. Which turned the whole thing into a somewhat vicious circle: The more she told us how much she had given up for us, the less we wanted to hear it.

When parents put a price on their pain, demanding recognition for their sacrifices as well as acknowledgment of the other parent's shortcomings, children are left in a precarious position. Twenty-eight-year-old Samantha explains how her mother was forced to enter the workplace with few marketable skills after her parents divorced when she was two. "Basically her life ground to a halt for twenty years," she says. "I mean, she worked all the time and finally went to graduate school when I was in junior high, but in a sense, she has always made me feel as if she sacrificed everything for me. She would always say, 'I'd give you the shirt off my back,' but you know what that does? I never really thought about it until much later, but you shouldn't be telling that to your kid."

For Samantha, a childhood spent watching her mother work hard to support the two of them, along with a creeping guilt at their plight, has fired a fierce determination to maintain a level of financial independence in her own marriage. "It's funny," she says. "I don't fear adultery or abandonment—I fear not having money. Or constantly fighting about money." Very quickly after getting married, Samantha insisted on opening up her own checking account and splitting the bills evenly. "All my married friends think it's crazy that we have separate checking accounts, that it's a bad sign the way we divide our money, but I say to them, 'You know, do what works for you.' Of course, our money is our money, but I'm still making sure that I'm taking care of myself. I told my husband that we need to be making two hundred thousand dollars before we have children," she says. "He thinks I'm crazy, but I had this figure in my head to indicate when I would be ready. It's not an emotional benchmark—it's practical. I still believe that money problems rip apart a marriage like nothing else," she points out. "And I don't ever want to resent my kids. My mother made me feel so damned responsible for her angst. My husband always says, 'You won't resent your kids,' but you know, I may. That's my fear, because marriages you can end; it's difficult and painful, but with a child, that's permanent."

Samantha's plan makes perfect sense to me. After growing up in an uncertain world of broken promises, fallible parents, and economic ambiguity, money offers the best bet for security. Money we can depend on in a way that we can't rely on people; money we can see and touch; money makes us independent. That's why I also make silent deals with myself: Never depend on someone else to support me, either financially or emotionally. Always make sure I have a place to live in case a relationship falls apart. "If we ever decide to have children, maybe we should draw up a contract beforehand," I say teasingly to my boyfriend. "Just to make sure we're on the same page about our responsibilities as parents." My boyfriend laughs. I'm only half-joking. My thinking? At least then, maybe, we have negotiated out of love, rather than hostility. Because I know that as thin cover for the passions brewing around a breakup, a divorce settlement, especially from a child's perspective, is mainly an emotional contract. Our parents may have been in charge of dividing their assets, but we were often the ones left carrying the scorecards of guilt, blame, and gratitude; and sometimes we end up carrying these scorecards into our other relationships.

When the conflict of divorce continues into the adult years, we are not given the space to heal. The not-so-subtle message in their behavior is that they hate each other more than they love us. By the time we reach adulthood, many of our parents have become increasingly numb to the ways in which their actions still bruise, perhaps believing that we have developed a thick skin over the years. "It's so weird for me, because my parents' divorce just never seemed to end. They could never let it go. It is only in the last three years, since I stopped talking to my dad, that it has started to get better, mainly because my mother has nothing to talk about with me now. Believe me, she would love to talk ad nauseam about my father," says one thirty-year-old woman, shaking her head. "It took more than twenty years to end." Another twenty-five-year-old woman discusses how her father wouldn't even say hello to her mother when they were forced together at her sister's wedding, being too wrapped up in his own hostility to even make an attempt to be civil. "Maybe if my parents could get over their divorce," she says, sighing, "I could too."

II

Broken Homes,
Broken Hearts

Life seemed all
loss, and what was more
I'd lost whatever it was
before I'd even had it

—Thom Gunn, "Autobiography"

4

Kiss Childhood Good-bye

WHEN I WAVED GOOD-BYE to my mother on that autumn afternoon thirteen years ago, I knew even then that day would mark the end of my childhood more than my first date or going off to college ever could. I no longer had a mother, at least in the everyday sense of the word, and as a teenage girl, the implications of this loss were staggering. I felt as if I had stepped through a looking glass, and from the other side everything looked wavy, warped, and completely surreal.

Alone, lying in bed that afternoon, I considered the possibility that my father, unwilling to raise a daughter on his own, might keep on driving and never return. Did I really believe this? I don't know. All I knew was that one of my parents had left me, and so who was to say the other one wouldn't too? I don't know how many hours passed, but it wasn't until after dark that my father's car finally pulled back into the driveway, the roar of the engine cutting through the silence. When I ventured out of my bedroom, I found him settling in at the kitchen table with a plate of leftovers. I stood watching his profile from the doorway, and that's when it really hit me: Everything was about to change.

When I think back to the year or so immediately following the divorce, I see my father's face closing down into a stony mask and hear the faint strains of the radio behind the shut door to his bedroom. When he thinks back to those years, he tells me now, he remembers a brooding adolescent always on her way out the door. Just as my father carefully avoided exposing any of my raw emotional nerves, I did the same, both of us seeking a relative safety in suppression. We were, for a while, simply two roommates living in the same house, rotating around each other but not connecting. Instead, we each dealt with the divorce privately, in our own separate ways.

Faced with so many bare rooms, my father set out, with a single-minded urgency, to wipe away all remaining traces of our former life. I watched helplessly as he rearranged what furniture was left and pulled up the carpeting my mother had chosen, muttering all the while that he had always hated carpeting. For three months my father laid down tiles in the family room, his white T-shirt damp with sweat as he slathered grout between the cracks with a feverish intensity. He decorated his bedroom walls with sailing photographs, and snaked a hose through the window to fill up his new water bed. He tore down the cartoon wallpaper that lined my sister's old bedroom, wallpaper that I had picked out and helped to paste up before she was born. I can still picture the brightly colored figures carrying balloons. In its place, he put up a simple floral pattern more appropriate for what was to be our new "guest room," although we rarely had guests.

Not that I blame him, then or now, for systematically dismantling the home I had always known. He needed to blast the slate clean, to remake the house as his and his alone; he certainly didn't need daily reminders of what no longer existed. We were, however, in two different places on this matter—while he was almost forty and eager to distance himself from the past, I was thirteen and felt every change as an irrevocable loss. I felt like I was fast disappearing into the distance, set loose as the ties to my past were cut one by one. I believed there was a safety in objects, that they represented concrete markers of my history, my identity, my place. Without them, the home that wrapped around me was at once familiar and foreign, and I wandered through the disconcerting patchwork of rooms, trying to figure out where I fit in.

My father's manic energy finally simmered down into a rather nondescript depression that inscribed itself in subtle ways. He seemed distant, the sarcastic wit that had always made me laugh gone somewhere subterranean. Unable to deal with the visible signs of his suffering, I found solace in my friends' homes. On the occasional evenings we spent together, my father and I sat in two rocking chairs in front of the television, hardly speaking, like an old retired couple.

But it was just the two of us, and we only had each other. One night, not long after the divorce, I came home and found my father in bed, curled up with burning stomach spasms. "I need to go to the hospital," he groaned, painkillers scattered across the bedspread. Not knowing whom else to call, and too young to drive him myself, I dialed my mother's number, and she rushed us to the nearest emergency room. As my father was carted away, my mother and I sat mute under the harsh fluorescent lights of the hospital waiting area, surrounded by general hysteria. Later, after my father had been secured in a hospital bed, an intravenous tube taped to his arm, my mother said good-bye to me outside the doorway of his room. I stayed, holding my father's hand until he was released. We took a taxi home.

Nevertheless, for the better part of my adolescence, I was angry at my father, partly because I was a teenager, and he was the easiest target at whom to direct my rage; partly because I felt he had isolated himself within his own fortress, and my anger was the only way I could get through; partly because he was only one parent instead of two. I can't identify the point when our relationship changed. I can only say that it did. Somewhere along the way, both my anger and his reticence dissipated, and we reached a new level of understanding that hadn't existed either before or immediately after my parents divorced. I will never forget how, in the midst of final exams during my first year of college, my father sent me a cardboard box filled with CDs, chocolates, and books. Or all the times he rearranged his work schedule to take care of me, even driving four hours when I had my wisdom teeth out a few years ago, so he could pick me up from the dentist.

Today, my father and I are very close, the type of closeness engendered by going through a difficult situation together and coming out on the other side. My father never remarried and still lives in the same house I grew up in. I constantly beg for him to move, but he assures me that he's content staying; I worry about him anyway. Sometimes I wonder why this is so important to me now, to see him leave this house of memories, and the best answer I can come up with is a selfish one: I guess a part of me feels guilty for leaving him alone, although we talk regularly, sometimes for an hour or two. He is often the first person I ask for advice, on everything from relationships to career choices; he sends me vitamins and magazine articles he knows I'll find interesting. I love my father, and although he isn't the type to say it, I know how much he loves me.

Still, it wasn't until the divorce had passed from crisis into fact that my father was able to fully step in and offer me a stable source of love and guidance; for those years in between, he wasn't always available. "You raised yourself," he says to me now with regret, and while I realize how hard it must have been for him to suddenly be thrust into the role of both mother and father—especially since he was dealing with his own hurt at the same time—a little voice in my head can't help but reply, "*You* were the only parent I had. What other choice did I have?"

Consider these images: A six-year-old girl sits and listens as her mother recounts the problems in her broken-up marriage, down to sexual incompatibilities. An eleven-year-old boy wraps his thin arms around his mother's neck at night while she cries on his shoulder after his father leaves. A seventeen-year-old girl steps in to run the household, paying all the bills and making sure her younger brother and sister arrive at school on time, because her mother is too exhausted from working two jobs. I heard many such stories, and despite the differences in their ages when their parents divorced, more than *two-thirds* of those I interviewed said the same thing—"I had to grow up too soon, too fast."

Divorce performs a powerful alchemy on our maturity level. While separation may bring about a cease-fire in the daily fighting between parents, the changes that accompany divorce make us vulnerable in different ways: Some children find themselves moving out of their family home, wrenched from their friends, and starting over at a different school in a new city. Familiar furnishings vanish, and money can suddenly become scarce. Says one twenty-seven-year-old woman, whose parents fought bitterly during their divorce when she was seven, "At one point, I tried to hide the living room furniture just so we would still have couches and chairs." Her action covers up a deeper truth: With the family in upheaval, many children feel defenseless and alone. In a relatively short period of time, all of our attachments—whether to people, places, or objects—are to some degree severed.

I know that after my family was bisected down the middle, my father and I spent a couple of years flailing wildly from the cut. At first, we didn't quite know how to interact with each other, how to function as a father-daughter pair, rather than a family unit. Like many children and their suddenly single parents, we had to struggle to reestablish our relationship according to new ground rules. With one parent taking on the everyday responsibilities of two, children become doubly reliant on a parent to fulfill several roles, from caretaker to disciplinarian, even if they didn't occupy these roles before.

"In the beginning, of course, there was complete devastation and fear after my mother left," says thirty-six-year-old Helen, who lived with her father after her parents divorced when she was thirteen. With her mother gone, Helen found herself entirely dependent on a father who had been mostly distant during her childhood. She explains:

> Before the divorce, it was the typical setup: My mother would threaten us kids with "You wait until your father gets home!" if we were acting out, so he was the person we were fearful of. We didn't see him very much. He was the man; he was the rule-keeper. But as things started to come up after the divorce, my relationship with my father started to change. Unlike my girlfriends at the time, who had their mothers around, my father got involved in those girl things. When I got my period, he felt the need to sit me down and talk to me, and I can't imagine what that must have been like for him, because at that point, I don't think he really knew me. My father had to take me to my first gynecological appointment and I'm sure his head wanted to pop off. But it didn't. He sat there and took it like a mom. Little things like that made me realize how hard he was trying to be a good dad. We just had to share things that most fathers and daughters don't share. He is my best friend to this day. I love him with all my heart, for being the kind of dad he was, and for who he helped me and let me become.

Children left in the care of a loving and supportive parent often credit that parent with giving them the emotional security central to their happiness as adults. "I think my mom did an amazing job of raising two boys on her own and working full-time. No matter what efforts my dad put in, if it hadn't been for my mom, my brother and I would have been complete disasters," says twenty-five-year-old Evan, whose parents divorced when he was four. "My mom was very busy, but every night she would come home from work, make us dinner, and the three of us would sit down and eat by candlelight. That was very important, to have that time so we could each talk about our day, and we kept up the tradition until I left for college."

But as our families are hurtled into an uncertain world, such routines can be difficult to sustain. And the absence of limits, mixed with hurt and loneliness, can set up an inviting backdrop for self-destruction. I remember sitting on the floor of my friend's bedroom shortly after my parents divorced, the late afternoon sun slipping between the slats of drawn blinds, gulping tequila out of the bottle. Heavy lids, liquid dazed. I start to giggle, drunk, plastered for the moment, finally. I remember how I loved the feeling of being numb, not caring, of losing myself to the spinning, falling. And by the time I was fifteen, I was regularly turning to alcohol to medicate my pain. Twenty-seven-year-old Sandra explains that she engaged in a similar disappearing act after her parents divorced when she was eight years old:

I started shoplifting, skipping school, experimenting with drugs. I became extremely defiant and unwilling to participate in "the family." I started becoming more insecure. I felt freakish, and I sought approval from my peers more than my parents. I guess I had a need to identify myself. Why had this happened to me? I needed to know why my life was different. And it made me angry. It's hard to say what the direct effects were, but I do know that virtually every aspect of my life had changed somewhat. When everything you know, trust, and depend on suddenly disappears, you are left facing emptiness and despair. It's impossible for your life to continue on unchanged.

For older children especially, who are more likely to feel the tension of before and after caused by divorce, the markers of progress can seem as if they've been knocked swiftly out of place. Twenty-three-year-old Lance, whose parents divorced when he was fourteen, points out, "I don't feel like I grew up in a divorced home. I felt like I had a great growing-up experience, up until my parents separated." With slivers of memory, Lance describes the house he lived in until he was thirteen years old: A backyard with a garden. Bicycles lying across the front lawn. A living room where his friends could hang out and play Nintendo. Rooms filled with the booming, and sometimes overbearing, voices of his father and older brother. "I loved that house, and I still do," he remembers. "I felt like a family there."

After the divorce, his family split apart, with Lance and his mother moving into an apartment across town while his brother and his father moved elsewhere. His mother suddenly seemed help-less—both financially and emotionally—and without his father around to act as disciplinarian, Lance admits she had little control over him. "My dad and brother used to demand all the attention when we were living together, and so I was a silent person in my house," he explains. "But then, there I was, suddenly the man of the house, and very soon kind of like the boss of the house." Mean-while, his father was going through his own adjustment to the di-vorce, and dropped out of Lance's life for a brief spell. "I felt like I didn't know him, like he was a complete stranger," he explains. "I had no idea where he was living, what he was doing, and didn't even really care, because he seemed so strange. It was like he had started a whole new life without me. In reality, that wasn't true. He just needed time away, I guess."

Divorce often puts the needs of children and parents at opposite ends of the spectrum, at least temporarily. While the chaos of di-vorce intensifies a child's wish for routine and guidance, separating parents are in the process of slicing the threads that once held their marriage, and by extension the family, together. "This is Crazy Time," Abigail Trafford writes in a book geared toward divorced men and women. "It starts when you separate and usually lasts about two years. It's a time when your emotions take on a life of their own and you swing back and forth between wild euphoria and violent anger, ambivalence, and deep depression, extreme timidity and rash actions. You are not yourself. Who are you?"

When a parent is unable to contain the strong emotions involved with discarding a previous identity, many children may find themselves echoing this very same question. Divorce acts as a door from one type of reality into another, and many parents walk through transformed. They have lost a partner, a fact that may threaten their position among friends, family, and the community; they may be anxious about being able to stay afloat financially and overwhelmed with taking on the role of single parent, wondering how they will manage alone; or they may get swept away by the thrill of liberation, eager to explore their new independence. "The divorce was definitely liberating for my mother," says thirty-year-old Leslie, whose parents divorced when she was five. "I think my mother felt like she had to live a certain life with my father, and it was incredibly unfulfilling for her. After the divorce, she moved us to the city. She was a pretty woman in her thirties and it was the seventies. She had a boyfriend who was so different from my dad. He was a producer. He wore gold chains and was really fun. And my mom had fun; for the first time, she kind of kicked up her heels and had fun." Meanwhile, though, Leslie was often left alone with a baby-sitter.

Unless left in the care of a loving guardian who continues to provide authority and guidance, children must align their responsibilities and identities in relation to their parents' behavior; these responsibilities can be psychological, such as comforting an abject parent, or more practical, such as cooking dinner, cleaning the house, and taking care of younger siblings. Regardless, the "natural order" of our childhood can seem thrown out of whack. Instead of following the rules of development—venturing gradually away from the hearth, scurrying back, then venturing farther still—children of divorce are often left without a psychological compass. For these children, divorce pushed them "out of time," and out of sync with the typical demands of childhood. While inside their feelings of responsibility and realizations about life seem to rapidly age them beyond their years, on the outside they are constantly reminded by their bodies and their environment that they are still children. Stuck in a developmental limbo, they alternate between their real and assumed ages, never quite belonging in either one.

Dana, whose parents divorced when she was seven, says her experiences dealing with stepfamilies and custody battles at an early age set her apart from her peers as she was growing up. At twenty-two, she has already been married and divorced. When she was seventeen, she met her husband, who was almost seven years her senior, and before she graduated from high school they were already engaged and living together in their own apartment. At the time, it seemed like a progression that made sense. "I always felt older than other people my age. In high school I had older friends, and when I met my husband I thought he loved me and I was ready to start my own family," she says. "Looking back, I realize I thought I knew everything, when really, I didn't know anything." After three years of marriage, during which time she worked to support them both while her husband attended graduate school, the relationship started to fall apart until they agreed to divorce.

Living on her own for the first time, Dana is now consciously trying to reverse her mental age and enjoy her youth. "I have adopted this attitude to have fun in life. Don't even worry about what other people are saying or how you look to them. But even so, in my head, I still feel like I'm thirty-two instead of twenty-two," she says, pausing to think about it. "Everything I've been through makes me have a different perspective on life and what it means. Most of my friends who are in their early twenties think, 'Oh, I'm free. Let's have fun.' And I agree with that, but I can't help but feel that you also have responsibilities. You have to take care of yourself, and if you're in a relationship, you have to take care of other people."

Obviously this notion of childhood—the belief that children inhabit a separate realm, a place of hope, fantasy, and innocence bound only by the mysterious crisscrossings of the imagination—is for the most part a social construct. Parents can and do bedevil a childhood in many ways: They can emotionally, sexually, or physically abuse their children. They can lose their jobs, fall ill, or die. Divorce is only one of the many possible disruptions that can occur during childhood, but in recent decades it has become by far the most common. "There is no perfect childhood," says one twenty-nine-year-old man whose parents divorced when he was fourteen. "Part of childhood is losing your innocence and realizing all is not right with the world. This realization may come earlier when your parents divorce, but it will come to all eventually." And that's true. But for many of us, who were forced by our parents' divorce to mature before we were emotionally ready, our developing sense of security was stunted, impacting the way we approach relationships and take on responsibility as adults.

Taking Charge: Anxiety and Responsibility

For twenty-six-year-old Cynthia, whose parents divorced when she was twelve, childhood was dramatically cut short by the changes that ensued after the divorce. "I really jumped from being this baby princess to having no freedom—freedom in terms of being able to do what I wanted to do," she says. "We moved within a year of the divorce, away from my father and his family. I was in the middle of eighth grade, so that was kind of awkward; I eventually made a couple of very close friends, but overall, I always felt really out of place. I felt very vulnerable. My mother was such a wreck that I couldn't do any of the rebellious things that might have helped me adapt; I was so scared it would push my mother over the edge, and my brother and sister would be left all alone; or that if I did something wrong, nobody would be there to pick me up."

During most of Cynthia's teenage years, her mother construed her attempts at independence as a betrayal, submerging her daughter's desires beneath her own goals. "She made it a mission to get remarried, so she would say to me, 'You have to take care of your brother and sister next weekend, because I have to go out and find someone so we can have a family again and be whole and be supported,' " Cynthia says. "She had her own issues she was struggling with, but I think there's something really dangerous in telling that to your kids."

Because of her mother's anger over the divorce, Cynthia was unable to engage in any of the traditional adolescent struggles between parent and child. "Anytime I tried to voice any opposition, basically anytime I would complain about her not being flexible, she would tell me that I didn't want her to have a better life. She would tell me I was just like my father, which was really horrible, because in the same breath she would say my father was the most horrible person on earth. If I wasn't agreeing with her, or doing exactly what she wanted me to do, then I was against her, and therefore on my father's side," Cynthia says. "I just had this sense that everything I did was going to have serious repercussions, and I still do. I can't do enough, and if I let someone down, it's an enormous deal." As soon as she was old enough to leave for college, Cynthia distanced herself from her mother and continues to keep her at arm's length. "I kind of stopped sharing with her. It's been weird," she says. "We just don't connect a lot of times because I'm on the defensive with her."

Mothers or fathers ravaged by bitterness over their divorce often make for volatile parents. Their animosity slides around them like a veil, making it difficult for their children to communicate with them. Melinda, twenty-eight, strings together a glimmering row of phrases to describe her mother before the divorce: Nurturing. Happy. Fun. Silly. Outgoing. Girl Scout leader. Her mother liked to throw wild dinner parties and sleep late on weekends. But after her parents divorced when she was seven, her mother succumbed to a deep depression:

> She basically had a nervous breakdown. She began to drink heavily all day, staying in bed crying, and went down to ninety pounds from a hundred thirty pounds. She was unable to care for us, and I did a lot of cooking and cleaning to

try to hide this. I was afraid we would be taken away. My grandparents figured out what was going on, and my grandmother took care of us. They wanted to have my mother hospitalized, but they didn't. Later, my mother became very angry and would have fits of rage, breaking and throwing things. Meanwhile, my father had moved in with his girlfriend and remarried within months after the divorce was finalized. By all accounts, he was having a great time. Family friends would spot him in nightclubs and restaurants. It got so bad that the weekend visits with our father dwindled because my mother threw fits of rage each time. When we returned to her, we would be subjected to endless interrogation, especially about my stepmother. We learned to answer with what she wanted to hear.

At first, I was concerned and protective of my mother—so worried about her. But when she started to have these episodes of rage against my father, but directed at me, I felt terrified of her. At times, I hated her.

Faced with such hostility and pressure, many children, like Melinda and Cynthia, are left without a safe outlet to release their fears and anxieties about the divorce. "I knew I was 'supposed' to hate my father, but I never did. I craved his love and attention and wanted very much to please him and gain approval," explains Melinda. "I wanted him to rescue me from my deranged mother. He was very rational, while my mother was irrational. He always seemed to be able to define some reality I felt more safe in, even though I knew he was not preoccupied with love or concern for us."

When bitterness, depression, or grief overcomes our parents after divorce, their emotional decline can appear to have no limits: The house may deteriorate into disarray; dishes pile up in the sink, and the dinner hour slips by without notice. They may lose interest in their appearance, or might turn to drugs and alcohol to ease their pain. Confronted with a parent who is so obviously miserable and wanting, many children may take on a more adult role, not only out of necessity but out of choice as well. Taking charge can provide a child with an aura of importance, with a secure niche in an insecure family, though it is often lined with self-doubt, for this intense pressure to keep things together is usually not accompanied by any specific guidelines.

Twenty-four-year-old Corinne, who was left to care for her alcoholic mother after her parents divorced when she was six, recalls, "My mother would go on these drinking binges. I remember asking her one night where she had been and she said, 'Just staring at the road.' I loved her and felt so bad for her. She became a lost soul, and in a way, a child. I became the adult. While my friends liked boys and music, I liked cleaning the house, baby-sitting for money, and staying at home. I was proud of my morals and values, although these were a result of lying and covering up for my mother. I guess I was proud no one knew. I was looked up to as being 'strong,' when really, I was insecure."

These are the children who could qualify as the success stories of divorce. From tumultuous homes, they emerged accomplished, well-behaved, and eminently responsible. But their performance, while notable, often hides a pain that numbs them to the pleasure of their achievements; this is particularly true for those who grew up feeling that making others happy was the only way to win a parent's love. "I think for some reason, after the divorce, I began to strive to be successful in lots of things, particularly school," explains a twenty-four-year-old woman, whose parents divorced when she was seven. "I also never argued. I was very supportive of happy, calm situations. I was literally perfect: straight A's, all the awards, perfect attendance." Another woman adds, "I felt I had to be perfect for someone to love me, so I tried to be the perfect daughter, student, friend."

When children of divorce must redefine their roles within their revised families, an identity based on competence and control is often the most appealing option. Furthermore, adopting more responsibilities can have its benefits; some studies show that taking on a moderate caretaking role as a child can lead to more capable and compassionate behavior in adulthood, especially among women. But, as psychologist Mavis Hetherington found, the placing of excessively high demands on daughters can also ignite feelings of self-doubt, depression, low self-esteem, a lurking sense of failure, and apprehension about performance and personal adequacy in young adulthood. Compared with girls whose parents stayed together, daughters of divorce, especially those with extremely emotionally needy mothers, are more likely to fall into a category that Hetherington refers to as "competent at a cost."

Although these women developed a fine-tuned sense of social responsibility, Hetherington found it was often saddled with elevated levels of depression and low self-worth that slid into their dealings in the home and at work. "I have this great need for reassurance, which I think comes from moving around so much as a kid, and my mother being so stressed all the time," says twenty-nine-year-old Caitlin, whose parents divorced when she was two years old. "Just recently I've had two ego blows at work, and I'm obsessing about them in a way that's so out of proportion to what happened. It's entirely this feeling of not measuring up. I'm a failure. I'm fat. I'm a loser. I get so mad at myself and wish there were a switch, or I could just tell myself, 'Well, they're wrong,' and move on."

In the long run, when children bear the weight of such a heavy load of problems and concerns, the experience informs their relationships once they enter adulthood. Thirty-eight-year-old Barbara, whose parents divorced when she was fourteen, is still trying to work through her tendency to put other people's needs before her own, a habit she picked up in childhood. "At various times growing up, I saw both my parents go through nervous breakdowns and always felt myself picking up the slack on some level. My mother would always say, 'We're more like friends than mother and daughter.' That was like the kiss of death. I was the oldest, so there was always this push and pull, this intense bonding matched by an equal level of resentment," she says. "But what that has translated into, for me as an adult, is being very good as a support person. I'm very good if someone needs help on a project, whereas what I kind of crave inside is to focus on my own achievements and my own personal goals without feeling like there's something selfish in that. There were no solid boundaries when I was growing up, and it is very difficult for me to say to someone, 'That doesn't feel comfortable,' or 'That isn't appropriate.' I'm very good at absorbing injury."

Girls, who are culturally groomed to be caretakers, typically fall into this pattern of hyperresponsibility more often than boys, who are generally encouraged to break away from their parents—especially their mothers—and seek independence outside the home. At the same time, since single parents are usually mothers, they may more readily lean on their daughters for emotional support than on their sons. Nevertheless, boys can feel the same weight of responsibility in taking care of mothers who are having trouble dealing with a divorce.

Thirty-three-year-old Henry suddenly found himself acting as the default "man of the house" at the age of fourteen. "When my parents divorced, I think my mother was still very dependent on my father, even though the quality of their relationship was godawful," he explains. "She had some college education, but she was basically a homemaker. We had just moved, and my father was working, so for him the transition after the divorce was much smoother, whereas with my mom that wasn't the case. I had to take care of her, because she didn't really know her head from her behind. So I assumed that role of buying the car and moving into the house and all that other stuff. She kind of lost it the first couple of years."

As an adult, Henry is determined to find a woman who can take care of herself. "One thing I look for is someone who is strong emotionally. I think I'm a little more sensitive on that issue than other people," he says. "For example, I'm definitely more drawn to professional women. I'm more attracted to women who are college-educated or beyond. It's always been a marker if I can go out to a social gathering or out with friends and feel comfortable with the woman I'm with—that she can navigate herself in a social situation without necessarily having me right next to her." He adds, "But there's definitely been a pattern in my relationships. I've gotten involved with women who on the surface seemed strong and sturdy, but I feel like I can't lean on them emotionally. I realize it's a much more complicated issue—it's not just about who I'm with, but that I need certain conditions before I can open up enough to take those steps."

When the events that follow divorce affect our feelings of security and self-worth, they also shape our capacity to form satisfying relationships as adults. After a childhood of taking care of others, some may continue to be drawn to emotionally dependent partners; others may go in the opposite direction and look for a partner who will take care of *them*. Still others equate depending on someone else with disappointment, especially if taking care of themselves is what they know best.

Taking Care of Ourselves: Independence and Self-Sufficiency

In describing her family life before her parents divorced when she was fourteen, twenty-six-year-old Anne recalls, "I wasn't particularly close with either parent. What I mean is that if I had questions about sex, boyfriends, drugs, and general teenage stuff, I would ask a friend, not my parents. They'd occasionally ask, 'What's happening in your life?' and I'd give the normal, noncommittal answer—'I don't know.' I guess it was the normal teenager-adult relationship."

But after the divorce, with her mother working three jobs to support the kids and her father disappearing out of sight, Anne's relationship with both parents went from normal to nearly nonexistent. At the age of fifteen, she started working, too, and remembers coming home at night to a quiet house, her mother either already asleep or still at work. "I didn't see my mother too much between the ages of fourteen and eighteen. Sometimes I'd go through a normal day without even seeing or talking to her. Basically I was alone a lot at home. My sister did her thing. My brother did his thing."

Left in a home that was basically fend-for-yourself, Anne became extremely independent and self-sufficient. Unlike the independence earned by the child who assumes the role of caretaker, the self-sufficiency developed when a family splits into a group of loosely joined individuals after divorce is based on the belief that survival is strictly personal. The lack of parental involvement can take many forms, from physical exhaustion that prohibits one from spending time with one's children to withdrawal as a way to mourn privately the end of a marriage. Since children often take their cues from the adults around them, many, having learned not to depend on their parents for guidance, will close themselves off too.

For thirty-one-year-old Steve, part of his sense of isolation came from being the only boy in a family of women. "I feel like my mother was very worried about raising a boy on her own—like if she coddled me, I wasn't going to grow up to be a *man*. So there wasn't a lot of affection," he says. "Unlike my sisters, I wasn't physically comforted when I had problems. My mother was always there for me, and I always felt like she was rooting for me, and our relationship now is great. We talk about a lot of stuff, but every now and then, I find myself expressing some hidden anger toward her. I'll even say to her, 'I don't know why I'm acting like such a jerk.' I think it comes from this sense of abandonment as a kid, but at the same time, now I'm like, 'Jesus, my mother was twenty-six with three kids,' so I understand her position."

As members of the family drift apart, home provides little pull as a refuge for children. Twenty-nine-year-old Jeremy, whose parents divorced when he was twelve, spent the first couple of years following the divorce living with his mother as she spiraled down into a deep depression; then he moved in with his father, who had remarried. As the aftershocks of the divorce rippled through their small town, both sides of the family were embroiled in the feud between his parents, making it impossible for Jeremy to ignore the hostility around him. Every time his uncle—his mother's brother—and his father ran into each other at the local bar, they would get into a fight; when his parents passed each other on the street, they would make an obscene gesture at one another. "I guess I sort of stood alone," he says. "As little kids, my sisters and I were supposed to act like adults, but my parents weren't really acting like adults, and everyone was pointing the finger—or giving each other the finger, I should say—and it all seems very childish now that I look back. But my grandpa, to this day, will not talk to my father, even though they both still live in my hometown."

When family life becomes disjointed, with parents acting like children or retiring to the sidelines of a child's life, notions of discipline and authority can fade away. With his entire family caught up in the divorce, Jeremy was left to essentially raise himself. "I matured on my own terms," he says, recalling how he became something of a troublemaker. "For a while there, I was on a one-way track to graduate from parole school. I fought with other kids, pulled pranks on teachers, got in trouble with the law a couple of times," he says with a laugh, then quickly adds, "Nothing malicious. I just had no respect for authority. And puberty didn't help. You have a million other things on your mind, and your parents are as moody as you are. At some point, I realized that my happiness was going to depend on me, since I wasn't getting much support from anyone else."

Although Jeremy now prides himself on his self-sufficiency and ambition, qualities he says he owes to his parents' divorce, the same self-reliance prohibits him from getting too close to someone. "It's like this blind shutter I can't get through," he says. "Maybe I can never open myself up like that." When children are left to their own devices, without the safety of family support, their hard-won autonomy can mask a deeper insecurity and sense of rejection.

"Because I never really had a father, I became a very independent person, and that independence has really helped me in my career," says twenty-seven-year-old Sonia, whose parents divorced when she was five. At the age of sixteen, Sonia left Asia and emigrated to the United States by herself. But her tough exterior, she admits, belies a more vulnerable interior. "I think there will always be some weakness inside of me, a part of me that yearns for love and reassurance. I feel like my father really never cared about me, and right now, I don't even know where he is. I used to go out with a lot of guys, but my relationships never lasted more than three months. I had all these promiscuous relationships that weren't very stable, and looking back, I see now that I was insecure." Contradictory as it may seem, many of us beam qualities of strength to the outside world *because* we feel so susceptible to being hurt. When divorce erodes at our sense of safety, being fiercely independent, we tell ourselves, is our best protection from ever feeling lonely or wounded again.

Adolescence: Love, Sex, and Divorce

In my own personal developmental time line, my parents' divorce butted in somewhere after I read my first Jackie Collins novel—a dog-eared copy my friends and I secretly passed around—and before I experienced my first kiss. After going through my parents' separation, though, the prospect of harmless flirtation had lost some of its luster. Thirty-year-old Megan, whose parents also divorced when she was thirteen, says she felt exactly the same way.

> I ran across my seventh-grade photograph recently, which is completely horrendous because I'm in the middle of puberty—but I have this big smile on my face. My eighth-grade picture, though, I look like someone died. It's just funny, these captured moments in time, and the difference between the two photos, only a year apart. It was so weird for me to look back and see that. That summer between seventh and

eighth grade, when my parents announced they were getting a divorce, I felt like I had gone from being a kid just taking those first steps toward adulthood to, boom, you're an adult. I really felt like it happened instantly. It wasn't like I had a chance to discover all those things that kids have to feel their way around and learn. I learned way too much about adult relationships way too fast. It felt like I was past all the flirting and dating of junior high, and I hadn't even done it yet. I just remember that all that joy and innocence of going to your first dance was gone.

When parents break up just as teenagers are exploring their own way through love and sex, the lessons of their parents' ending marriages have an instant and striking effect. Dating and young romance no longer offer the same kind of magic when parents are in the thick of dividing up property and bemoaning their broken union.

By the time we hit adolescence, most of us have one foot out the door already. Our horizons are expanding, our hormones are raging, and our peers are infinitely more important than our parents. We all know that the teen years are rarely a golden period in the personal history of parent-child relations. Goals clash, with teenagers intent on testing their freedom and independence and parents frantically trying to set down rules and limits to keep them in the fold. Yet, although adolescents may seem to lose interest in their parents, the stakes change when their parents seem to lose interest in them first.

Thirty-two-year-old Molly, whose parents divorced when she was fourteen, says the stress associated with her parents' divorce almost blended in with the trials of being a teenager. "I even remember saying this at the time: Adolescence is such a living hell in general. It's so traumatic, and you're so awkward and everything is a problem, so in a way, my parents' divorce sort of fit in with everything. If you're going to have a time of your life that's full of uncertainty and upheaval and all sorts of weird feelings, fourteen is probably the perfect age. Changing body. Changing life. In a way, my attitude was 'Just pile it on! Keep it coming!' Not to be flip about it, but that was basically my attitude—'Oh, geez, another stupid thing my parents are doing to make my life miserable.' I couldn't get out of the house fast enough. I think I had a lot of random anger. I can't even explain it, but overall I was angrier, more aggressive. I was very distracted and couldn't pay attention to anything."

Along with all the physiological changes, teenagers must meet a number of psychological challenges as they develop their own autonomy, start to form patterns of intimacy, and forge a sexual identity. And when a parent is also primping for dates, staying out late, and exploring romantic options at the same time, it can be, at the very least, disconcerting. "I hated the parade of boyfriends who came through there, sorry divorcés with toupees, paunches, these on-the-make middle-aged singles who went through women like my mom like they were nothing," says one woman whose parents divorced when she was thirteen. Another woman remembers how embarrassed she used to get when her father would openly grope his much younger girlfriends in front of her.

For twenty-five-year-old Cheryl, whose parents divorced when she was two, the ideas of sex and unconditional love became intertwined during her childhood, and only as an adult has she started to disentangle them. "My mom didn't have a lot of time for us. I knew she loved us, but I was always jealous when she devoted time to a relationship. I wanted to have that time with her," she says. When her mother became involved with a serious boyfriend, Cheryl didn't know how to compete. "And so, in a really mental-case kind of way, I think in some ways I oversexualize my relationships now, or rather, sex becomes too much of an issue. If it's a sexually intimate relationship, that's the hierarchy, the type of attention that rules over any other kind of attention. Mistaking sex for love, I guess that's the problem. Maybe that's just the model I saw. I saw my mother giving attention to a relationship in a way that I felt excluded."

Parents, when they start dating, can inadvertently provide their children with an early education in sex. "There was a certain sexualization in my household," says Cheryl. "My mom was really open and we learned our bodies were beautiful things, but there was *too much* open sexuality in our house, to the point where I would come home from a weekend at my dad's house and find blankets and pillows and underwear on the floor. And I would think, 'Oh, Mom is upstairs in the bedroom,' and I knew what was going on, and that attention was something I wasn't getting."

While a parent's sex life can be disturbing, it can also be interpreted as a model for the way intimate relationships should unfold, pushing us into promiscuity. Thirty-eight-year-old Malcolm, whose parents divorced when he was fifteen, says his views on sex and love were shaped by his father's swinging single lifestyle after he and Malcolm's mother split up.

"It seemed like he couldn't get enough women in bed," he remembers. "He belonged to this organization, Parents Without Partners, which I think was just a feeding ground for this kind of thing. He really went out with more women than I could count. When I was living with him, sometimes it was just night after night of different women. There were many mornings when he would wake up sober and laugh to me that he had no recollection whatsoever of the woman sleeping in his bed. At the time, I thought it was kind of funny, but it definitely affected my attitude about how guys should be in the world in relation to women. Right along with my romantic notion that there was a perfect woman out there for me was this idea that a regular guy has sex with as many women as possible, as often as possible."

For years, Malcolm viewed frequent sex as a means of validation, rarely questioning his motives. Only later did it become apparent that sex had in fact become simply the most available outlet for his insecurities. "On the one hand, with my romantic ideas, it was very important to have a woman say she loved me, but because of my suspicions, the only way I could believe a woman loved me was if she was having sex with me. At a really fundamental level, I felt that every episode of sex was a demonstration of my value, of my love-worthiness, even if no one was saying I love you. I became visible because a woman was finding me sexually attractive and enjoying sex with me, so that meant I was okay. It didn't last, though. As soon as it was over, I felt the need to have it happen to me again."

Divorce has long been associated with a loss of innocence. Over a hundred years ago, Henry James's novel *What Maisie Knew* depicted the experiences of a young child of divorce in order to illustrate the death of childhood. In the aftermath of their divorce, six-year-old Maisie shuttles between two particularly malicious parents, who shamelessly use her as their messenger to carry their sharp verbal lances back and forth; they each pry information about the other from her lips, then vent their anger on her as proxy. Confused and alone, Maisie deliberately starts to pull back, playing dumb to her parents' probing questions and demands for loyalty. "She had a new feeling, the feeling of danger; on which a new remedy rose to meet it, the idea of an inner self or, in other words, of concealment."

Of course, growing up today is much different than it was a century ago. As social critic Neil Postman argues, the divide separating childhood and adulthood has been fast disappearing in recent years, dissolved by our easy access to the parade of sex, violence, death, rape, AIDS, and genocide that lies only a click away on the television screen. Yet, most of us learned more about fear from watching our parents threaten and insult each other, and more about anxiety from seeing them go through nervous breakdowns and withdraw than we did from any movie of the week or episode of the nightly news. We discovered that our parents were not superhuman but flawed and imperfect, or worse.

Even against our modern backdrop, James's description of how divorce erodes a child's innocence still applies with startling relevance. When we say we had to grow up too soon, too fast, what we usually mean is that with our parents no longer our protectors, we became pretenders. We tried to act like mini-adults, even though we still harbored the needs and insecurities of children. We tried to act like our peers, even though we felt burdened with a cynicism and gravity of someone two or three times our age. We had to parent our parents, and at the same time, parent ourselves. We were thrown out of the province of childhood, and some of us remained lonely wanderers for many years. Others adjusted by sewing together a new version of self to fit the circumstances surrounding them, but the seams were often loose; we worried the emperor had no clothes. "In my worst moments, I still crave being a child with absolutely protective parents," says one woman. "My main problem now lies in this sense of emptiness, this lack of safety, that feels as if it is somewhere in the core of my being."

There are consequences when adulthood is not the true north of childhood, and all we are left with is a spinning needle. I see it in myself. Growing up was not a steady, upward climb, but more of a jagged rise and fall, and I have spent much of the past thirteen years trying to figure out how to act and feel my age. I certainly don't look back at my youth through a haze of nostalgia. But over time, I'm starting to catch up with myself, to tie together the loose ends of my identity. When I say this to one thirty-one-year-old man, he smiles and nods. "Truthfully," he says, "I haven't faced anything as unpleasant as growing up since. It just gets better every day."

5

Part-Time Parents

AT NIGHT, I used to sit on my parents' bed and watch my mother smooth cold cream over her face and neck at her black lacquer vanity table. She'd gleam for a moment like something moonlike in the darkness before she gently wiped the cream off with a tissue; the vanity mirror would glow, dappling the blue walls of the bedroom with splashes of light. It was all so soothing, like being underwater where the sunlight splits into something soft and silent. I thought she was the most beautiful woman in the world, and I loved her more than anything. When she was finished, she would come and wrap her arms around me, smelling faintly of lemons and Joy perfume, then tuck me into bed. It was our nightly routine, down to the kiss on my forehead as she sat on the edge of my bed and pulled the covers underneath my chin. It was a routine that simply existed, outside of question or doubt—and that, I realize now, was the beauty of it.

When my mother moved out, her black lacquer vanity table, the one I always viewed as a necessary player in our nightly drama, went with her. And that wasn't all. Gone were the womanly scents, the makeup bottles strewn across the bathroom counter, the high heels and purses piled in the closet. Gone was my favorite dress-up gown—a filmy blue, floor-length number with metallic embroidery and delicate rhinestones around the bodice; it was packed up, along with an entire rack of clothing that I was finally on the brink of fitting into. Gone were the boxes of photographs, the mixed-up chronicle of my family history.

Vanity tables. Dresses. Perfume. These are only symbols for a loss too painful to put into words. Because as soon as we lived apart, the mother I once watched, while dreaming of womanhood, was gone, and she was never coming back. In my mind now reside two mothers: The one I grew up with for my first thirteen years, the mom who helped me get ready for school, put my report card up on the fridge, and listened to the details of my day; and the one who replaced her, taking me out once a week for brunch and maybe some shopping afterward. They are separate and distinct, as is my relationship with each of them.

I saw my mother almost every Sunday. I can still picture the mid-morning scene: Me, sitting at the kitchen table in my pajamas, clutching a cup of coffee and trying to shake the sleep out of my eyes. My father, already up for hours, starting on his second, or maybe third, cup. Phone rings. Air goes thick. I pick up the receiver, hear my mother hesitate on the other end, her hand triggered to hang up if, by chance, I'm not the one to answer the phone. "Hi, Mom," I say. Dad gathers up his cup and busies himself at the sink. Mom and I briskly make plans; my father listens, trying to appear casual, but he picks up the pertinent details, and within minutes, the car keys are in his hand. "Will you be home for dinner?" he asks. "I'll try." And poof, he is gone in ample time to avoid any accidental driveway encounters. Even though his car is noticeably absent when my mother pulls up, she sends my sister toddling to the front door, just in case.

I admit, sometimes I wasn't up for these visits. They seemed like odd appendages tacked on to real life. There were Sundays when all I wanted to do was lounge around the house, or go out with friends, or just be; other times, I would look forward to these get-togethers with my mother, forgetting the artificial conditions of the visit long enough to enjoy her company. But then she might ask about a friend I hadn't spoken with for years, or get my current boyfriend's name all wrong, and I would give her a tremulous smile and feel the distance between us. Guilt, hope, hurt, anticipation, and numb disappointment all rumbled underneath and around this weekly visit, but on the surface, we pretended this awkward situation was anything but.

Visitation. What a formal word. Reminds me of something antiseptic, of hospitals and prisons where visitor and visitee are separated by glass walls and wire netting. In a sense, though, this *is* the atmosphere of a visitation. After all, the supposedly organic relationship between parent and child—a relationship usually composed of a million small, insignificant moments throughout the day—is suddenly crammed into an imposed structure that only lasts for a brief burst of time.

In short, a part-time parent is a contradiction in terms: How do you reconcile the fact that someone who helped to bring you into this world is not there every day to guide you through it?

With divorce, one parent almost always bows out of our daily lives, changing our relationship forever. In most cases, the parent who leaves is the father. Close to 90 percent of children lived with their mothers after divorce, according to 1980 Census figures. In my own research, the percentage was lower, though still significant: Of those I interviewed, 72 percent named their mothers as their custodial parent, 6 percent named their fathers, 11 percent had joint arrangements (although the mother often retained physical custody), and another 11 percent said that, at some point during their childhood, they switched residences (usually leaving their mothers to go live with their fathers).

Visits with a parent can create pressure on both sides: Parents may not know how to act in this new position as outsider to their children's lives; children may not know how to handle spending time with a parent whom they feel they hardly know. "I remember feeling super-awkward a lot of the time. I didn't know what to say, and he didn't seem to know either. So we'd sit a lot in the car, and he'd say, 'Talk to me,' and I wouldn't know what to say. I felt like I still adored him, but from afar," says thirty-one-year-old Erica, whose parents divorced when she was three. "There was also a big issue with him being late to pick us up; he was late a lot, and even though I kind of understood it was just work, I couldn't help but feel like an afterthought. Or a burden."

For twenty-eight-year-old Irene, whose parents divorced when she was eleven, these visits were too much to bear. She had never felt particularly close to her father, even before the divorce. "I remember it feeling very contrived when we would visit him—we would go to the zoo or eat lunch—and I think I finally told my mom I didn't want to go on those forced visits anymore. The emotions seemed forced as well—nobody was comfortable." Within a year after the divorce, her father had remarried and moved across the country, and Irene rarely saw him; in the last five years, she tells me, they have almost lost touch completely. "I spoke to him two years ago to tell him I was getting married, and that I didn't want him to attend the wedding, although I did want him to meet my husband. I invited him to come visit me, but he hasn't called me since."

Many fathers, like Irene's, start to fade from their children's lives. The 1981 National Survey of Children found that among adolescents aged twelve to eighteen, including both children of divorce and those born to unmarried parents, 52 percent of those living with their mothers had not seen their fathers at all that year, and only 16 percent saw their fathers as often as once a week. These strained relationships usually continue into adulthood, and a 1989 Gallup poll found that only 31 percent of adult children of divorce felt close to their fathers, as compared with 77 percent of those whose parents were still married and lived together.

When a parent is not living in the same house with us, our

relationship with that parent may take on a formal quality. "We didn't see my dad that often growing up, so when we did, he made it a point to do fun stuff. We went to Disney World and amusement parks, and he made up for his lack of being with us by doing really fun stuff. So, of course, it was great," says thirty-three-year-old Kenneth, whose parents divorced when he was four. "But I never had the emotional extremes with my father that I did with my mother, partly because our time was limited. We didn't have that kind of emotional honesty, and all that's good and bad about it. While on the surface it seemed like a terrific relationship because we didn't lock heads and fight a lot, we also had kind of a fake relationship because I didn't feel like I had the ability to do that."

Meanwhile, back at home, Kenneth's mother openly expressed her hostility toward his father, which complicated his own feelings toward him as he got older. "As a child, I knew I missed him and wished I could see him more, but I wasn't really fully conscious of that until high school and college. Then I realized he wasn't a part of our lives and had resentment toward him for that," he says. "And my mother, she pounded any resentment and hurt I had toward my father with her anger toward him, so I was kind of brainwashed to . . . not hate him, because that's kind of a hard word to say, but think less of him. I have only recently been able to separate how much of my feelings came from my mother."

Anger is a common response when a parent leaves, and it can sometimes be our ally, allowing us to vent our hurt and frustration and force a parent to take notice; it can also clear a path for discussion. Twenty-four-year-old Victoria, whose parents divorced when she was sixteen, says she was furious at her father when he left. After the divorce, her mother, who had suffered from bouts of depression throughout Victoria's childhood, became even more withdrawn. "My mother couldn't really raise three children by herself and there were no other relatives helping out," Victoria remembers. "She would confide in me, more than I think a sixteen-year-old could handle. More than I could even handle now. I could see that she was trying to pit me against my father, but I was bitter toward him for my own reasons. Not necessarily because he hurt her, but because by hurting her, he hurt my brother and me—he knew my mother was depressed and he still left."

For almost a year, Victoria refused to see or talk to her father. "There were a few times when I didn't really yell, but I raised my voice and I got pretty emotional right in his face and blamed him for everything and told him how his leaving affected each one of us," she says. "Those were the first times I ever saw my father cry. He would listen and he would say he was sorry, but he never tried to rebut anything. When I did see him I wouldn't eat around him and I knew that used to piss him off, so I had my own little control game going on there. My brother saw my dad a lot more than I did—almost every weekend, and I used to skip weekends all the time. I'd fill up my schedule with activities and then say, 'Nope, I'm busy.' I spent a couple of years just beating my father down because I felt so beat down." As time passed, though, Victoria's anger started to diminish, and now she and her father have become close, reaching a level of openness in their relationship that wasn't there while he and Victoria's mother were married. "Now I think I can say anything to him, and sometimes I shock him with my brutal honesty; but I feel comfortable telling him how I feel, and he usually responds."

With effort, some noncustodial parents can admirably perform their roles from a distance. Twenty-six-year-old Alex, whose parents divorced when he was eight, says that his parents even struck an unusual bargain the year following their divorce. Instead of shuttling their children back and forth between their two separate dwellings, Alex and his brother stayed put, while his mother and father each rented an apartment nearby and rotated in and out of their family home. "They were fantastic," Alex remembers. "They continued to live in the same town and share custody after that, and my father in particular never made an issue out of the fact that my mother functioned as our 'primary' custodian."

Alex typically saw his father twice a week and every other weekend until he left for college. "My father always coached my soccer teams and came to virtually every game I ever had through high school," he recalls. "All of my friends' parents were married, but in almost all of their cases, they had investment-banking fathers who were never around anyway, so they thought my father was so cool because he came to all the games; their fathers never came." Now engaged to his girlfriend of four years, Alex is looking forward to having his own children. "I hope to be a parent like my father was after the divorce," he remarks, "one who is willing to do anything for my kids and who is involved in their lives."

When noncustodial parents maintain frequent contact, their children are better able to isolate the divorce as an event between their parents. Although Alex's parents were no longer married, this fact did not significantly interrupt his relationship with either parent. But for the most part, I found that after divorce, parenthood was no longer a partnership, but a one-person show, and many speak of even questioning the meaning of the terms "mother" and "father." As twenty-two-year-old Jillian, whose parents divorced when she was twelve, says about her father, "I resent him being a 'father.' I guess he will always be my 'daddy,' but that's the last thing I remember him as. Next thing I knew, we had split apart, and suddenly now he expects to be a 'father.' Sometimes he knows so little about me, while at other times we are practically the same as we were fifteen years ago. I'm just not as willing to give him a claim to my life as I once was. Not out of spite. He just doesn't know enough about me anymore. If divorce does anything, it makes 'men' out of 'daddies.' "

In interviewing others, I found that within the confines of a part-time relationship, four patterns of interacting emerged in the way parents approached their roles after divorce. Naturally, these patterns are somewhat dictated by a parent's personality; but while divorce may not single-handedly cause these behaviors to occur, it often erects obstacles in the parent-child relationship—such as hostility between two parents or physical separation—around which relationships develop. In turn, the level and quality of involvement a parent maintains have lasting impact on a variety of aspects of our lives.

The Distracted Parent

I am sitting in a dimly lit bar with twenty-seven-year-old Keith, a lean, soft-spoken man whose parents split up before he was even born. He starts out by telling their story: They married in college and were together for a rocky couple of years of breaking up and getting back together. While his mother was pregnant with him, his father started having an affair with a mutual friend of theirs; his mother responded by doing the same. They tried to work things out, he tells me. They even decided to drive across the country together to start a new life in another city, but they only made it outside state lines before his father turned around, alone, and his mother continued on. "I think when I was born, my father wasn't even at the hospital," Keith explains in an even voice. "I think my mom's boyfriend was there instead."

The table between us is made out of wood, and carries the carved initials and slogans of patrons past. When I ask him about his relationship with his father, Keith runs a finger across a deep groove on the surface. He shifts and takes a sip of his drink, slightly uncomfortable, before moving into his memories.

He didn't meet his father until he was six years old, just after his mother's long-term boyfriend, whom he had considered a father figure, moved out; Keith had held the door open while the moving men carried away the boyfriend's belongings. "Then, one day, my mother just said, 'Your father is coming today.' A man came by, this tall guy I had never seen before, and after that point, he was in our lives, but only marginally. My sister and I would spend summers with him," he says. "I didn't really know what was going on most of the time. I would just go here and go there. But I think once I started going to visit him during the summer, that's when I started to really miss having a father. I'd come back, and I think I just felt abandoned. I resented him. I had fantasies of moving in with him. I never imagined my parents getting back together, because I had never seen them together, but something was missing. I felt that, and the older I got, the worse it got. You know, you're like a puppy when you're a kid. You just want to follow your dad around."

From September until July, Keith wouldn't hear from his father, their contact rarely spilling beyond their planned visits. Meanwhile, his life at home only increased his longing for his father. "It was a bit chaotic. My mother was only twenty-four when she divorced, with two kids, and so she worked a lot. We were always kind of poor. We moved around a lot, lived in a lot of bad neighborhoods, plus I was the only boy in the family and I think I felt misunderstood," he says. "I think imagining living with my father became a form of escapism. I viewed living with him as some sort of promised land where everything would be better. But in reality, he didn't seem to take much of an interest in maintaining a relationship with me, and that hurt me a lot."

As psychologist Judith Mishne points out, this sort of idealization of an absent parent—whether the absence is caused by death, divorce, hospitalization, or emotional withdrawal—is not unusual. Without the everyday action between a parent and child to illuminate the relationship in the light of reality, she writes, "the shadow of the absent but existent parent" inspires the child to paint that parent in shades of grandeur. The abandonment meanwhile strikes a profound blow at a child's self-esteem. Children often harbor images of reunion with a distant parent that are fat with illusion and daydreams, but when such reunions occur, they don't always live up to their hopes.

When Keith was a sophomore in high school, he decided to move across the country to live with his father. "I felt like I didn't know my father at all, so I figured if I didn't get to know him now, I never would," he says. "My mother was upset, and it was very hard to go. I felt really guilty, but it was something I had to do. So

I went out there, and basically, I felt like the bastard child—my father had remarried, and my stepmother's very bossy, very annoying, a real busybody. She's like the classic stepmother you hate. She would set up all these little rules, leaving notes around the house like 'Clean the bathroom.' She got on my case constantly—'Get a job,' 'Go outside,' 'Wash the dishes'—and I couldn't stand it. I found it really oppressive. I felt like I couldn't be myself. My father and I would do things together, go camping and fishing, and it was nice, but I always felt a little uncomfortable, like we didn't know what to say to each other. I always had this nagging suspicion that maybe he didn't like me. The only time he showed any emotion was when I would argue with my stepmother, and then he would step in and tell me to shut up. We never really argued otherwise, which is why I felt he could care less."

There were periods of anger against his father; there were periods of reconciliation. Now, he says, he has resigned himself to the fact that his father has always been a remote figure in his life. "I used to pretend I didn't need my father, although I did. Now that I'm a grown man, I don't need him anymore," he says. "It still makes me sad, of course, that we have such a weak relationship, but I don't need a father anymore," he reassures me. "I really don't." But the absence of his father still pulls, like a ghost pain. "I think, growing up the way I did, people came and went a lot," he says, rubbing the back of his neck. "Not just my father, but stepfathers, and my mother's boyfriends. I got used to people moving, moving on and leaving. I think in my mind, I put up a block that's hard to get past. I say to myself, 'They're not going to be around forever,' so I'll hang out and enjoy myself, but I never expect anyone to stay around."

A Distracted Parent quietly accepts a position on the fringes of his or her child's life, appearing too preoccupied or disinterested to play an active role. "My relationship with my father during adolescence was very difficult. I was mad at him for a long time; it was always that my father never had enough time for me," says thirty-one-year-old Steve. "He was working really hard, and he got remarried and had a new family—and that was very difficult because I had some big-brotherly feelings for my half brother and half sister. I was very protective of them and loved them to death. At the same time, when I would go to visit my father, I felt like the babysitter. I was the hired help. I would go there and literally spend most of my time doing chores around the house."

When Steve graduated from high school, he invited his father to come to the ceremony. "I got a limited number of tickets to the graduation, and my mom said, 'Who are you going to invite?' And I said, 'Well, I want my dad to come.' Her response was 'He doesn't deserve the ticket.' But I drew the line, getting a lot of anger from my mom for insisting that he come, and then I invited my father and he said he couldn't come because it was too expensive to fly up for the day. I couldn't believe it. I was furious."

By far, the Distracted Parent was the most common one I encountered during conversations with others. If our culture has become increasingly obsessed with time management and efficiency, with squeezing in as many activities in a given day as possible, divorce adds another complication. As parents—and later, children—juggle their commitments, careers, and personal lives, scheduled visits may lose out to other priorities and obligations. "Honestly, we spent a lot of time in day-care centers," remembers twenty-eight-year-old Tom, whose parents divorced when he was three. "So that was the big joke at the time—that we flew across the country to go to day care. Sometimes we went to baseball games and Dad would eat peanuts and drop the shells on the ground and yell real loud at the umpires. I loved that. I stood on my seat and yelled at anything that moved."

As an adult, Tom now regrets the fact that he has never really had a strong male figure in his life. "I've definitely always felt that I missed some male-role-model stuff. It's hard to put in words, but I've always felt it's pretty obvious that I was raised by a female—pretty much exclusively. The best way I can describe it is that I've always been pretty close to friends who have good fathers. I've always felt like I try to siphon stuff out of other guys' relationships with their fathers. I'm always searching for a male role model. I do wish there was some way to bring me closer to my father. I wish I could have spent more time with him along the way. Now, I say I love him, and I do, but in all honesty I barely even know him. I know that he rides horses and loves baseball. That's about all."

While they aren't searching for male role models to emulate, girls also look toward their fathers as they develop their sexual and feminine identities. Fathers provide their daughters with what author Victoria Secunda calls a "dress rehearsal" for their future heterosexual relationships, and when a father doesn't give his daughter the attention and love she craves, it can affect the way she relates to men. "I've definitely always had father issues," admits twenty-eight-year-old Samantha, whose parents divorced when she was two. "When I was in high school, I actually dated someone who was ten years older than me and was a friend of my mom's. It was very scandalous, but I have always been attracted to older guys."

Samantha remembers waiting outside her house for her father to pick her up for the weekend, then realizing he was never showing up. "I remember saying, 'Mommy, Mommy, where is he?' Those were really awful times," she says, her easy smile dimming for a moment. "My mother once told me that on my father's list of priorities, I was below playing basketball and laundry. This was according to her, but I was eight years old when she told me that, and it stuck with me. My mom kind of created this universe for me where it was 'You and me against the world, kid.' She used to actually say that to me. So I grew up really feeling that way—like everyone else was out to get us, including my father and his parents, and my mom was the only person I had. Everyone else was wrong and Mommy was right." She thinks for a moment, then adds, "My dad was a piece of shit, no doubt about it, but was he really as bad as my mom portrayed him to be?" She shrugs her shoulders. "I don't know."

Although she viewed him as the enemy, and says that she was firmly on her "mom's team" until college, Samantha often found herself trying to win her father's approval. "With my father, I always wanted him to be really proud of me. Whenever we'd see each other, since we didn't have this warm father-daughter relationship, I would just try to impress him with my SAT scores or my awards. Whatever I could do to say 'See? I'm worthy. See? I'm good.' I find that, even today, I still want to please him. With my mom, I act much differently. I'll flat out tell her no, or hang up on her when we're fighting on the phone, or just be mean in a way I won't ever be with him."

Thirty-seven-year-old Valerie, whose parents separated when she was nine, also sought her father's praise growing up. She describes her adolescence as "very, very difficult years." Although she was relieved that once her father moved out the fighting between her parents stopped, she was also left in the touchy position of being her father's favorite within the family. So, while she fought constantly with her mother, who absorbed the brunt of her teenage rebellion, Valerie continued to idealize her father. "When I spoke of him, it was often in these laudatory terms about his being an artist, but deep down it was false, because I rarely saw him," she recalls. "As if to make up for that, I wanted to become an artist, just like my dad. The truth, though, is that I missed him. I didn't have a father to help me define who I was becoming. I was very thin, shy, and bookish."

Valerie eventually confronted her father for his lack of involvement in her life growing up, and addressed the deep-seated insecurity in her relationships with men that traveled with her into adulthood. Over the years, Valerie has realized she doesn't have to act a certain way to be loved. "I think it counts for a lot that at this age, I'm still single. Several of my closest friends are too, even though they grew up in two-parent homes, but in my case it has taken me until now to learn how to successfully navigate a relationship in terms of being secure enough to clearly say what I do and don't want from a relationship. And mean it. I think for too long, I—the little girl in me, I think—looked to be accepted by men for my 'niceness' instead of 'This is me; love me or leave me.' "

Although the situation is much rarer, some mothers who relinquish custody of their children then wander to the outskirts of their lives. Mothers and their children—especially their daughters—are portrayed by our culture as sharing a primal bond, one that goes beyond rational explanation. "Nothing is more absolute or unquestioning than a mother's love, which is a gift freely given, a last of last resorts to a troubled soul," writes Diane Ackerman in *A Natural History of Love.* "Even serial killers have mothers who love them." When mothers give up their children, the cultural punch behind their departure renders it one of the most scarring forms of rejection around.

Twenty-two-year-old Laura moved in with her father when she was fourteen, after her mother took up with a hard-drinking boyfriend. "Basically my mom chose a guy over me and made it clear that she had no interest being a mother anymore. She doesn't call me. I always have to initiate contact. She doesn't give me any financial support—not for school, or clothes, or anything really. I'm doing good just to get Christmas and birthday cards," she says. "So of course I have trust issues. If you can't trust your own mom, who can you trust? If someone who brought you into this world can't love you the way they're supposed to, then how can someone else? Every day I pray that I will not be as cold as she is and that I will be one hundred times the mother she was."

In her memoir *Fruitful,* Anne Roiphe observes: "My oldest daughter, who spent the early years of her life without a father, has divisions in her self that come from early father loss. Substitute fathers are fine but memory lingers and wounds like that don't easily heal, and while I can't measure the damage I know it's there. It influenced her choices. It made her doubt her lovableness. It warped something." Distracted Parents, in their absence, pass down one lasting legacy: the sting of rejection that we carry with us always.

The Controlling Parent

Thirty-two-year-old Jonathan, whose parents divorced when he was nine, describes the visits with his father as dangerous. "We would usually spend the weekend up at his country house, and we didn't know anyone else or have any friends there, so we were very isolated," he says. "There was very little stimulation there for an adolescent kid, and so it could be kind of dull. My father would make us go on these long hikes, and we used to jog together, too, but whenever there were any complaints that this was maybe not the most fun thing to do, he would explode. I remember once complaining that I had a lot of homework to do, and I guess I mentioned it twice, and that was enough to set my father off on this huge rage—that if I didn't want to be there, I should just leave and never come back. There was a sense that we had to perform for him. We were there *for him*."

Although involved in their child's life, Controlling Parents refuse to be flexible or to compromise about their visitation schedule, and often blow up at any request to do so. "My father never really acknowledged that I had a life," says thirty-two-year-old Alice, whose parents divorced when she was four. She remembers the first time she stood up to him. "It was the day before Thanksgiving, which I usually spent with my dad, and he wanted me to come up that afternoon. But I was in tenth grade, and I really wanted to go to the parade with my friends. So I asked if I could take an early train up the next morning. I even promised to get there before he woke up. He said no. I decided I was going to go out with my friends anyway. I called him from a pay phone and said, 'I'm not coming this afternoon,' and he cursed and screamed and hung up the phone. He said, 'I want you here by five o'clock, or don't bother coming tomorrow,' which was the way our conversations usually went when I did something he didn't want me to do. But this was the first time I didn't give in."

It can be difficult for children of Controlling Parents to carve out a space for themselves as they shuttle back and forth, especially if their parents don't get along. "It wasn't about not *wanting* to see my father, it was about trying to balance out my life," Alice says. "My parents hate each other so much that they never tried to make it easier for me to go between the two of them; they just wanted to make it as inconvenient as they could for each other." Many children see their parents' need for control as being fueled by resentment over the divorce and the push to the periphery that often follows. Like Alice, twenty-five-year-old Frank says his father was hypersensitive about his role as a weekend parent. "I wasn't scared of him, although he was intimidating. I just remember this eruptive, explosive temper, where he'd say, 'You're going to respect me. You don't know how lucky you are to have a father like me.' I had to be there at eight o'clock sharp on Friday evening, or the whole weekend would be ruined; he would harp on why I couldn't be there on time. He was always apologetic about not being around so much, and I didn't really get it. I would always say, 'Hey, it's fine, I'm concentrating on my own life and it's no problem,' but he couldn't get past that. My mom would make decisions about where I would go to camp and things like that, and my dad would get furious. He wanted his own market share as to what decisions were made. He always brings up that he wasn't given a chance to be a father."

Some parents will even employ threats and scare tactics to direct the time they spend with their children. Says thirty-year-old Megan, whose parents divorced when she was thirteen, "My father used to say that he didn't have the money to pay child support, and then it became my sister and I weren't fulfilling our obligations to him. He wanted to have dinner with us at least two nights a week and spend every other weekend together." Furthermore, these visits with her father were highly unpleasant; he was authoritarian rather than supportive, and although Megan wanted to make a connection with him, his behavior often discouraged her. "My father would lecture me on the 'real world.' These weren't discussions. These were one-sided monologues where my father would lecture and I'd sit there silent," she explains. "Sometimes it was humiliating. Mostly it was like Chinese water torture—long and dull. One time he said to me, 'I am telling you that you're ugly so you don't learn to use your feminine wiles and be deceitful.' It's hard enough when your body is growing fast and your hormones are raging, but then to have your own father intentionally destroy your self-esteem . . ."

By forcing their demands, rather than working to develop a relationship based on trust and affection, Controlling Parents leave their children feeling that they are viewed more as property than as individuals. Unless these children confront their parents and create new terms for their relationship, they can grow accustomed to smothering their own needs and desires as adults. Says Alice, "I always tried to keep peace on all sides, which is an issue that I'm still trying to work out. I've always been a real pleaser, doing what my parents want me to do, instead of just saying 'This is what I'm going to do and both of you have to deal with it.' My relationship with my father dramatically improved once I left for college, because it was no longer 'Okay, you have so much time with your mother and so much time with your father.' At that point, I didn't have time for anyone."

The Lonely Parent

When parents are devastated after a divorce, their needs may overwhelm visits with their children. As thirty-eight-year-old Barbara remembers:

Before the divorce, Dad was preoccupied with work, money. We mostly bonded around television sporting events. He was never very affectionate and lost his temper easily. He always had a bad back or something. But he could also be funny, entertaining. He loved music, and on family vacations he would teach us to dance—I learned how to cha-cha with him.

But after, my dad was devastated. I remember seeing him cry and my feeling very helpless. He was kicked out of the house and went to live in this rented house with two other divorced guys, each of whom had half a bedroom. They had this card table, not enough silverware, and a toaster oven. It was totally depressing. We would get together on Sundays. They were usually confusing, guilt-ridden occasions. He seemed kind of pathetic to me, and often I didn't want to go. My siblings and I would go to his house, maybe go to a movie, eat, sit around, be depressed, wish we were home, feel sorry for him, talk about the divorce. Mostly I remember it being awful. We hadn't spent that kind of concentrated time with him when he lived at home, and there was no basis for this kind of relationship or interaction. It sucked! He seemed to need something from us . . . reassurance that we still loved him? I don't know, but it was all pretty anxiety-provoking.

Faced with a parent who is living alone, children often feel a great deal of guilt and responsibility, despite the awareness that they have not caused the situation and that there is nothing they can really do about it. "I always felt uncomfortable around my father, like I had betrayed him in some way. I felt guilty, even though I knew the divorce wasn't my fault. I just wanted to make him happy and was always trying to please him," explains twenty-five-year-old Maureen, whose parents divorced when she was seven. When her mother decided to move to another city five years after the divorce, Maureen was crushed. "How could we leave my father? I think I resent her even to this day for that. I felt such an obligation to my dad, and she was forcing us to leave him, to hurt him. Her reasoning was mostly financial—we were moving to be closer to my grandparents—and she almost put the blame on my father, saying he couldn't provide enough financial support for us to stay. Leaving him was the single most difficult thing I've ever done."

When a noncustodial parent is also battling with mental or physical illness, alcoholism, or drug addiction, these feelings of concern can be intensified. For thirty-four-year-old Daphne, her parents' divorce when she was twelve hit her with a double whammy: Her mother suffered from manic depression, so Daphne couldn't live with her, but at home she felt emotionally abandoned by her father, who seemed more focused on his new girlfriend than on his daughter. Daphne usually saw her mother, who was living with her grandparents in another town, every other weekend. "We held hands and hugged a lot," she recalls, describing their visits. "Just breathing her smell, holding her. It was in a way more difficult than having a parent die, I felt. When a parent dies, you grieve and move on. But when our visits ended, I would grieve us being apart all over again. Mondays were a nightmare. I wouldn't or couldn't get out of bed. I'd be ill, cut school, and just stay in bed, crying, trying to recover from the loss again. I missed her for all those 'motherly' things—she wasn't there for my first training bra, my first period, the sex film at school. All those things I didn't have her to share with me, and I missed her and hoped she was doing okay." A few years ago, Daphne's mother passed away, two weeks after the birth of Daphne's first child. "She died the day she received the first baby pictures," Daphne explains. "In a way, I felt she hung on long enough to see my daughter. And then knowing I'd be okay now that I had my own child, she let go."

When our parents can't fully share in the major milestones we encounter during childhood and adulthood, they leave behind a gnawing gap. But this longing becomes even more complicated when a parent abandons a child after divorce, losing contact entirely.

The Disappearing Parent

Twenty-six-year-old Anne, whose parents divorced right before she turned fourteen, remembers that her father called her shortly after he moved out to ask her what she wanted for her birthday; that was the last time she ever heard from him. When people ask her today if she has any desire to contact her father, Anne's answer is always no. She explains why:

> For whatever reason, my father left and stayed away, and he has missed what I consider my growing years: He was not there for me when I graduated from high school and left for college; he was not there for me when I had problems with boyfriends; he was not there for me when a friend of mine committed suicide; he was not there for me when I found out I was pregnant and needed to make a life decision; and he was not there for me when I got my bachelor's or master's degrees. If he reentered my life now, what would he be there for? And is it okay with me, knowing what he's missed? I don't think so.

A parent who abandons a child leaves behind a welter of anger, confusion, hurt, and embarrassment. Since he was eight years old, twenty-six-year-old Peter hasn't seen his father. "I don't remember having any relationship with the man. He was never really there," he says. "I remember being in high school and when people would ask me if my parents were divorced, I would just tell them that my father died when I was very young. It was easier to tell someone that than explain my parents were divorced—because even divorced parents still have contact with their children. This man didn't, and to me, he was dead. I was and still am bitter toward him. I have felt that way since I can remember and that will never change. My brother always said that if he did show up at our door one day, he would just tell the man that our father died when we were children and slam the door in his face. And I would do the same."

Just as with children of Distracted Parents, those children who have been abandoned by a mother or father must grapple with intense feelings of loss and rejection, coupled with longing. Although Peter never missed the father he had—a father who stayed out all night drinking and was deeply in debt—he did miss the presence of a father figure. "I think I looked at other kids and saw how they were with their dads and wanted that. I never realized it until I was in high school, and then one day it just hit me. There I was, not involved in sports or anything, because I never had anyone who was investing their time in that with me. I still regret missing those years. Even today, there are certain things my friends know; they know about cars, and I don't know anything about cars. I never went fishing or golfing or anything like that—all those things that fathers usually take their sons to do."

Parental abandonment produces a lot of questions: Why did they disappear? Where are they? What are they thinking? These are usually questions that were too painful to deal with as children, but may increasingly spring up as adults. Twenty-seven-year-old Janet, whose parents divorced when she was seven, saw her father during regularly scheduled weekend visits for the first year after her parents divorced, then he disappeared from her life. "It's blurry, and I can't quite figure out what happened. But this I remember: I asked my father if we could switch the days of one of our visits, because a friend of mine was having a surprise party, and he went completely nuts," Janet says. "He said, 'I can't deal with this. This is unacceptable.' I never saw him again after that, amazingly enough." Shortly after the fight, Janet moved with her mother to a different state, and in the following years, her father never attempted to contact either her or her brother; he also refused to pay child support.

Growing up, Janet handled her father's absence by pretending it didn't bother her. "I started to feel angry, instead of feeling abandoned," she remembers. "I just felt pissed off." Like Peter, when Janet's friends asked about her father, she told them he was dead. "For ten years, I acted like a 'tough girl' who was simply baffled by my father's strange behavior, but was fine and able to function. I denied that my father's absence had any effect on me."

It wasn't until her father passed away while she was in college that Janet started to honestly explore how his abandonment affected her, acknowledging the hurt and sadness she felt and still feels. She also, for the first time, started to ask her mother and other relatives questions about what happened during and after the divorce. "One of the stories I hold on to involves a friend's father who ran into my father. They weren't great friends, but my dad said something to him like 'My kids don't really care about me. They don't make time to see me.' My friend's dad, I remember, was struck by how ridiculous that sounded. We were kids. But that little interaction is meaningful because it gives me an idea of what was going on in his head and why he couldn't even talk to my mom." Although her father's death means there will never be a reconciliation between them, Janet has let go of her anger, choosing to keep the good memories she has of her father from early childhood as she moves forward in her own life and her own relationships.

Forming New "Families": Friends, Relatives, and Mentors

What might have been a bleak holiday celebration the year after my parents divorced turned out to be a fairly festive occasion. My grandparents had flown across the country to stay with us for three weeks, and two of my friends had been able to slip away from their own families to come over for dinner on Christmas Eve. My grandmother made the same traditional holiday pudding she had been making for years, while my father experimented in the kitchen with more ambitious dishes like grapefruit-glazed chicken and persimmon mash. Instead of just the two of us, there were six of us crowded around the table, clinking our glasses together in a round of toasts.

Amidst the turmoil caused by divorce, I was lucky enough to have the anchor of friends and my grandparents to hold on to. My grandparents were always there for me, either by phone or in person on holidays; on a daily basis, my friends became my surrogate family, inviting me to eat dinner at their houses and even letting me tag along on their family vacations.

Indeed, many of those I interviewed expressed a deep affection for and loyalty to their friends that often surpassed what they felt toward their families; yet, precisely because friendships are so important when the family falls apart, a number of people added that they choose their friends carefully. "I don't have many close friends," says twenty-eight-year-old Marianne, whose parents divorced when she was seven. "I have to really trust someone before opening up to them and being able to confide my feelings, and it usually takes a long time for me to reach that point. But the friends I do have are very, very strong. I've had the same best friend since I was fourteen, and I know we'll always have a relationship. Even though she lives in a different city, we can pick up the phone after three months and it's as if no time has passed at all."

While friends can offer invaluable comfort and understanding, as peers they can never really take on the role of guidance that an adult can. In fact, psychotherapist Lillian Rubin identified the ability to be "adoptable" as one of the major characteristics of children who rise above adverse conditions or abuse and become successful adults. Relatives, teachers, coaches, employers—all these people can step in and provide a crucial source of support during our childhood.

Twenty-seven-year-old Ross, whose parents divorced when he was five, found a mentor at a time when he needed him most. After a childhood of moving back and forth between his mother's and father's houses, as a teenager he started to express his anger in destructive ways. "I remember my first real best friend was this kid Brad who was really dangerous, and together we were like a match and gasoline," he says. "He really brought out all the anger I had toward everyone inside of me. I began lashing out. I wouldn't speak to anyone. I cursed at people, and I ended up going to jail," he says, explaining that he'd gone along with his friend to break into a neighbor's house. "I went to jail for a week, and my parents basically disowned me."

After Ross dropped out of college during his first year and moved in with his mother, his anger turned to depression. "Then I got really lucky," he says. "I met a guy who was fantastic and gave me a job. This guy picked me up by my bootstraps and told me I was an idiot right from the start, and you know what's interesting is that I believed him. He wasn't saying it as a criticism. It was almost like he was saying 'I can't believe what you're doing with your life. You look like a smart kid.' So I just sort of trusted him and I listened to him. He showed me how to run a business; he made me go to a good college. I mean, it was the first real relationship I had ever had in my life. He was a father figure and a friend, and it was unbelievable. I never had anything like that before. It was a real turning point in who I was."

We often try to seek out information from other sources, in order to learn what our parents can't or won't teach us. "My parents will never be parental figures. The problem is I don't really respect either of them enough to emulate them," says thirty-three-year-old Sean, whose parents divorced when he was seventeen. "My father is one of those parents where everyone's like, 'Your dad's really cool,' and he may be really interesting, but everyone else's dad is there for the soccer game, and my dad isn't. Both my parents in the abstract sound great, but I guess you crave what you don't have. When I see these families where Mom and Dad are still really happily married, and all the kids come home, and they have these big white Christmases, well, our family was never like that at all. And I don't think my dad ever gave me advice on anything, like how to shave or how to pick up a woman. I mean nothing like that. Ever. So, when I was a little bit younger, I used to seek out older men as role models. I've had these jobs where I've worked with someone who is about my dad's age and who intellectually and morally inspires me. As I've gotten older, though, I've realized that your mentor should actually be five years older than you, not thirty."

Our homes are the first place of socialization, the classroom where children learn to measure their own worth, follow patterns of behavior, and obtain the knowledge that will eventually guide them in their lives beyond the home. In *The Art of Loving,* Erich Fromm draws the distinction between conditional—father—love and unconditional—mother—love. Our parents—as a male and female pair—provide the yin and yang of our identities. They not only act as role models, but according to Fromm, exhibit two types of love toward their children that complement each other: Conditional love satisfies our desire for achievement, and unconditional love satisfies our longing for security. When one or the other is lacking, the framework of our interior design tilts.

"The one thing I missed during those teenage years was the kind of security I imagined a father would give a daughter," says twenty-eight-year-old Dawn, whose parents divorced when she was seven. "Almost every woman I know with an involved father is just in love with him. Their fathers become the yardstick for every guy they date. But for me, when I'd talk to my dad every once in a while growing up, he would ask about school, then say something like 'Well, just remember to keep your pants up and your skirt down.' That would be it. His words of advice. Had he been there on a day-to-day basis, I don't think he would have been so crass."

Now facing the prospect of entering her own relationships, Dawn believes that a childhood without a father has left her with some crucial gaps in her knowledge of men.

"I don't know what it's like to have a male figure with whom to share things in a mature sense," she explains. "One of my close friends, her parents have been married for almost thirty years, and I used to be amazed by her family dynamics. Her mother has her role, her father has his role, and the kids have their roles, and you see how all these different roles interact with each other. And then I see how my friend is in her own relationships, how she recreates these roles. But for me, I can't recreate them because I just have no frame of reference. I haven't been in a relationship for a long time because I don't even know how to handle the male ego, how to relate to men. I look at my friends who grew up in a two-parent household and most of them are in pretty healthy relationships for the most part, and my friends act just like their moms do toward their fathers, in a very nurturing way. I don't want to say 'subservient,' because that has a negative connotation, but in a way that allows a man to be a man."

As if it were an onion, I can peel back the layers of my confusion about how to conduct a relationship one by one. Underneath the obvious absence of a close-up model of marriage lies another glimmering doubt, burning yet elusive: That maybe it isn't just my home, but me, that is somehow all wrong.

Although I would have been loathe to admit it as a teenager, I missed my mother terribly when I went out on my first date and attended my first dance; I missed her during all those times when I desperately needed to talk to another woman because I felt that my father, as a man, just wouldn't understand. Whether my mother could have offered me the guidance I wanted, I will never know. What I do know is that I don't have to travel very far into myself to realize there is a part of me that, no matter what the circumstances, will always feel somehow deficient because my mother essentially missed out on those years when I was growing up. I feel there is a block between my mother and me, born not only out of her distance from my life but also because I, too, pushed her away. Sometimes I find myself today searching for the mother's love I lost, in the praise of a boss or the arms of a boyfriend; the words and embraces of others, however, are usually inadequate approximations of a parent's love.

I still experience a brand of discomfort when faced with the little reminders that just as she lost a central place in my life, I lost a central place in hers. At my mother's house, I sleep on the pullout couch, and surrounded by her clutter, I realize it is a clutter that doesn't belong to me, that has no relation to me whatsoever. I don't know the stories behind the stain on her striped couch or the row of white seashells on the mantel. I notice that among all the framed photographs of my sister and my mother, candid snapshots from their daily life, there is only one picture that includes me—a professional, posed photograph of the three of us taken when I was twelve years old, before the divorce. I examine my feathered hair, the pink-striped Jordache sweater, the wide smile—all preserved on Kodak paper, all from another lifetime.

6

New Roles, New Rules:
Siblings and Stepfamilies

HOLIDAYS ARE THE WORST.

First, there is the question of splitting up Christmas Eve and Christmas Day—Dad usually gets the former, and Mom the latter, although every year, the exact schedule continues to be a source of some anxiety, debate, and the occasional snafu. Like the year my mother casually informed me that she had bought a plane ticket to New York for the holidays, as if our family could allow for such spontaneity, and I had to tell my father that, sorry, my Christmas was booked; to which he rather grouchily announced that he wanted to come visit me, too. So, on Christmas Day, my father appeared at my door for his shift, just minutes after my mother had left. I didn't even have enough time to change the sheets on the pull-out couch.

For the past couple of Christmas Eves, though, my father and I have gone to his girlfriend's house for dinner to celebrate the festivities. The tree twinkles in the corner of her living room, candles flicker their warm light, and an elaborate spread covers the dining room table. I wander among the friends and relatives who chat in clusters in the kitchen and on the couch, and although everyone is friendly, I can't help but feel a little bit like an outsider: My place within this close-knit group is unclear. At the end of the night, my father's girlfriend's children and their cousins, all of whom are roughly my age, exchange gifts—a tradition of playing Secret Santa that dates back to when they were young. I watch from the sidelines, feeling slightly envious of their history together.

The next morning is a blur of activity. My mother drops my sister off at the driveway of my father's house, and the three of us open presents and eat lunch. Before we know it, we are jumping back in the car to see my mother for more presents and dinner. As soon as we leave, my father goes back to his girlfriend's house for Christmas dinner, which her own children are having with their father. By the time the holidays are over, and I am back at my apartment, I am ready to collapse from all the activity and from the strain of taking on so many individual disguises, so many different layers of identity: I am my father's daughter, my mother's daughter, a boyfriend's daughter, a mother's boyfriend's daughter, and a big sister. But where do I belong?

Where do I belong?—this is frequently the lament of a child of divorce. Anthropologist David Schneider once described family as a mother and father living under the same roof as their children, and without the clean simplicity of this increasingly outdated definition, the typical divisions among these positions in the family often became blurred: We had one parent taking on the tasks of two; stepparents who had more of a day-to-day role in our lives than our biological parents, who probably were spending more time with their new spouses' children than with us.

We all have prescribed ideas of the way families should act, points of reference where our cultural notions and personal expectations intersect. And the reality of divorce doesn't always fit in. Says twenty-eight-year-old Denise, whose parents divorced when she was two, "My father had a slew of girlfriends while I was growing up. I can't even count how many there were, and of course, since we saw him on the weekends, we were always thrown together with the girlfriend of the month. Looking back, I realize that I hated it, but at the time, I was just so happy to be with my dad. But it was just not normal, schlepping to stay at some girlfriend's house. Or staying in my dad's bachelor apartment while he went out." She repeats emphatically, "That's not *normal*."

Without her father as a regular part of her life, Denise grew to depend on her older brother to fill the empty role her father left behind. "My brother in a sense became a father figure to me," she explains, "although he doesn't really know that. I have yet to bring that up with him. My dad was never the typical dad. When he calls, he doesn't even say 'It's her father calling,' but 'This is Bill,' like we're buddies. He thinks it's funny and cool, but it's really not. So, growing up, I really cared what my brother thought, not my dad." But when Denise's brother left for college, he distanced himself from her life. "He left, not just physically, but by detaching himself from our family. I had always felt like we were on the same page. We were a team, and it really hurt. He left me holding the bag, and I just felt so abandoned. I still do." She adds, "I have a father. I have a mother. I have an ex-stepfather. I have a stepmother. I have all this. But I don't really have a family."

When the family framework breaks apart, many of us land in this constant state of the ephemeral, where nothing and no one seems safe from disruption. All the roles—and all the rules—have changed, leaving each member scrambling to adjust.

Sibling Relationships

Brothers and sisters: They can be our best friends or our archrivals or a little bit of both. The relationship between siblings can have more ups and downs than a seesaw over the course of a lifetime. But regardless of how we view one another, we share the unique distinction of growing up surrounded by the same characters and going through similar family dramas. When we talk about divorce, however, we usually cast it in terms of parents and children, without really taking into account how siblings are affected by the change in the family dynamic. When all the roles within the family are shifted, new pressures are often placed on the bond between siblings. Like Denise, younger siblings can start to depend more on older siblings; likewise, older siblings can feel more responsibility toward younger ones. "My parents never reassured us in words or actions that they would always care for us. I literally thought I might any day be out on the street," remembers one twenty-nine-year-old woman, whose parents divorced when she was seven. "When I was about ten I started telling my sister I would get a job as a waitress and support us both. We were close before, but after the divorce, my sister and I clung to each other, and I tried to protect and reassure her."

I found that, in many cases, the stress of divorce tends to exaggerate whatever relationship already exists between brothers and sisters. Siblings who were close before the divorce may form a tight, united front, turning to each other for support; some may drift farther apart; still others may bring the hostility they shared before the divorce to a fever pitch. Our parents' needs and behavior following the divorce contribute to the direction our relationship with a sibling takes, especially in determining the extent to which a sibling becomes a pseudo-parent.

Peer as Parent

On a humid Saturday afternoon, my mother calls me with an emergency: She has to go to work, and asks me to take care of my sister for a few hours. I'm sixteen years old, and while I bridle at the idea of being a default baby-sitter, I agree. My mother suggests we go to the pool in her town house complex, and an hour later I'm lying on a lounge chair, sweating, surrounded by yelping children. The scent of chlorine and suntan lotion hangs heavy in the air, and I'm cranky; this is not my idea of a good time. I keep one lazy eye on Caroline, who is splashing around in the shallow end of the pool, and finally decide it's time to get a soda. I kneel by the edge of the pool and curtly instruct my sister not to move.

When I return a few minutes later, she is nowhere in sight. A shudder of apprehension travels across my skin, and I jog around the perimeter of the pool. Right before I'm about to go into a full-fledged panic, I spot Caroline with another little girl in the deep end of the pool. With a fury out of proportion to the crime, I march over and start to yell, "Get out of the pool right now!" My sister, who is only five years old, scrambles out, dripping onto the pavement as I storm back to the changing rooms. "I told you not to move!" I fume, throwing clothes on the bench, packing up our bag, whirling around like a virtual hurricane. Caroline creeps up behind me, her face stricken, and puts a hand on my arm. "I'm sorry," she says quietly. "I know it's not easy for you to take care of me." That stops me in mid-whirl, and I bend down and give her a hug, reminded that I am the adult to her child.

It is not a comfortable place, this undefined role somewhere between parent and sibling, and I'm afraid that at times I wasn't very good at it. Sometimes I would snarl at my sister indignantly when she was being too insistent, or sigh with impatience when she was just acting her age. I didn't always keep my promises, distracted by some obligation to my friends, to boyfriends, to myself, and I felt terrible when I saw her disappointment. Although our eleven-year age gap made me protective of Caroline from the day she was born, the divorce added the new dimensions of guilt and need to our relationship.

The absence of my sister from my daily life was perhaps the worst fallout from my parents' divorce. I missed watching her grow up, and that is a loss I will always carry with me, along with a sadness and a sense of responsibility that seem bottomless. I remember all too well how my sister, at the end of our Sunday visits, would clutch my leg. "Why do you have to go?" she would ask, her round face looking up at me, covered with tears. "Why can't I go with you?" I remember how, if I simply bought her a candy bar, she would thank me until I would give an exasperated laugh and say, "Enough already!" and then she would apologize, convinced I was angry at her. While I may have been suffering, too, I believed my sister was the greater casualty; that this deep-seated uncertainty spawned by my parents' divorce had somehow entered her muscles, her blood, her heart. And while I did the best I could to help her through it all, it was never good enough.

For a few years, things got a little twisted around. When I brought a boyfriend with me to visit during a college vacation, my sister refused to acknowledge him. If I got within a few feet of him, she would squirm her way between us. If he and I held hands, she would grab my hand away with a territorial "She's *my* sister." In private, she demanded to know whom I loved more; I would try to explain that there were many kinds of love, that love did not have to be mutually exclusive. "I will always love you," I told her. "You're my sister." But she wasn't buying it, worried as always that she could be quickly replaced in my affections.

Older children often end up taking care of their younger siblings, either out of choice or necessity, but it's a shift that effectively turns the balance of power upside down. Sometimes single parents, overwhelmed with their responsibilities, will explicitly hand off the discipline of younger children, forcing a relationship that may be too close for comfort. One twenty-eight-year-old man describes his relationship with his younger brother after the divorce as pretty rough; as the oldest male in the household after his father left, he was put in charge of keeping his brother in line. "My brother definitely acted out, and my mom, who couldn't handle him physically, made me the enforcer," he says. "It was a terrible thing to do, though I suppose it was either that or let him run wild."

Even today, when my mother is worried about my sister, she calls me for advice; when my sister argues with my mother, I intervene on her behalf. I act as her defender, her court of appeal. It can all start to seem like a bizarre brain teaser: If a parent persuades us to act as a parent to a sibling, then who is the real parent here? Who is in control? Says thirty-one-year-old Steve, "My father didn't fight with me the way he fought with my younger sister, mainly because I have no problem going for the throat. My sister, she doesn't argue very well, and he would get her to the point where she was so frustrated and upset that she would start to cry. My father came down on her like a ton of bricks. So when he complained about her behavior, I found myself coming to her defense. I would say, 'You know why she doesn't want to talk to you? You frighten her. You scare her. You bully her.' When they fought, my father would come down so hard on my sister, I used to have to step between them and say, 'Hey, stop attacking her!' "

When one sibling takes the position of enforcer or protector of another sibling, it is not always a welcome transition: Older siblings may resent their extra responsibilities, while younger children may not be so willing to accept their new "parent." Lydia, twenty-three, was seven when her parents divorced, and with her mother working extra hours to support the family, her older brother stepped in as her de facto parent. "My brother became my father, in the sense that he took care of me, gave me an allowance, and grounded me. I had to ask his permission to go out," she says. Overall, Lydia didn't appreciate her brother's attempts to play the heavy. "I had tons of problems with this relationship because while he tried to be my father, and expected respect like a father, he was still my brother. He still played video games, but he would get mad like a parent." Resentment is met with resentment, joining siblings in a cycle that can strain their relationship.

Becoming a replacement for an absent parent is often too much for an older sibling to handle, both physically and emotionally, and taking on such a burden of responsibility is typically out of sync with their own developmental needs. As a result, when older siblings finally leave home to pursue their independence, they may not want to look back at whom they are leaving behind.

Thirty-three-year-old Sean, whose parents divorced a year before he left for college, says that it took him years to repair his relationship with his sister, whom he left alone with their mentally-ill mother when he went off to college. "My sister is five years younger than me, and when I left, there was a lot of guilt involved," he explains. "My mother was getting much sicker, but my excuse was 'I've taken care of her for this many years, now it's your turn.' She had a lot of anger toward me, and my dad, for leaving her with this. When I was growing up, we didn't have money problems, but after the divorce, my sister had to work all the way through high school to support my mother. She was going to inner-city schools and living in the projects because my mother would get her paycheck and go out and buy champagne and caviar to celebrate, instead of paying the rent. So I had this terrible guilt that I kind of stuck her in this situation. We've been able to work through a lot of issues and laugh about the past. Now we're very close. She lives four blocks away and we see each other all the time. But I see how guilt drives a lot of what I do, in all aspects of my life." For me, as my sister has grown older, I've come to depend on her for support as much as she used to depend on me. I sometimes wonder if we would have been so close if the divorce never happened. But the way our relationship changed is only one possible outcome after parents split up. Just as the belief that love is a scarce commodity can bring siblings closer together, the rupture caused by divorce can also intensify competition for a parent's love, driving siblings apart.

Old Rivalries

In *Born to Rebel,* a study of the impact of birth order on personality, author Frank Sulloway draws on Darwin's "principle of divergence" to explain why siblings brought up in the same family are often opposites. In nature, diversity allows species to compete for scarce resources, and according to Sulloway, the same strategies can be applied to families, where siblings are competing for parental love and attention. By developing disparate abilities and interests, siblings attempt to carve an individual niche, and by doing so, avoid competition. Following with this line of thought, divorce can potentially draw out these basic desires to curry favor; with only one primary parent, who is usually preoccupied by the stress of divorce, and time spent with the other parent limited to shared visits, sibling rivalry can grow fierce.

In any family, the complexion of each child's relationship with a parent is unique, as such factors as age and personality shape alliances within the family into a constant shifting of "favorites." These loyalties can become explicit in divorce, especially when the competition takes place in two separate homes. In spiteful divorces, when children may learn that rejecting one parent will win them favor with the other, it is not unusual for siblings to choose different parents to side with, creating another battleground for winning their parents' affection. As one thirty-six-year-old woman recalls, "My sister and I became split along 'Mom's favorite' and 'Dad's favorite.' Whenever we argued, my sister would tell me to go live with my father. It hurt, because he didn't want me to live with him. I knew that, and besides, I probably wouldn't have lived with him anyway. But the truth of that quip hurt."

Thirty-one-year-old Erica, whose parents divorced when she was three, also felt like she stood alone growing up. "I was jealous because my mother really favored my sister in a lot of ways; she wants a ten-speed bike, she gets one, and I get some three-speed clunker. My mom has just always gotten along better with my sister. Always. Other people have noticed it too, so it's not just paranoid fantasy on my part," she says. "I always felt different—I had no relationship with my dad, my sister and mom were close, and they always took sides against me. My sister would provoke me, really subtle and sneaky things, until finally I would haul off and hit her. And my mom, who hadn't seen anything, would say, 'You're so mean.' At the same time, though, it was pretty clear that I was the big sister, and she looked up to me, so over the years we've just gotten closer and closer. We can say, 'It was crazy growing up,' and laugh about it now."

While time and maturity can diminish rivalry between siblings, the position adopted within the family after divorce can have an impact that lasts long past childhood. Thirty-two-year-old Joseph, whose parents divorced when he was seven, says that as the middle child of three, he became his mother's main emotional support, while his brother and sister constantly acted out. "My role after my parents split up was to be the 'good' kid," he explains. "I became the one to keep everything from going awry. I had to protect my mom. It wasn't conscious, of course, but it was obvious." Today, he finds that he easily falls back into that position in his intimate relationships with women. "In my twenties, I had this ongoing pattern of meeting women who had serious daddy issues; they needed someone to come in and be the perfect 'daddy,' to protect them from everything and be infinitely strong and caring and concerned. And that really pushed my buttons. *Ding. Ding.* She needs me, therefore I believe she loves me. If someone doesn't need me, I can't believe she loves me."

As in Joseph's case, brothers and sisters can behave in opposition to one another; for instance, if one becomes overly defiant, the other may act overly compliant. The variety of roles children may assume within a single family make clear how different the experience of divorce can be for siblings. Nicole, thirty-three, tells how each of her four siblings responded in a different way following her parents' divorce when she was eight. While she became the "good daughter," graduating with honors from high school and throwing herself into extracurricular activities, her siblings responded in other ways:

My older brother graduated from high school, had drinking problems, married at nineteen, and became a father. I was a mother to my niece at twelve years old. My older sister was busy partying and being a delinquent, so we weren't close. She and my older brother were pretty violent to each other, so I just stayed away. Because they weren't around much, I became responsible for looking after my younger brothers. They would tease me, disrespect me. They didn't want to listen to me, so we fought a lot—we were the neighborhood show every week. I often wonder what my siblings would say about the divorce. I bet their feelings would be the same, but how we came upon our reflections would be quite different. . . . Five different stories, even though we lived in the same house.

Sometimes, siblings will actually split up, with one moving out to live with another parent, a choice that can further incite hostilities. Jeremy, twenty-nine, lived with his mother immediately after his parents divorced when he was twelve, but after a couple of years he decided to move in with his father. "I couldn't take the dumb-ass boyfriends my mother would bring home. They'd come over and try to be friendly and I would tell them to buzz off. But when I left, my younger sister, who was very close with my mom, despised me. She felt betrayed. It has taken up to this point to get to a decent level with her. Two years ago, she came to visit me and we got into a huge fight. She was very emotional about why I left her, that she had to stick it through with my mom by herself. I walked away from her back then, and she had a lot of bad blood about that."

When parental love is not perceived as a given, but as a matter of divided loyalties, even the passing of time cannot completely fade away the belief that love is indeed a competition. Says twenty-nine-year-old Ross, whose parents divorced when he was five, "I was over at my brother's place just the other day, and my mother called. He was on the phone with her for a while. After he hung up, I asked him if he wanted to go grab some dinner, and he said, 'Well, I have to see my mother tonight.' I said, 'What do you mean *your* mother?' And he said, 'Well, you don't like her anymore, so she's *my* mother.' He was dead serious too. It just goes to show you that in my family, the love was so doled out in increments that it was almost a fight to get any of it." Siblings, however, usually compete for a parent's affection on a level playing field. But when a parent becomes romantically involved with someone or remarries, the game changes entirely.

Stepfamilies

Around two years after my parents' divorce, my father started dating. His first girlfriend was perfectly pleasant, but not exactly warm, and our interaction rarely extended beyond the courteous nod when she would come over to the house. As they continued to date, though, and got more serious, I started to feel, well, threatened. When the three of us were together, she would often talk for my father, using the imperious "we" that, very clearly, did not include me. She wanted to get married and have a baby. And from the sidelong glances she sent my way, I definitely got the impression that I did not play a part in the future familial bliss she envisioned.

After returning home from a summer away at camp, I noticed my father's girlfriend was no longer coming around. When I asked him about it, he shrugged and replied, "It just didn't work out." Only later did I learn from my grandfather, the purveyor of family gossip, that she had handed him an ultimatum—her or me—after he refused to leave me at home alone or drop me off at my mother's for a week so the two of them could get away for a romantic vacation together. While I was grateful to my father for choosing me, the mere fact that he was asked to make a choice left me cold. What if, next time around, he chose differently?

Although neither one of my parents ever remarried, most divorced people eventually do—about two-thirds of the women and three-fourths of the men. In 1985, there were 4.5 million two-parent households that included at least one stepchild, a figure that doesn't even take into account those parents living with a significant other or not having custody of any children. Yet, with remarriage, the ties of family become ever more convoluted: Connections between parents, stepparents, stepsiblings, and half siblings intersect and can potentially tangle. With each person struggling to define his or her place within a reconstituted family, the period of transition can be rough; and in fact, about 20 percent of second marriages dissolve within the first five years, a failure rate significantly higher than that of first marriages. Some parents embark on what sociologist Andrew Cherlin calls a "marital career," remarrying several times.

Twenty-seven-year-old Olivia, whose parents separated when she was three, didn't realize how traumatic a divorce could be until her mother left her stepfather when she was sixteen. "They were married for five years," she explains, "and although I didn't think of him as a father, he was still a part of my family. It was pretty devastating when my mom told me she was leaving him." She remembers the scene, and the shock she felt. "My stepfather was a total wreck. I have this memory of him sitting on the couch in the living room, talking and crying, telling us how they were going to split up all the furniture and appliances. Everything seemed to be crashing down. A couple weeks later, we had to move to a much smaller apartment that had mice and was in a crummy neighborhood. And even though I was fairly close with my stepfather, our relationship just stopped. This person who had been a parent to me in many ways basically disappeared from my life."

If going through one divorce gives pause about the permanence of relationships, experiencing two or three divorces magnifies these doubts. As one twenty-year-old woman points out, her experience watching marriages come together and fall apart has made her a bit of a relationship expert to her friends. "Well, let's see," she explains. "My mother has been married three times, and her husband now has also been married three times, and my father has been married four times and his latest wife has been married six times. I learned quickly that the definition of family isn't the same for everyone. I guess all this change has made me more cynical about relationships—I still firmly believe that everyone will leave you in the end. I don't look at myself as a pessimist, but as a realist."

Many remarriages do last, and sometimes when families are

patched back together through "steps" and "halfs" they work out wonderfully. Thirty-year-old Ben, who was eight when his mother remarried, says that he has always viewed his mother and stepfather, George, as his parents. "There's really no pre-George moment for me, because they started dating when I was three. I have a few spotty memories of before my mother remarried," he says. "I remember being dropped off at KinderCare because she had to work and being miserable. I remember driving around in a blue car. But this is funny—up until college, I thought my mother wore a black dress at her wedding. I have this vivid image of her at the altar in a black dress, and then we were flipping through some wedding photos, and of course, it's so absurd, and I told her about this image I had. My mother was like, 'My God, honey, what were you going through that day?' and came over to hug me. How's that for an image? They become less vivid as you grow older."

The image of the black dress notwithstanding, Ben and his stepfather got along immediately. "George dealt with everything very well, and sometimes I can't believe how he dealt with it as well as he did," he says. "You know, sometimes as a kid, you say hurtful things without really meaning to, little things like 'My dad's stereo is better than yours.' I don't think I ever said anything like 'You're not my real father.' I knew I didn't have to be part of the bargain. I didn't have to be totally loved with all his heart like his own son. It could have been 'You're Kevin's son, and I'll support you and certainly love you.' But he really went way beyond what I think is the bargain of being married to a woman with a child." When Ben was eighteen, he decided he'd like to be legally adopted by his stepfather. "The day I said I wanted to be adopted was the happiest day of his life. We love each other very, very much."

Ben, who hasn't seen his biological father since the adoption went through, no longer makes the distinction between the terms father and stepfather. "Throughout high school, I told people that Kevin was my father and George was my stepfather. But in college, with the name change that came from the adoption, I never bothered to explain the difference except to close friends who wanted to know," he says. "They always just thought I was part of this perfect family because George and my mom would come to college to visit, and they're great, fun people. We can go out until two A.M., just talking and eating dinner. Even during high school, I would come home and my friends would just be up talking to my mother. It was that kind of family, so I never felt the need to point out that I was adopted."

Some stepparents can supersede a biological parent in giving a child love, affection, and financial support; these children live in the comfort of an intact, two-parent home. But for many children, the formation of a new family is a rocky road that either ends in a separate peace of sorts or merely affirms that intimate relationships are fraught with conditions. For, if marriage is considered a tricky proposition these days, the challenges of remarriage are even trickier.

Stepfamilies start with handicaps that don't usually burden biological families. The primitive stirrings of belonging start on the surface, and when children grow up in a loving family—with two parents at the helm—their physical similarities to each side of the family are usually celebrated. A child has her mother's eyes, or her father's musical talent, her great-grandmother's temper, her great-grandfather's hair. Every genetic echo whispers that the children belong, that a shared history unfolds within them. "This knowledge rids us of anonymity," writes anthropologist Robin Fox. "We are not dropped into the world without a history."

Yet, whereas families grow together as a unit, a functioning organism bound together by the same stories, stepfamilies are grafted together with people who have different histories. Therefore, the entrance of a stepparent usually involves a difficult transition for children. With their position within the family suddenly threatened, they can feel left out or forgotten, their precious ties with one parent now compromised by a new spouse or a new family. Having already struggled to reach a plateau of stability after the divorce, these children are required to go through another period of chaos and adjustment when parents remarry—but this time, with a relatively unfamiliar element introduced into the mix. Lost in a swamp of divided loyalties and silent contests for affection, many feel flung to the sidelines of the family. "I felt very, very shut out by my father's remarriage," says one thirty-year-old woman. "I wasn't invited to the wedding and always felt like I was not a truly welcome part of my stepmother's new family. Rather, I was there because I had to be; it was the 'right' thing to do. Even though she did make every effort to include me in things, to raise me, I just always felt like she thought I was an extension of my mother. I felt totally in the mass of mutual resentment between my mom, my stepmom, my dad, and the extended families."

As in all relationships, an attitude toward a stepparent can evolve, although it may take years to do so. Younger children tend to be more accepting of a stepparent, while adolescents have an especially hard time adjusting to the presence of a new adult within the family. Thirty-three-year-old Tammy, whose parents divorced when she was five, had mixed feelings about her mother's remarriage eleven years later. "I was very happy for my mother, but not particularly open to my stepfather," she explains. "It was just strange having a man in the house after so many years of just the two of us. Plus, he was a very backwoods type of guy, and I was very liberal and wanting very much to get out of my hometown and into the world. Now we are great friends, but that took a long time."

Sociologist Patricia Papernow has outlined seven stages that stepparents go through in the process of moving from "outsider" to "intimate." In the first stages, a stepparent can grapple with fantasies about repairing a broken family, only to end up in a state of confusion and alienation when his or her attempts are spurned. In the middle stages, more sustained interactions take place between stepparents and their stepchildren, and finally, in the last stages, after the role of the stepparent has been established, both sides reach a level of intimacy, comfort, and "authenticity." According to

Papernow's observations, such a cycle can take anywhere from four to twelve years, with some stepfamilies never reaching the last stage. Because of this cycle, growing up in a stepfamily during childhood often means existing in a constant state of flux until each member has adjusted to his or her new role in the emerging "family."

Relationships with stepparents varied widely among those I interviewed, with feelings ranging from fierce love and respect to disgust and hostility, from mild affection to cool indifference. Sociologist Penny Gross found a similar assortment when she asked sixty teenagers between the ages of sixteen and eighteen, all of whom had at least one remarried parent, to specify whom they considered family. Almost a third continued to name both biological parents as their family. Thirteen percent named only one biological parent and a stepparent, and 28 percent named both biological parents in addition to at least one stepparent. Finally, a quarter of the respondents named only their custodial parent, considering themselves part of a "one-parent family." In most cases, these teens were still struggling with the introduction of a new stepparent and had poor relationships with their noncustodial parent, usually the father. They felt excluded by their father's new family, and suffered the most distress of all those she interviewed.

When a part-time biological parent becomes a full-time parent to someone else's children, it can be a terrible blow, further increasing a child's sense of hurt and isolation. Thirty-eight-year-old Barbara says that watching her father take care of someone else's children on a daily basis, when he was such a peripheral part of her life, was one of the most painful things she endured after her parents' divorce. She never felt like a part of his new family and didn't get along with either her stepmother or her stepsiblings. "My stepmother spent my father's money like it was water. She was a Home Shopping Network addict—she used to tape it. She didn't like to cook, clean, or eat real food. She consumed mostly instant coffee and weird plastic food like squeezable cheese. I thought my stepsiblings were trashy. The eldest daughter was a cheerleader, the middle son a football player, and the youngest son a heavy-metal guitar player," she explains. "When my stepsister got married, my dad walked her down the aisle, and I flipped out. I got really drunk with my boyfriend at the time, and I cried. . . . I resented them all because my dad lived with them and not with me." She adds, "And guess what? After fifteen years of marriage, my father and his second wife divorced, and all of her kids stopped speaking to my dad—even that daughter he walked down the aisle. Even though he had played doting grandfather to her child for years. He was really hurt by that."

If divorce intensifies rivalry between biological siblings, the competition between stepsiblings during a remarriage can reach explosive proportions. A child's old place within the family hierarchy can be completely shuffled with the advent of a new set of siblings. Twenty-eight-year-old Marianne, whose parents divorced when she was seven, found her mother's remarriage four years later difficult to handle particularly because she fought bitterly with her stepbrother. "My stepfather had two sons who were in the same grades as my sister and I. My stepbrother and I would get into physical fights, and when something happened, I would tell my mom and she would get upset. So my stepfather blamed me, on more than one occasion to my face, for their marital problems. I'm not sure if my stepbrother and I were dealing with the oldest-child syndrome or what, but my mom would get mad at my stepbrother, and he would get mad at me in return; he punched me a few times in the face, and I would get bruises. My stepfather told me I was egging him on, and his solution to the whole situation was to hit his son whenever he hit me. My mom eventually divorced him, and the truth is, I always felt he was my mother's husband and not my stepfather anyway. My sister had a completely opposite view, but me personally, that's the way I felt."

Stepsiblings may find themselves trying to establish their legitimacy within the patchwork of their family, jockeying for a parent's attention and support and trying to guard what they feel is their rightful territory from being invaded. "I remember going back to visit my father in my old house and finding my toys. My stepsisters told me that those were their toys, but I recognized the toy box," remembers thirty-three-year-old Jane, whose parents divorced when she was four. "I even found my mother's handwritten recipes on my stepsister's dresser in my old bedroom." Several of those I interviewed told similar stories of stepparents taking away their belongings and giving them to their own children, or otherwise making their preferences clear. Twenty-two-year-old Dana, whose parents divorced when she was seven, describes a childhood marked by sparring with her four stepbrothers. She remembers the first day living with her new family.

"My father had gotten married while I was visiting my mother, and I remember arriving at the airport, and my dad picking me up with this woman I had never met before," she says. "The very next day, my dad went to work, and my stepbrothers and I were roaming around the house, and they started teasing me, calling me fat. I wasn't used to that. I started crying, and went outside on the porch to try and compose myself, and that's when my stepmother walked out and said, 'Well, you know, you are fat.' I hated her from that moment on. I didn't think I was worth anything for the longest time, mainly because of my stepmother. She always seemed to care more about her own children," she says. "And my stepbrothers and I were so hateful to each other. We would say things like '*Your* mother didn't pay child support this month'—I mean really awful, hurtful things. There was just a lot of hostility in our family. We all had different last names, so we would always argue, saying this is the so-and-so house, not your house."

Many adult children of divorce trace their insecurity, low self-esteem, and lack of confidence not to the divorce itself but to a parent's remarriage that left them feeling passed over in favor of a new spouse. As adults—especially those with parents who remarried right away—they still feel replaced in their parents' affections. Thirty-three-year-old Jackie, whose parents divorced when she was thirteen, says her father went so far as to disinherit his four older children in his will in favor of his new children. "He never bothers to buy, or make, gifts for us, for many years now. Once he said to my mother when she pleaded for help in dealing with my brother in one of his many crises, 'I can't come and help, I have a family now,' meaning, of course, his new nuclear family."

Especially for a child who has developed a close relationship with a parent after the divorce, his or her remarriage may seem like a "demotion." This is the way thirty-year-old William remembers it. Up until his mother moved in with her boyfriend when William was six years old, it was just the two of them; his parents divorced when he was two, and he has no memories of them together. "I had a very close bond with my mother, because she was determined to make it work as a single parent. I would say, if anything, she was too involved. She was overly concerned about our relationship," he says. But after his stepfather entered the scene, their relationship changed. "It actually did a hundred-eighty-degree turn," he says. "All those years, I was my mom's primary relationship, and when you're a kid, you don't think of it in those terms. It was just my reality. But suddenly my mother had a second shot at a 'real' family, and that became her number-one priority. So, whenever there was a problem, her priority was to preserve the family."

To make matters worse, William and his stepfather did not get along. "He didn't physically abuse me, but he singled me out, and to this day I don't really understand why," he says. "My mother, well, she kind of turned a blind eye to any conflict. I had a lot of problems with my older stepbrother, and my stepfather always took his side. He was bigger than me, and I remember one time we had this huge confrontation, and he punched me in the face. I got a black eye." William laughs without mirth. "But *I* got in trouble. I actually ran away down the street that night. I didn't want to be at home."

William felt like he had no support at either his mother's house or his father's house. Along with his persecuting stepfather, he had a stepmother whom he describes as a nasty woman, a cocktail waitress his father met in a bar and quickly married. "It's like the Joey Buttafuoco story," he comments, grimacing. "It's just so ugly." Every weekend, William was dropped off at his father's house, with five strange stepbrothers and stepsisters, and left to fend for himself. "My relationship with them wasn't antagonistic, there was just nothing there," he says. "We didn't have anything in common." Since his biological parents lived in the same school district, all of William's stepsiblings, from both homes, attended the same high school, adding another twist to his feelings of alienation. "It was like we were this broken family for the entire school to see," he says. "Everyone knew the situation, and they knew that my father and his second wife did not have a real solid marriage. We were not exactly the poster family for happy domestic bliss," he remarks. "I didn't have the same last name as anyone but my father. My mother had taken her new husband's name, and all the kids had their own fathers' surnames. Then one day, I found out that my father's stepkids had my last name too. My father had adopted them legally, but I was never told. I figured it out myself."

Sometimes parents have more children when they remarry, and the birth of a half brother or sister can cause a further sense of isolation and confusion about identity. The half sibling is what is sometimes called the "hub" of the family, turning a temporary family into one that has more staying power, and often the stepfamily becomes more integrated after the birth of a child. Nevertheless, once half siblings enter the scene, it can be difficult for children from a divorce to figure out their place in the new configuration. Now they may feel like they are part of a past that doesn't quite fit into the present; they carry half the characteristics of an ex-spouse, unlike their new sibling, who is the product of an intact marriage.

Kyra has a framed photograph of her father that he gave her one Christmas when she was five years old, shortly before her parents divorced and her father moved out. On the back, he had written a short letter, explaining that he was leaving. As a five-year-old, she fumbled with opening up the frame, and when she did, she wasn't able to read her father's tight cursive; it wasn't until she was eleven that she found his letter again, but by then, the divorce was old news. Both of her parents were on the brink of starting new families with new spouses: Her mother had remarried, and shortly after, gave birth to Kyra's half sister. A year later, her father remarried and had a son. "Some coincidence, huh?" she comments wryly.

Although Kyra loves both of her half siblings, she spent most of her childhood caught between two families, feeling like she did not have a real position in either one. "I think I was mad at my mother for remarrying and having another child. I felt like she was trying to start over again . . . to get it right this time," she explains. "My mom, my stepfather, and my sister made this cute nuclear family and I didn't really work in the picture." So, as a child, Kyra strived to belong in other ways. She worked hard at school, eager to win approval. "That made me feel good," she says. "Worthy." But still, the doubts would crawl in. She battled with a low self-esteem, and tried extra hard to smooth over any rough spots between her parents. "I remember my stepfather and my mother arguing about the fact that my father didn't pay child support as they did the budget. My mom always wanted to take my father to court, but whenever I thought that was going to happen, I would throw a tantrum. I'm not sure why, but I felt like we didn't deserve his money. I didn't want to be a burden on him. I wanted to avoid putting any pressure on him at all, probably out of fear that he wouldn't love me anymore."

Kyra, now twenty-eight, falls between her parents' two mirroring nuclear families, entrapped in a sort of timeless limbo. "Lately I've taken to spending holidays in my apartment instead of visiting my mother's family. I've done that for the past three Christmases," she says. "I just don't want to be reminded of what I'm missing or of what I think I'll never have. Sometimes, when I'm really feeling sorry for myself, I'll wish I were adopted. I imagine that at least that way both parents would want me. But I know that's silly."

When we are stripped of the essential sense of acceptance provided by our families, we lose the grounding for our relationships. Any sense of home is torn asunder, and after a childhood of feeling like we don't belong, we can become emotional nomads as adults. Twenty-eight-year-old Aaron, whose parents divorced when he was two, spent the length of his childhood alternating between living with his father and living with his mother and stepfather. During the course of his childhood, he lived in a total of ten different houses and went to seven different schools. "I adapted to this lifestyle of always having to start over," he says. "In some ways it was hard, and in some ways I found it nice. I mean, I find myself today affected in the sense that I'm always restarting, moving somewhere else and just starting over. I'm just uncomfortable with long-term relationships." He adds, "I just wish I had a place I called home, a place with a reservoir of self-affirming history."

III

Rebuilding Relationships,
Rediscovering Love

But nothing's lost. Or else: all is translation
And every bit of us is lost in it
(Or found—I wander through the ruin of S
Now and then, wondering at the peacefulness)
And in that loss a self-effacing tree,
Color of context, imperceptibly
Rustling with its angel, turns the waste
To shade and fiber, milk and memory.

—James Merrill, "Lost in Translation"

7

Looking for Love

I USED TO BELIEVE the recipe for love was simple: Proceed with caution. At face value, this is not necessarily a bad rule to love by, but in my case I have often taken it to its utmost extreme. At some point, love requires risk, a leap into the unknown, and too many times I've found myself turning away at the precipice. Not to say that I'm not interested in romance—some might say the opposite is true—only that over the years, a definite pattern has emerged in my affairs of the heart. Except for a few, brief flings here and there, which I can count on one hand, I have been involved in almost back-to-back long-term relationships since the age of fourteen; the shortest one lasted two years and the longest one lasted five.

When I look back, almost all my relationships started in an eerily similar way: We meet casually as neighbors in a college dorm or through a mutual friend, without any of the awkwardness and pressure of a first date. We stay up until the pink hues of dawn color the sky, just talking. He calls every day to ask how my day went, listening raptly as I recount the details. He surprises me by bringing over takeout from my favorite restaurant when I'm sick. He's kind and sweet; he adores me. Soon, we are inseparable. Only after I've felt the first tingling of trust, after he's given a declaration of his love and devotion, do I fully venture into the realm of intimacy. It's all very comfortable, and more important, all very safe; I'm secure in his affections long before I ever dare to reveal mine.

Falling in love may temporarily melt the sticky hold of my fears, drawing me into the flush of the moment, but once the initial high of togetherness has subsided, the doubts start to crawl in. They always do, and that's when the trouble starts: I'm jealous about his past relationships, unwilling to share him with even the memory of another girlfriend. The fledgling trust I once felt starts to disintegrate. I need constant reassurances that I'm loved most, and I hate this show of weakness on my part. If his attention starts to slip, even for a night, I retreat into silence. If he comes home late from work, I probe with seemingly innocent questions about his whereabouts, wondering if he was really working late. Every mysterious phone number scribbled on a piece of paper is a clue of betrayal, every wandering glance a signal of a cheating nature. Even though my suspicions are proved incorrect time and again, the warnings still crowd my mind. "Be careful," I tell myself. "Things are not always as they appear. The people you love are not necessarily who you think they are." I wonder if I should stay. I wonder if I should go.

"You would know if you were in love, if he was the one," my friends advise me when I voice my doubts. And although I'm not saying that love at first sight doesn't happen, or that there aren't relationships where two people instantly click, I'm not so sure I possess the radar to *know*.

How can I trust my love, let alone his? I do the best I can. I lay traps and orchestrate tests as a means of gauging the safety of my heart; if he doesn't pass with flying colors, he gives me one more reason to leave, and if he does pass, well, the reassurance is fleeting. It's an exhausting exercise, and I waste more energy than I would like to admit tormented by some treachery that hasn't occurred and most likely never will. Before I know it, the scenarios of heartbreak have dripped their slow poison, and I begin pulling away until there is nowhere to go but out, at least the way I see it. I want to make sure I am always holding the reins of rejection firmly in my grasp, and although it is not very admirable, a part of me is relieved to be calling the shots. I'm the one saying "I don't *need* you." But the truth is I'm frightened by the demands of intimacy, the irrational fever of passion, the increased vulnerability that all come in love's messy package; all those variables that are impossible to predict or capture, although I certainly try.

When it comes to my fears about love, I know I'm not alone. Romantic love is a slippery stretch for us to cross as we grow older. Several expert theories try to explain the travails adult children of divorce encounter in their intimate relationships: Children who grew up as witnesses to their parents' divorce may be more open to the possibility of divorce themselves, even expecting that their marriages and relationships will eventually fail. Without a healthy model of intimacy as reference, we may internalize a skewed picture of marriage that we unwittingly recreate through our own behavior and in our choice of partner. In some cases, ongoing family conflict may push young adults into early, unstable marriages as a means to escape their homes; this is particularly the case when divorce lowers children's economic status and impedes their educational opportunities.

Then there are the cracks that are less obvious. In an ideal world, a child grows up within the comforting embrace of a loving family; this foundation of emotional security gives us the ability to form healthy connections with partners, with our friends and colleagues, and with ourselves. But when divorce deprives children of what British psychiatrist John Bowlby refers to as a "secure base," they are often left to start from a place below ground zero in their adult relationships. Attachment theorists, like Bowlby, have observed that infants and small children develop levels of trust and resiliency based on the treatment they receive from a parent or other primary guardian; those who receive inconsistent care often become clingy and apprehensive, while those who are routinely ignored or rejected will withdraw into themselves. If left unchecked, these behaviors—commonly defined as "anxious-ambivalent" and "avoidant"—run the risk of no longer acting as responses to a particular person or situation, but as general attachment patterns with which to approach all relationships.

Finally, regardless of how it plays out, divorce sends a message that we absorb early on: Intimate relationships are a shaky proposition. Beyond our parents' experience, we see divorce everywhere—among friends, colleagues, other relatives; in movies and on television; in the media accounts of high-profile divorces that stream through the pages of magazines. As a result, overall attitudes toward love and marriage have become increasingly laced with caution. "Statistics and experience show that marriages are unlikely to last," remarks one twenty-seven-year-old whose parents divorced when she was two. "So it seems like it would save a lot of heartbreak not to marry at all."

In fact, statistics show how rapidly the demographic profile of marriage has changed in the past twenty-five years: Between 1970 and 1993, the median age of those entering a first marriage climbed from twenty-one to twenty-five for women and from twenty-three to twenty-seven for men. In that same span of time, the marriage rate dropped by 40 percent, dipping to a thirty-year low. Among those between the ages of twenty-five and thirty-four, over one-third had yet to go to the altar—three times as many people as in 1970. More and more of us have created our own alternatives to traditional marriage: Some choose to remain single, and by 1993, there were as many people living alone as there were married couples living together with children. Others take a detour on the conventional road to marriage by moving in together, creating "invisible" or "trial" marriages that serve as either an intermediary step before getting officially hitched or as the final frontier of commitment.

Although we each confront love in our own way, our behavior is often shaped by two opposing impulses: fear and desire. "Somehow this idyllic vision of marriage, children, and stability has seeped into my head, and I think maybe I can do it too," says one twenty-five-year-old woman. "On the other hand, I think maybe I'll get married when I'm eighty, so my chances of divorce are that much lower." The search for love may be as old as the pyramids, but during our lifetimes we have become all too aware of just how rugged the journey can be. We have statistics. Odds. Tales of marriages gone wrong. Our fears are grounded in fact, and our uncertainty fleshed out by memory.

Will I end up like my mom? Will I end up like my dad? Will I fall out of love with my spouse? Will my spouse fall out of love with me? After years of relying on myself, how can I possibly entrust my heart to another? At the same time, if we didn't receive the proper love and attention from our families as children, how can we not grab at every chance for love as adults? We long for intimacy, yet the belief that it will be pulled away—or worse, used as a weapon against us—always lingers. If love is supposed to be a blissful, overpowering event—an emotion strong enough to rise above the threat of divorce—how do we explain the misgivings that creep into a relationship? In an age of divorce, how can we possibly adhere to Plato's notion of the perfect union, where two lovers lose themselves in each other to form a perfect whole?

"How do you even know if you love someone or not?" asks a twenty-eight-year-old man whose parents divorced when he was twelve. "I have an idea of what a relationship should be, but it's like Utopia, this imaginary thing. It seems like it will never be obtainable."

Words cannot truly convey the range of emotions that are roped under the heading of love, and I certainly won't attempt to hazard a definition here. But while the task of defining love is an impossible one, we can consider how we approach and shy away from love as a way to understand the issues divorce raised during our childhood. After hearing from more than a hundred adult children of divorce, I found that people fell mainly into three groups: the Wary Investor, the Commitment-Phobe, and the Nester. These categories are neither mutually exclusive nor rigid definitions, and often we can switch between them or show evidence of more than one of these behaviors in our romantic relationships.

Wary Investors

Wary Investors find a middle ground between fear and desire in the promise of a safe bet. Armed with the knowledge of how relationships can go sour, we choose our romantic ties with serious deliberation, carefully assessing a partner's strengths and weaknesses in hopes of rewriting the past. As twenty-two-year-old Evelyn explains, "Every relationship I've been in I view in terms of marriage; if I can't see being married to the person, it's not worth my time. I don't put up with much in a relationship—no second chances." Her point of reference, of course, is her parents' marriage, which ended in divorce when she was eight. She can still remember crouching by the closed door of the basement, listening to their arguments. "I have never seen my parents as miserable as they were during the last part of their marriage. My father has since told me that he couldn't stand living with my mom anymore," Evelyn recalls. Now engaged to be married, Evelyn is still struggling with a few remaining qualms. "My greatest fear is that I'll get divorced," she explains. "That is, I don't want to get married to someone who will make me miserable. I have found someone who makes me happy and lets me be myself; we've been together for five years, so I think he's okay, but I still get afraid sometimes when I think about it."

Wary Investors' faith is won by degrees, and trust must often be earned over time. Every situation can become another chance for partners to either prove their dedication or expose their flaws, and as Evelyn says, there are usually no second chances. "I don't know if you do this," says thirty-three-year-old Sean, "but I throw up all my barriers at first. I put up these hurdles. I want the person to go through an obstacle course. Meanwhile, the other person is probably thinking, 'What the hell is going on?' I will say all sorts of outrageous things, and if she decides she doesn't ever want to talk to me again, I think, 'Well, then, she's not worth the trouble anyway.' My sense is that I'm very, very difficult in the beginning, and after someone puts up with the crap in the first few months, then it's fine." He pauses, then adds, "Until the ultimate breakdown later, which is for much bigger reasons. But at least they jumped over all the hurdles."

For some, setting these emotional booby traps is a symptom of more than merely testing a partner's mettle; they also represent a quest for unconditional love, the kind of love a child usually craves from a parent. If a partner doesn't walk out the door when we show our worst, then maybe we can let down our guard just a little, though not enough to open ourselves up to hurt. "My idea of a good relationship is one where the man adores me and is exuberant and consistent in demonstrating his love," explains thirty-three-year-old Jackie. "Ideally I would love him the same way in return, but in reality, I think it works best if I love and respect him, but not too much—less than he loves me. I feel much more comfortable in a relationship if he loves me tremendously, but I love him only to the point where he can't hurt me unduly if the relationship ends. I love my husband very much—enough, I think, to have a good, stable, devoted marriage—but not so much that I would ever lose my identity in him or be completely devastated by the loss of him." Like Jackie, many Wary Investors view love as only one stroke away from loss, and therefore they invest, but not too much.

Twenty-seven-year-old Keith admits that after a childhood of watching loved ones come and go, he chooses relationships where he can maintain full control of his emotions without exposing himself to any real threat of heartbreak. "I always halfway expect the women in my life to take off any minute, and I find myself wondering how relationships will end even as they start. I guess I find it hard to believe that these people actually love me, or that they even really know me," he says. "I fall for women who are elusive and skittish, so it could never work out; but I become seriously involved with good women I care very much about, and become close to, but who usually don't turn my world upside down. I end up in semi-intimate relationships, but the birds aren't singing, so I always keep one foot out the door, ready to make my escape. This, of course, impedes intimacy, but makes the breakup, when it comes, more bearable. I guess I always expect rejection, so I have learned to become detached in general."

To some extent, whether our parents are divorced or not, we are all afflicted by what I call the "perfect-partner syndrome." We long for someone who will embody every quality we desire, satisfy our every need, love us without faltering; in short, we want a sure thing. It is a seductive solution to easing our doubts: After all, if we can form a perfect fit with our partners, with no rough edges, perhaps we can successfully avoid the conflict and dissatisfaction that tarnish a relationship. The quest for a perfect partner, however, can serve to further hinder our search for intimacy. Twenty-eight-year-old Aaron says that his tendency to find flaws in his partners has unhinged many of his past relationships. "I'll find some imperfection in the person I'm dating—usually not just one—and I'll become obsessed with it," he explains. "I can't find any way around it. It could be her voice, or her attitude toward life, or some physical aspect. Maybe she is too aggressive or too submissive. You know, she can't win, or maybe I can't win with myself. Maybe my expectations are too high or it's just a defense mechanism. I'm afraid I'm going to go on like this, just seeing one woman after another, but never really finding someone."

Unfortunately, love holds no guarantees, and surrounded by what-ifs, many of us become stuck in an agonizing halfway house of commitment. Our relationships sag under the weight of constant appraisal and scrutiny. "I've been dating my boyfriend for five years, and most people I know might have gotten married, or at least made some sort of move," says twenty-eight-year-old Danielle. "But I guess I have this general cynicism. I think when my parents divorced I learned that men, and people in general, let you down. I just don't believe in relationships, and I'm not sure that any of them are 'meant to be.' I don't even believe myself when I'm in a relationship. I analyze everything and intellectualize a lot, and I can't stand to feel out of control. I guess I would need to trust and believe that the other person is real and deep-down good; but you know, my boyfriend is the epitome of all that, and I'm still scared. So maybe what I need is not something another person can give me. Maybe it's me. I need to get to the point where I can say it's not so scary." But fear is a powerful deterrent, and sometimes it can prevent us from getting close to someone at all.

Commitment-Phobes

Steve, thirty-one, has never been involved in a romantic relationship that has lasted longer than three months. Cramped in an overstuffed chair at a café, his voice barely rising above the reggae music that blasts through the speakers, he describes his fear of commitment.

"I get really nervous and uptight in dating situations. I've had some serious anxiety attacks," he begins. "Once I spent the weekend with a woman, and I'm standing there in the underground parking lot waiting for my car so I could take her home, and suddenly I had to get out of there. It felt like a millennium had passed before the attendant brought my car around. We got in, and she's trying to hold my hand, but I keep pulling it away. After I dropped her off, I remember it was this beautiful, sunny day, and I was roaring through the streets feeling like a million-pound weight had been lifted from my chest." He stretches out his legs and shifts into another position before continuing. "I know it's me," he says. "I know I'm a lunatic, and I know I get crazy. It's such a cheesy thing to say to someone 'It's not you. It's me.' But in my case, it really *is* me. Their expectations are not unreasonable—my anxiety is unreasonable. And I can't really talk about my feelings. I can talk about them in the abstract, like we're doing now, but when it's happening in the moment, I get nuts. I'm just very, very quick to pull the rip cord or push the panic button."

While Steve has developed several close, lasting friendships with women, the prospect of romantic intimacy sends him reeling. "I'm not antimarriage," he points out, "but I think about it almost in terms of saving for retirement. Sometimes I think that when I'm old and by myself, I'm going to have these horrible lonely Sundays where everyone is off with their families. But for me, that's not a reason to get married. The reason should be that you love someone and can't imagine being without them. And the fact of the matter is that there hasn't been a lot I can't handle on my own." After his parents divorced when he was three, Steve retreated into self-reliance, basically raising himself. "I think as a kid I had this sense of abandonment, of not having people there for me. There were pieces of me that were closed off, a lot of cauterized emotions that I don't want to open up," he says. "It was good, because it made me independent, but at the same time I think a large part of the reason I've never been in a serious relationship is because I'm used to digesting problems on my own without looking to someone else."

For children who grew up equating independence with survival, intimacy poses a direct threat, echoing back to a time when they looked for support and none was forthcoming; often these children had no choice but to take care of themselves, especially if a parent was aloof, unavailable, or abusive. "I never thought that I needed anybody," says twenty-seven-year-old Ross, who spent his childhood shuttled between his mother, father, and grandparents. "When I was a kid I had to survive, and surviving meant I *couldn't* need anybody because there was no one to rely on. I could only be with me. And that has affected my relationships dramatically. I've never really been able to open up to a woman and really love them and be loved. I'm afraid that if I open up to someone, I'm just going to get crushed. I'm not a kid anymore, but I still have those kid feelings." He reveals that he's recently been trying to work on some of these fears through therapy. "I would love to have a real partner, someone I could talk with about my problems, where I could say 'Help me out here.' I would love to raise a family; that's what I really, really want, but I know I'm not ready to do that yet. I know I can do it, but it takes time."

For many Commitment-Phobes, the problem is not necessarily that they don't want to commit, but that their fear of vulnerability effectively smothers their desire for love; their hearts don't open quite so easily. Getting close is inextricably linked with getting hurt, and so a mounting level of attachment raises a warning flag. Twenty-six-year-old Peter, who hasn't seen his father since he was eight years old, says his greatest fear is that he will be abandoned; so, in a defensive move, he will leave first. "Honestly, I know that I will end relationships for weird reasons," he says. "I had no excuse to break up with my last girlfriend. She was smart, sweet, and gorgeous. I said I wanted to be by myself, but really, I think I was just afraid that if I committed to her, she would end up hurting me. I don't know how to describe it exactly, but maybe we broke up because I started counting on her for security, and I didn't like that feeling."

When protection is the primary goal, fear often eclipses desire; the past overshadows the present. Twenty-five-year-old Katrina, who came home from a vacation when she was seven years old to find that her father had moved out and all the furniture was gone, links her fear of intimacy to her distant relationship with her father as a child. "I literally get terrified around men when it comes to dating. I fear being disappointed—and it has to be because I constantly saw my dad disappointing my mom, and then me," she explains. "The one thing I always heard was 'Your dad doesn't care enough about you kids.' Dad always had more important things going on: One time when I was a kid, he forgot my birthday, and I just remember we rushed to the toy store and he waited while I quickly picked out a present. Today we are not close at all. We talk out of obligation, but my mom still has to push my dad into helping us kids out."

Commitment-Phobes often see the contradictions in their behavior; they don't want to be abandoned, so they abandon; they don't want to have their love cast aside, so they avoid relationships entirely. But the need to distance themselves is not always rooted in rational thought. Rather, panic and discomfort become almost physical responses that go beyond explanation, knee-jerk reactions we learned from experiencing hurt as a child. Even though we are grown up, and have different resources at hand, old habits are hard to break. As one thirty-year-old woman says, "I spend so much psychic energy pretending things are going to happen that I don't want to happen. But I'm not at the point anymore where I would be staying at home, sobbing, and that's what's so bizarre. I envision that I would fall apart, freak out, be lying prostrate on the ground if someone left me, when the truth is I would probably be fine."

Creating a stable base is one way Commitment-Phobes gain the confidence to not only give but receive love. Thirty-year-old William says that for a long time he used to hide behind sex as a way of avoiding serious relationships. "I was absolutely terrified of letting anybody in. I became incredibly promiscuous, but it would literally be a onetime thing. I wouldn't even consider going out on a second date. I think that came from this feeling of rejection growing up, of never being accepted. And I didn't ever want to revisit those feelings again, so it was the old 'I'll reject them before they reject me.' It would be strictly sex and that was it," he says. Ultimately, though, as William gained both financial and emotional security from his career and a tight network of friends, he allowed himself to enter into his first long-term relationship, which recently ended on amicable terms. "Those old feelings are still there—they are definitely still there—but I'm getting better. During those earlier years, even though I said I wanted a relationship, I couldn't handle it. I was lonely and not wanting to get close to anyone at the same time. Those years were really hard."

For now, William is choosing to remain single, but this time his decision is not based on his fear of intimacy. "I haven't wanted to rush into another relationship right away, even though my last relationship was good," he says. "For the first time in my adult life,

I've enjoyed being alone. I have a dog. I look forward to turning the key to my apartment and stepping in. I feel very, very comfortable in it, and I never had that feeling growing up or during my first few years. This is the first place I view as a real home."

Nesters

As outside the rain furiously pelts against her window, twenty-six-year-old Cynthia talks about her recent engagement to her boyfriend of five years. Her apartment, which she shares with her fiancé, is cozy, filled with hanging plants and issues of *Travel & Leisure* magazine. When I ask her if she's nervous about getting married, she thinks about it for only a moment before answering. "I met my fiancé in college, and it was kind of whirlwind. We were seeing each other seriously the minute we met. So sometimes I think, 'I've never been a dating adult.' That's scary. Part of me wishes I could let go for a year, but I couldn't. It would make me crazy. I guess that's the problem: I'm scared he wouldn't come back. I wouldn't be able to deal with him seeing other people," she says. "But I'm not really scared of marriage, because I've always known that I wanted to be married. I know I want to have kids. And I knew that if I kept waiting for someone I didn't doubt, it was never going to happen, because it's not the other person I doubt, it's me. Like I'm not good enough or something."

After Cynthia's parents divorced when she was twelve, her life descended into chaos. She was forced to move to a new town and start at a new school, and her parents fought viciously over child support, frequently bringing her into the middle of it. Her mother was devastated by the divorce, and as the oldest of three, Cynthia was left with the responsibility of taking care of her siblings; meanwhile, her relationship with the father she once adored grew strained. Shortly after she left for college, her mother remarried, and Cynthia is still struggling to figure out where she belongs in this new family arrangement. "My stepfather lived in a house with my sister, and he's a father to my brother. When my sister fought with my mom, he was the one who would step in and ease things over," she points out. "But I never really had a relationship with him, and now they've built this home together. It's my sister and my brother's home, but it's not mine. It's my stepfather and my mother's home, but where do I fit in?"

Unlike Commitment-Phobes, who spurn relationships for fear of getting hurt, Nesters eagerly enter relationships with the highest hopes, often looking to find the attention and security they didn't receive as a child. "I never had a family, with Mom and Dad together, and it's difficult for me to accept the reality that my parents are so distant from my life," says twenty-one-year-old Julie, whose parents divorced when she was four. "I've always wanted to get married young and have kids before I turn twenty-five. I think I've always looked for a way out, wanting to start a family of my own. But I'm also scared I'll ruin it, that I won't know how to have a 'correct' family when I do marry." Some Nesters succeed in finding a caring partner able to provide the support they crave, and they enter into marriage carefully, with their eyes open; others, however, are steered by their need to feel wanted, to satisfy their yearning for love, that they will hang on to relationships that are destructive or deficient, too afraid to let go even when their needs are not being met.

Thirty-one-year-old Erica, who recently divorced her husband of almost eight years, is starting to explore the reasons why she married—and remained married to—an emotionally abusive man. As with many Nesters, who tend to climb the ladder of attachment quickly, Erica's relationship took off at full speed: Within four months they had moved in together, and not even ten months after they met they were married. "It felt really nice to have someone there to come home to. I hate being alone," she admits. "This is one of the big things I'm trying to get over now. Everyone laughs at me, because if I'm alone for five minutes, I have my cell phone out, calling someone up to talk to. But I think it's because I was alone a lot when I was a kid—if not physically, then alone in my head."

As Erica puts it, she and her husband instantly clicked—but in a bad way. "In my marriage, this was the dynamic," she explains. "He would flip back and forth between being the greatest guy, really supportive. He would cook dinner for me and the whole nine yards. But on the other side, he would constantly berate me: I was stupid. I was corrupt. I was evil. It was my fault children were starving in the Amazon." She grimaces. "That's kind of exaggerating it, but not really. And I would believe him. I cried a lot. I felt—and I'm still not sure why—an incredible responsibility toward him, like I had to take care of him. If he was in a bad mood, it was because of something I did. My husband knew all the right buttons to push with me. He was totally incapable of taking responsibility for anything, and I am the type of person who takes responsibility for everything. *Everything*," she emphasizes. "My boss can walk down the hall with a funny look on his face, and I think I did something wrong. It's always me."

After almost eight years of marriage, Erica finally worked up the courage to ask for a divorce. Looking back, she sees how her deep-seated desire for love and acceptance dictated her actions. "With my husband, I was able to fool myself into thinking we had a real relationship. I could make myself believe this was really love, because I wanted it so much and didn't know any better. Granted, I was only twenty-two when I got married, but even so, I just never realized how important it was to choose the right person—and that you do choose. Love is not something you fall into. I didn't realize that you could say no and be selective and not take the first person who looks at you, because it's better than no one. To be honest, I just felt like I didn't have a say in the matter. When my husband asked me, 'Are we going to be together for a long time?' I didn't feel like I could say no. Or maybe. Or 'It's too early to tell.' I had to say yes."

For many Nesters, choice is not the issue: When love seems like a train with only one stop, you better get on or risk being left behind. Being loved by someone—never mind whether we love them back—is paramount. By the same token, any perceived threat of losing that love, even one as seemingly insignificant as a peculiar glance cast in our direction, is seen as a personal failing on our part. *What's wrong with me? If only I could figure out the magic formula that would make the relationship work.* In some respects, since only nonstop reassurances of love can offer total security, Nesters are always on the run. As twenty-five-year-old Maureen explains, "I'm constantly afraid that I might do something that will make my partner not want to be with me anymore. I feel like I'm trying to please them, so they are happy and will want to stay with me. I have such a fear of being alone that I rarely act like myself in a relationship. I just do whatever I can to please my partner."

Like children who blame themselves for their parents' divorces, Nesters believe that the success of a relationship is within their control—that by being good they can stop anyone from ever leaving them again. When their relationships do end, old feelings of loss and rejection may be painfully reawakened.

Twenty-eight-year-old Marianne, who had broken up with her longtime boyfriend a few months before we spoke, is still struggling with the process of letting go. "It's very hard to handle, even though we hadn't been getting along and had grown apart; we started dating when I was eighteen and had become different people with very different values. At the time I was willing to work it out, but now I think I stayed in an unhealthy relationship longer than I should have because, as a child, I always wanted to fix things and make them better. I was so scared that conflict was bad, that it led to bad things, so I would hold a lot of feelings inside. That's what I was used to. I probably would have stayed longer if he hadn't put a stop to it," she says. "There was never any cheating, any physical abuse, or anything serious like that, but when we were together I was always nervous, always expecting to be hurt by him cheating or lying. Even now that we've broken up, I'm still asking him, 'Where were you last night?' and he tells me, 'None of your business.' He could have just been at the gym, but I still want to know. A part of me thinks, 'Maybe he'll come back,' but the other part says, 'No, even if he does, you can't let him hurt you again.' "

Love—both finding it and letting it go—is not easy for anyone. At some point, almost all of us, whatever our family background, experience shades of fear about being hurt or abandoned. It is the nature of intimacy for our hearts to alternately hide and seek, and these three profiles I've described could be broadly applied to many others whose parents are not divorced. Being careful about committing to a partner, choosing to be alone, or wanting love are simply ways of behaving that are neither "right" nor "wrong." In the end, it's not how we approach love that's important, but why we make the choices we do.

In speaking with others, I have begun to realize that certain romantic patterns are not permanently engraved into our being, although sometimes it may seem like they are. Says forty-year-old Tara, "I used to date men who were intelligent, witty, oh yes, and incapable of making a commitment. Man after man cast me aside when he was through with me. Finally, I got it together at age thirty-three and met a wonderful man and now I work hard at my marriage, because I don't want my son to know divorce."

"I got over my suspicions," agrees twenty-four-year-old Victoria, whose parents divorced when she was sixteen, "and it had a lot to do with my boyfriend reassuring me. He keeps telling me, 'We're not your parents,' and he's right." She mentions that they are planning to get married in the future, but haven't yet set a date. "I was thinking about not getting married for a long time because I believed that marriage did not mean that you were more committed to someone than if you didn't get married. I thought, 'A ring around my finger is not going to make me want to be with you and want to work things out—my love and desire to preserve the relationship is what's going to keep me with you.' " She pauses. "I guess the whole sanctity of marriage meant nothing, especially knowing that both my parents had extramarital affairs. But my boyfriend has started to put back the beauty in marriage, and it's a good feeling."

As for me, I still have moments of panic, but I have slowly been able to notch up my ability to trust and to dampen my initial flight instinct when I hit a bump in a relationship. When I'm upset with a partner, I don't immediately resort to tight-lipped denials that nothing is wrong. I am now better able to see the bridge that carries a present hurt into the past, and to stop myself before I cross it and revert to a child's defenses. Trust and realistic expectations can be cultivated over time, and with the help of healthy relationships. And by confronting the past. Because when intimacy becomes a mirror that reflects the past, we become trapped in its prism of waiting and wanting, our relationships dictated by the experiences of childhood. By exploring our fears, and where they come from, we take the first step toward viewing love on our own terms, and not the terms set by our parents.

8

Difficult Passages:
Coming to Terms with Our Parents

MY PARENTS WERE BOTH TWENTY-FIVE YEARS OLD when I was born. I mention this only because, for as long as I can remember, in that way we arbitrarily set guideposts in life, turning twenty-five stood as my own personal marker for entering adulthood. As a young child it seemed like a nice number, plump with cyclical significance, and back then I couldn't wait to hurry up and reach that magical age when I would finally arrive at some eagerly awaited future.

A few months before my twenty-fifth birthday, my boyfriend of almost two years proposed, slipping a diamond engagement ring out of its black velvet box and onto my finger. This was not exactly a surprise: We had been living together for a year and often discussed the possibility of marriage. Still, four hours later, gripped by sheer panic, I took the ring off and placed it on the dresser. "This doesn't mean anything about us," I pleaded with him, unable to look him in the eye. When he remained silent, I added lamely, "I just need more time." One glimpse at the stricken, bewildered look on his face told me that I was asking too much; that I would have to make a decision, and fast.

But as winter melted away into spring, I was no closer to

making a move in any definite direction; when the conversation turned to marriage, I could only turn to evasion. Our relationship was starting to show the strain. I knew I was acting unreasonable: One day, I would feel confident enough to walk down the aisle—enthusiastic even; the next day I retreated, my doubts and anxieties about marriage winning out. God, it was a mess. I was a mess. I started to have trouble focusing at work, straggling in late in the mornings and bolting out early in the evening. My coworkers were taking me aside, whispering, "Is anything wrong?" to which I would smile brightly and reply, "No, I'm fine." I couldn't express exactly what was wrong to myself, let alone to anyone else. All the while, applications and travel books continued to pile perilously high on my desk, ample distractions from the fear that I was not ready to turn twenty-five. Not yet.

But, of course, turn twenty-five I did. On the day of my birthday, I woke up with a tightening in my chest. It was a bright, silvery morning in May, on the brink of summer, with only a damp tingle of heat in the air. Sunlight entered through a pair of fluttering white curtains. My boyfriend's parents had invited us to spend the weekend at their house, and I had happily left behind my cramped apartment, with all its confusing clutter, for somewhere clean and uncomplicated. I lay in bed in their guest room, staring at the ceiling, breathing and listening. The absence of sound was unfamiliar: No car alarms. No swish of tires. No bangs and bumps of city living.

I was twenty-five years old and confused. Unlike my parents at the same age, I was not married with a house and a child, making me feel somehow unofficial; at the same time, when I considered these options, the memory of my parents' divorce hovered over me as an unmistakable warning. I was twenty-five years old, and by my own complicated set of reference points, I was no longer a child, but an adult capable of making the same mistakes my parents made. I didn't know where to turn, which way to go, even what I wanted.

When I finally wandered into the kitchen for breakfast, a surprise was waiting for me. My boyfriend and his parents were sitting around the table, chatting, and we exchanged a round of good mornings; the kitchen was the way I always imagined a kitchen should be: cozy and filled with light, the scent of coffee threading the air. And there on the counter was a chocolate frosted cake. My boyfriend's mother got up and lit the spray of candles on top as the three of them, grinning and slightly off-key, started to sing "Happy Birthday." Following their murmurs of encouragement, I blew out the candles, watched the smoke rise as everyone clapped, and then cut the first slice across the pink block letters of my name. There were hugs and presents, sweet bites of cake and conversation, and the entire time I felt so utterly grateful, so completely awkward, so unsure of how to handle this unexpected act of kindness that I ended up feeling, most of all, painfully self-conscious. I heard myself saying "Thank you" again and again, and each time it sounded more inadequate. This welcoming cloak of belonging with someone else's family weighed heavily, and I squirmed to overcome my clumsiness and make it fit.

Later, during the drive home, I said to my boyfriend, "Your parents didn't have to do all that."

He shook his head and smiled. "Are you kidding? They *wanted* to."

As soon as we arrived back at our apartment, I went over to check the answering machine, feeling a sense of urgency. I listened to the messages from my friends, my grandparents, and two from my father, all wishing me a happy birthday. Their sentiments faded away, overshadowed by one missing voice. My mother hadn't called me. I rewound the messages, hoping I'd skipped over it by accident. Nothing. It was almost eleven o'clock at night when I dialed her number and she picked up the other end of the line, sounding sleepy.

"It's my birthday," I blurted out, anger as my shield. "Were you going to call me?"

She made some excuses: She was going to call later. She didn't think I would be at home. But I could tell from the startled lilt of her voice that she'd simply forgotten. She started to ask what I'd done over the weekend, and after a few curt answers, I ended the conversation abruptly and hung up the phone. I stood there for a moment in the dark entryway of my apartment, which suddenly seemed much too small after a weekend away. My boyfriend had collapsed on the couch without either of us having bothered to turn on the lights, but from the streetlamp outside the window, I could make out the stacked newspapers in the corner, the dishes still waiting in the sink. My boyfriend fiddled with the remote control and the television clicked to life. The walls, as they say, were closing in; in that instant, I felt a despair so physical that I had to escape. Without a word, I walked out the door, letting it slam shut behind me.

It had started raining outside, but I walked around in circles anyway, finally sitting down on a building stoop, huddled, my arms folded across my stomach. A few minutes passed, then my boyfriend jogged into sight and quietly settled in beside me.

"I've been looking for you," he said. "Are you okay?"

I nodded.

"Did I do something?"

I shook my head. My hair was plastered along my cheeks, my clothes were soaked wet against my skin, and I almost wanted to laugh at the drama of it all, except that this intense loneliness was pulling me from the inside.

After a short silence, the only thing I could manage to say was this: "My mom didn't call to wish me a happy birthday." Even as the words came out, I knew that wasn't entirely it, and I could tell from his expression that he didn't really understand why this oversight, while upsetting, should send me flying into the night. And the truth is, my mother had never been one to make a big fuss about birthdays, either before or after she and my father divorced. I knew that.

But for one day, with my boyfriend's parents, I had experienced what such a birthday might have been like in a parallel world, an altogether imaginary world where my parents would have been happy together and we could have celebrated as a family around our kitchen table. But this other world was not—and never could be—my world. Instead, I was sitting in the rain on what had been a much-anticipated birthday, feeling terribly alone, yet unable to commit to anything or anyone. Just when I was supposed to cross the threshold into the future, the past came rushing up, tripping me from behind. And all I wanted to do was go backwards to a place that was not on the map.

I wanted to go home.

This sudden and intense longing for home, which appeared to come out of nowhere, rattled me to the core. But it also rattled me loose by forcing me to confront my mother about her absence in my life. As I've discussed in earlier chapters, on some level, whether subconscious or not, we all carry a script of how relationships should unfold: We expect our loved ones to guide us when we're confused, applaud us when we succeed, and comfort us when we're upset. When they don't act in a way that meets with our assumptions, we once again experience disappointment, hurt, and resentment—for their shortcomings not only in the present, but in the past as well. The loss of our families builds layer upon layer throughout our lives, with each transition or milestone we encounter and surpass— leaving home, our first job, entering into our own marriages, having children of our own.

Nevertheless, many of us find that when we experience these childhood emotions, the distance afforded by age allows us to examine the past with the increased capacities of an adult. For some, this shift in perception allows for a greater understanding of our parents and their choices. "My mom was so young when she got married—she had gone from parents who never gave her a chance to be herself to a husband who never saw her as an individual," explains thirty-eight-year-old Barbara, whose parents divorced when she was fourteen. "My dad's parents had also been very unhappy together, and I don't think he ever really learned what it was to be in a loving relationship until much later. And my mom was so frustrated in her attempts to express herself that her resentment wouldn't allow her to be in a position to give my dad what he needed. I always knew they were miserable together, but over the years I've been able to substitute a lot of the anger and resentment I felt toward each of them with compassion for the challenges they had to overcome."

For others, however, reviewing the past only brings up a full range of emotions we couldn't or wouldn't allow ourselves to feel as children. "I remember visiting my father and my stepmother when I was twelve, and I didn't speak; there seemed to be no point because no one acknowledged my presence. My stepmother wouldn't even set a place for me at the dinner table," says thirty-year-old Theresa, whose parents divorced when she was six. "When you're a kid, and you're being treated that way, you know something is wrong, but you can't put your finger on it. You can't speak up and defend yourself. But now that I am two years younger than my parents were when they divorced, I'm *disgusted* at their behavior. My mother was helpless in so many ways, and my father was a selfish bastard. Don't you think when your twelve-year-old daughter is silent that perhaps something is wrong? Sometimes I wish I could sit him down and ask him 'How could you be such a horrible parent?' It blows my mind."

Children have an incredible capacity to withstand certain emotional blows, partly because they do not yet possess the developmental facilities to process them. As we get older, however, old grievances can be dusted off and reexperienced through memory. As David Elkind, professor of child study at Tufts University, writes in *The Hurried Child,* "Now young people can conceptualize and attribute motives to their parents' behavior that they only intuited before. Many painful memories of childhood are resurrected and reinterpreted in adolescence. Hence, young people begin, in adolescence, to pay their parents back for all the real and imagined slights parents committed during childhood that were suppressed or repressed—but not forgotten." These suppressed emotions, when they surface, can be a heavy cross to bear. But once we've recognized how we've been affected by our parents' behavior, though, we can use confrontation not as "payback" but to challenge and negotiate our relationships with our parents so that we can progress in our lives without the dragging weight of the past.

As adults, we can also start to address the emotional injuries that our parents continue to inflict on us in the present: an empty seat during graduation, a birthday gift that is entirely inappropriate, or one parent's ranting against the other. "A couple of weeks before Christmas, my father called and said he was going to be in town, and he wanted to have dinner with me. He never called," says twenty-eight-year-old Marianne. "When I got back to college, I wrote my father a long letter about my frustrations and my feelings. There were a lot of little things that forced me to write that letter, things that showed his lack of commitment, promises he never followed through on. Afterward we talked for an hour. That was the first time we ever talked about hurt feelings between us." Several others mentioned similar events that triggered them as adults to approach one or both parents.

Twenty-six-year-old Josephine, whose parents separated when she was six, says it wasn't until college that she started to recognize the anger and resentment toward her father that had built up during her childhood. Growing up, she saw her father every weekend, and they had a close relationship. "My father and I have always been friends," she says. "Even though I was living with my mom, he was, in a weird way, the more active parent."

When she was fourteen, Josephine decided to move in with her father and stepmother. "Initially, when I moved in with him, I thought I was doing the best thing for myself, and in a way, I guess I was getting back at my mother for all the craziness she put me through by constantly moving us around, and all her various boyfriends," she explains. But Josephine immediately felt uncomfortable in her father and stepmother's daily world. Her stepmother, who made it clear that she never wanted children of her own, gave Josephine the distinct impression that she was not welcome, labeling items in the refrigerator she wasn't to touch and complaining when she brought friends over; her father never intervened on her behalf. The two adults went away on long vacations together during the summer, leaving Josephine in the house alone. "My father really thought of me as being silent in high school, but I was only like that around him, because I felt like I was intruding on their space. When they were around, I tried not to be there."

For Josephine, it was difficult to let go of the idealized vision she'd had of her father as a child. "Before I lived with him, I thought my father was a god. He was my savior," she says. "I think you want to believe your parents are going to protect you, and when you realize they are just people, and they are not there for you, and may even do things that are selfish or that will hurt you, it's such a shocking revelation. And I had really put my father on a pedestal. He was the one person in my life I had felt like I could trust." Rather than blame her father for the tense situation at home, Josephine turned the blame on herself. "I thought it was my fault that things had changed between us after I moved in," she says. "But as I started to look back on what it was like living with him I realized that I was angry with him for not standing up for me."

When she was in college, a trivial incident became the breaking point for Josephine, unleashing her resentment into the open. She and her father had arranged to celebrate her birthday over dinner, just the two of them, and he arrived at the restaurant with her stepmother. "He told me she wanted to come along, but my stepmother seemed like she was in a foul mood," Josephine remembers. "She was silent, and when the steak she ordered came, she was unhappy because it was overcooked, so my father gave her his steak instead. I just remember watching that and thinking, 'My father would never do that for me.' It was something so minor, but when I left that night, I just felt angry." Later that week, Josephine met her father for coffee and told him how much she resented the way he had treated her growing up. "He admitted that he felt like he was caught in the middle between my stepmother and me, and by taking her side, he was basically trying to save their marriage," she says. "It made me feel better to get that out in the open, and it also validated what I had been feeling. It was important to know that his view of the past was the same as mine."

By addressing these issues with her father, Josephine was able not only to push their relationship to a new level of honesty but to obtain a handle on the past, allowing her to put it into perspective. This process often entails challenging a child's version of the past and seeing it in a new light of retrospection. While Josephine had to knock down her romanticized image of her father, thirty-five-year-old Bridget, whose parents divorced when she was almost two years old, had to do the opposite, coming to terms with a father who had been characterized as indifferent and cruel during her childhood.

From her mother, Bridget learned that her father was abusive, both physically and mentally, and was told that he wasn't worth knowing. When he sent cards to her in the years following the divorce, her mother returned them to him unopened. When Bridget was six years old, her mother remarried, and they moved to another state; she never saw her father again and had few memories to hold on to. As far as Bridget was concerned, she was living in a two-parent home, and she didn't have the desire to seek her father out. "Before I can really remember anything, my stepfather was in the picture. He became Daddy, and I was his little girl. He loved me, probably more than if I was his own," she says. "I always thought my father no longer cared, and so I wanted nothing to do with him."

When she was a teenager, however, her father died and Bridget discovered that in his will, he had named her sole heir to his estate. "I had to go back to his house—he had never moved out of the house we had all once lived in—and my room still had little kid's drawings hanging up. All these years, I thought he didn't care, because he never really tried to find me. So I guess it kind of hit me then that maybe that wasn't true," she says. "His housekeeper told me that he had never stopped caring, but he had sort of backed off, thinking that it was the right thing to do. It was a very difficult period after I learned that. I got very upset with my mother for a while." She pauses and then concludes, "My mother was absolutely right to leave him for what he did to her. I only wish I had been given the chance to get to know him and come to my own decision about him, and I regret that now."

As we enter into our twenties and thirties, we all start to redefine our relationships with our parents. This is a normal part of becoming an autonomous adult. But when our parents are divorced, this passage can be littered with additional obstacles. First, we must contend with examining our bond with not a parental unit, but two individuals with whom we have separate ties. Furthermore, in propelling our relationship with each parent to another level, we must deal with any residual hostility our parents have toward each other, as well as address any resentment and anger that is ours alone. We each face unique challenges in negotiating new terms for our parents' breakups—everything from setting boundaries to forgiving old grievances—but by steering the direction our relationship with a parent takes, we open the way for achieving stability in our lives.

Finding a Balance

Ever since her parents divorced when she was two years old, Cheryl has inhabited the two different worlds of her mother and father. After their divorce, her parents settled on a joint custody arrangement, and the visitation schedule was figured out with an almost mathematical precision. Although her mother's house remained her primary residence, Cheryl would see her father on alternating days during the week and every other weekend. On weekdays he would pick her up after school and take her to his house, where she would do her homework and eat dinner; right before bedtime, he would drive her back to her mom's house. When he moved to a town half an hour away later in her childhood, her father kept up the visits, making the commute to pick her up every weekend.

While her parents were not openly hostile, they drew sharp boundaries between them, which Cheryl had to negotiate on her own. Even today, they rarely speak or acknowledge the other's presence. At her high school graduation, her mother and stepfather were on one side of the hall, and her father and stepmother were on the other. She went back and forth, taking photographs with each family. "There was no standing together as a group and chatting," she says matter-of-factly. "They were two separate camps, and no one had any intention of bringing them together. Everyone was comfortable with the extremely uncomfortable situation."

But after Cheryl moved away for college, she started to feel the stress of juggling her two families. Since they lived in close proximity to each other, she found herself caught between two parents who both wanted to spend time with her. When she came home to visit, both parents would show up at the airport, standing a few feet apart, and she would greet them separately and then have to decide which parent she was going home with.

Sitting on the couch with her feet tucked underneath her, Cheryl describes her last holiday. "I had to go to dinner at my stepgrandmother's house, drive two hours that same evening to be with my mom at my grandmother's house, spend the night there, drive another half hour to my other grandmother's house, say hi to my cousins for a couple of hours and not really get to hang out with them because, boom, I'm off to the next place. It was *nuts,*" she says. "I was spending the night all over the place, living out of a backpack, and it was a real pain in the ass. I mean, I want to see everybody, and there are so many people to see when you include all the stepfamilies. I had a breakdown before I left, bawling my eyes out because I couldn't stand the pressure. I finally got to a point where I could slow down and say to myself, 'You don't have to do it all. You can make some choices here. For once, you need to think about yourself first.' "

At twenty-five, Cheryl is exploring her independence away from the constraints of her family, and realizing that she needs to set limits on how much she can do. Beyond matters of scheduling and time management, she is also trying to figure out how the emotional pull between the opposite poles of her parents' personalities has influenced her. "It's this question of 'Who am I?' Not in relation to my parents, but who am *I*," she says. "I've been trying to get on this road of discovering myself, and part of that process is looking at the past. I've really been trying to think back, and what I come up with is after the divorce, I was traveling between these two different worlds all the time. I was always playing by different rules, adjusting my personality to fit in. I felt like everything I did fell into one of those two molds." She sighs and sits up. "There were two people in my life who represented two lifestyles that I had to pass between on a regular basis and still do. My mom was really open and liberal, and my dad was pretty conservative. There was no gray area between my mom's personality and my dad's personality. She's on the West Coast of the cosmos, and he's on the East Coast," she says, using her hands, palms up, to show the distance between them. "Now I have to define my own life, and I'm finding that it's really hard to do. Everyone goes through it, I guess. For me, I always thought, 'I'm going to turn out like my mom,' or 'I'm going to turn out like my dad,' instead of turning out like me."

Defining our own lives can be especially difficult when we continue to be pulled in two different directions, both psychologically and physically, as adults. Twenty-eight-year-old Melinda, whose parents divorced when she was seven, grew up in an environment of constant hostility between her parents that has extended into adulthood; when she got married, she eloped, unwilling to deal with the prospect of inviting both her parents—who hadn't seen each other for the past twenty years, except in a courtroom—to the wedding. When her sister got married, she solved the problem by having two separate ceremonies. But despite Melinda's efforts to remain on neutral territory by conducting a painful balancing act, a few years ago the scales tipped, forcing her to create a new balance in her life:

When I was twenty, my mother told me she would disown me for attending the funeral of my paternal grandmother's second husband. Somehow, attending a funeral became a "crime" that she was willing to sever her relationship with me for. My father then told me *he* would disown me if I did not attend. I was a perfect daughter, a good student, and had done absolutely nothing wrong, and I was being forced to choose one of two "crimes," either of which would cause me to lose a parent. I chose not to attend because I felt my father was more rational and I would eventually be able to explain my decision to him.

After the funeral incident, my father didn't speak to me for a year. Finally I called him and we met, and for the first time, we openly discussed the divorce and our relationship. He was honest about his mistakes and tried to explain his intentions. We both apologized and agreed to put the past behind us and move on. We have had a good relationship ever since. In the last two years especially, my relationship with my father has gotten closer than it ever has before. We have now rebuilt our relationship from the ground up. For the first time in my life, my father calls me just to say hi, and I enjoy his company and value his advice.

In strengthening her relationship with her father, Melinda was forced to alter her relationship with her mother. She admits that although the two of them are close, their relationship is rocky as she sets boundaries that should have been in place long ago. "She still wants to rant about my father," Melinda explains, "and I have finally refused to participate."

Finding a balance between two parents means attaining strength and resolve in our own lives, which can be difficult to do if a parent refuses to change or acknowledge hurtful behavior. Explains twenty-seven-year-old Sandra, "My mother and I are not speaking as of very recently. She has made some decisions to insult my brother and my dad, so I came to their defense, and she said some vulgar things. She has no ability to talk politely, and I couldn't take it anymore, so I asked her not to call, E-mail, or write me. She is always starting something. She even calls her new husband by my dad's name. We have all moved on except her." As Sandra points out, sometimes to move forward, we need to leave a parent behind.

Cutting Off Contact

It wasn't until his own divorce a couple of years ago that thirty-two-year-old Jonathan started to question the quality of his family relationships and decided he was ready to make a change. "My divorce was sort of a shock to me, and I think the pain of that shock forced me into confronting my emotions for the first time," he says. "I started to reexamine all the major relationships in my life, including those with my mother and father. So I went to these people and told them I wanted things to change, to be more honest, and everyone responded really well except for my father, who threw a fit," he says. "The crux of it was that I wanted our relationship to go two ways, meaning I wanted him to be conscious of what I wanted, what I felt and where I was, instead of our relationship being dictated by what he wanted," he says. "He gave me a blanket apology—along the lines of 'I'm sorry for everything I did to you in your life'—but the apology rang a little hollow. He separates himself from his previous actions, like that was the 'old' me and this is the 'new' me. And he never elaborates on it, which makes me feel like there's no sense of responsibility. We went through a yearlong period of fighting and rapprochement—all the rapprochement was on my initiative—and finally I stopped approaching him."

For most of his childhood, Jonathan subjugated his own desires and personality to his father's desires: There was never any flexibility over their weekend visits, and little room for honest discussions. While his father was involved in his life, it was an involvement that rarely delved beyond the surface details of the everyday. "If someone had actually asked me if I had any resentment toward my father growing up, I might have said yes, but it wasn't really that conscious," Jonathan says. "I remember once in college saying to him, 'I would like to talk to you more,' which was probably recognition on my part that some emotional connection was lacking. But nothing really changed. We would still have these obligatory phone calls where we'd talk about the weather, and that was about it. And that type of communication extended into my thirties."

The last time Jonathan contacted his father was a disaster; he was in his father's town on a business trip, after watching an in-flight movie of a father-son relationship that resonated with him. It moved him enough that he decided to call his father after more than a year of silence between them, and they ended up having a nice chat over the phone; but when his father asked when they could see each other, Jonathan explained that he was only there for the weekend, and he was on business, so maybe they could get together on another trip. "Later on, I got a call from his wife, and she was all upset, and I gathered that after hanging up the phone with me, my father had concocted this elaborate plan on my part to ruin his day—I called to trick him into asking me if he could see me, just so I could turn him down," he says. "After that I was like, well, no good deed goes unpunished. I'll be careful when I contact him again, if ever."

Although it's not an easy decision to make, sometimes the best alternative we are left with, after too many years of hurt and disappointment, is to cut off contact with a parent entirely. Thirty-year-old Megan, whose parents divorced when she was thirteen, describes the incident that finally convinced her she needed to exclude her father from her life:

The last day I talked to my father was at my grandmother's funeral. When she died, my father wasn't even the first to tell us—my uncle told us. My father called us a few hours later, and he told us there wasn't going to be a funeral, she was just going to be "planted," and that was the end of the story. I was horrified. That wasn't what my uncle had said; he told us there was going to be a small graveside ceremony. It was the last straw. He'd lied and deceived my mother about child support, he'd lied and deceived me about paying for both college and graduate school, and now he was lying about my grandmother's funeral. I finally decided that, as an individual, the person known as my father was not someone I wished to associate with at all. Since then, I've gotten one or two cards, a letter, and a Christmas card in 1993. I pretty much don't think about ever talking to him again, although I'll admit that I'm envious of my friends who have good relationships with their fathers.

Tragic or emotional events can bring an unsatisfactory relationship with a parent into sharp relief. For thirty-three-year-old Jackie, whose parents divorced when she was thirteen, the murder of her sister flushed out her deep-seated anger at her father. In mourning her sister's death, Jackie could no longer ignore the grievances against her father that had built up in silence, grievances that her father refuses to address or acknowledge:

I now sympathize much less with my father and more with my mother. When I was younger, I essentially thought it was fine that my father left to try and pursue his own happiness. Now, particularly since he failed even in finding his own happiness—his second wife divorced him in 1989, and he suffered from depression and unemployment for a few years—I no longer believe that. The divorce caused too much suffering and destruction for too many people. I don't believe anymore that a parent divorces only the spouse. Invariably the parent divorces the children too.

Even though I treated my father lovingly until the last few months, I have long been angry inside about many things: His lack of support for my college education; certain scumlike behavior around the divorce, like inviting his second wife over to the family house while they were having an affair; disinheriting us four children in favor of his two children with his second wife; and most recently, refusing to allow my sister's estate to have been distributed as she would have wished—mostly to my mother—and insisting on taking half because he could legally.

I am now sick and tired of being the good, loving daughter. My sister's murder put many things into perspective, and I have been much less willing to just shut up about things that are wrong. So I have offended my father greatly by telling him what I think of his behavior, and we are avoiding each other. It is sad to have a bad relationship with a parent— a new, almost unimaginable thing for me—but I just don't really want a relationship with him anymore. I am happier in my day-to-day life not having to deal with him.

While Jackie broke out of her role as the good daughter to her father by putting distance between them, thirty-year-old Ben made it official by deciding to be adopted by his stepfather when he was eighteen. His parents divorced before he was two years old, and his visits with his father had always been somewhat tense. "My father drank too much," he says. "I can't tell any dramatic stories about violence or anything like that—it was more an intimidating sarcasm and distance that really made me afraid of him. I mean, I was a nervous bird of a kid."

Nevertheless, the decision to be adopted was not an easy one to make. "I have very, very mixed emotions about what I did when I got adopted, and I really struggled with it for a few years afterward.

It took me a long time to get over the guilt of what I'd done. The last time I saw my father at my family's attorney's office, he actually mentioned that he and I were very much alike. Our aloofness and sense of humor. The way we look. And he was right," he remembers. "But as a friend said, my dad had the fun part and my stepfather had all the hard work. Really, as far back as my memory goes, my stepfather's been my father figure in a meaningful way. But still, the argument was very powerful—there's just that biological connection." He waves his hand off to the side. "If he walked in right now, you would probably recognize him as my father. But I decided that I wanted to go through with the adoption, and when I told him, he said, 'Do you know what you're doing here? This is pretty final. It's going to be pretty hard to keep a relationship going.' And I said yes, I know what I'm doing. I've never seen him again."

I ask Ben if he wants to see his biological father again. "I used to want to see him, especially in the early years when the connection was stronger—you know, it's just like a breakup," he answers. "But I think it would have spun me around and dredged up a lot of feelings. Now, although it would still be incredibly difficult, I think I could handle it. As my mother says, you don't want people to pass on with any regrets of things you should have said or done, so if he does escape me for too long, I'll probably reach out and try to find him." Meanwhile, his father's presence, the possibility of a chance encounter or run-in, lurks in the back of his mind. "I always wonder at airports if I'll bump into him," he adds. "I scan the crowds, because you never know if he's going to be there."

Cutting off contact with a parent might be a necessary last resort, but it is often not an ideal way to leave things. Although our lives may be improved without the presence of a hurtful or abusive parent, there always remain the loose ends, the questions, and the issues that can't be resolved through silence. "I hate my father," remarks forty-four-year-old Simone, whose parents divorced when she was seventeen, after almost two decades of marriage. Her father's announcement that he was in love with another woman tore apart what Simone remembers as a pretty happy family life, and Simone basically stopped talking to him after he left. "He just traded us in for another woman who also had three kids," she explains. "My mother was totally devastated, and she had to be put on tranquilizers. She had never held a paying job in her life and now she had to take care of three kids and a mortgage. Her life has been utter hell for two decades. I have actually gotten more angry about my father's infidelity as I've gotten older, especially since I'm now involved in my own divorce over another woman. I do not trust men." She adds, "My father is now on his fourth wife, and she's the same age as me."

Disowning a parent also means giving up the chance for making peace with that parent and feelings of loss and rejection can continue to haunt us, especially if a parent easily accepts a place outside our lives. Says one thirty-one-year-old woman who hasn't talked to her father in five years, "I don't speak to my dad, and it doesn't even bug him. Maybe every now and then he has an odd moment, but he has never really tried to work on our relationship." Another twenty-six-year-old woman, who hasn't spoken with her father for three years, says, "I would have these spiteful little moments, like 'I'll show him'—he won't know what's happening with me, and one day I'll show up with ten grandkids. But then I got married, and he wasn't at the wedding, and I realized I didn't show him, he showed me again, because I still don't have a father."

Making Peace

During an hour-long conversation, twenty-nine-year-old Caitlin, whose parents divorced when she was two years old, mentions that she recently spent Thanksgiving with her entire family. Together. When I remark that I couldn't even imagine what that would be like, she laughs and says, "You never know. A few years ago I never would have thought it would be possible either. But it's grown positively warm. We have these family get-togethers now, and there's a lot of joking around the table, and everyone has an interesting life. We talk about who we are today. At the end, we're like, 'Wow, we're a family.' We sort of bonded."

A decade earlier, her family was being ripped apart by conflict. When Caitlin was seventeen, her mother sued her father for child support, mainly as a symbolic gesture. Her parents had gotten into an argument over money, and her father had refused to give her mother credit for having raised two children on her own, with only limited financial support from him. After the court battle, each member of the family descended into hostile silence. Caitlin finally took it upon herself to break through the barrier, shuttling back and forth between family members as she tried to get them to at least communicate with some civility. "Everyone hated me," she says. "I was in the middle. My brother was really outspoken in his disapproval; he thought I was weak for giving in to them. But I always felt like it was the right thing to do, even though I felt guilty about my mom, who felt the most betrayed, always so threatened and fearful that we would turn to my dad instead of to her, again maybe for financial reasons."

In working to bring the family back together, Caitlin started to address her own conflicted relationship with her father. Growing up she rarely saw him. "As a kid, it wasn't a realistic relationship. I guess there was a childhood's worth of idolizing and dreaming of a dad, and what a dad is, and I wanted a dad. I was just in love with the idea of a family, a normal, whole family," she explains. When she was fifteen, she moved in with her father for nine months, and she describes it as a nightmare; her father was going through his second divorce, and he was often unreliable and overly critical. "Now I understand my father's perspective to some degree, although I still don't totally trust him and am wary of getting too close. It just doesn't make sense that he could have been as ignorant as he claims to be about our financial situation growing up. Still, we talk on the phone almost once a week, and we do things together.

We have a pretty damned good relationship, and I very consciously built it."

Peace, by definition, comes on the heels of strife. Once we work through resentment over a parent's past—or even present—behavior, some of us are able to reach a new level of understanding and forgiveness. "There was a time when I felt like I didn't care about my father, and I would lay it all out there, all my anger," says twenty-eight-year-old Samantha, whose parents divorced when she was two. "I don't do that anymore. I feel like it's time to rebuild. When you just hate and hate and hate, you can't move beyond it, and that's it. You can only be bitter for so long."

The turning point, as Samantha remembers, was when she got engaged at age twenty-three and was forced to decide whether her father would walk her down the aisle. Sitting on her bed in her mother's home, she told her father over the phone that he might not be invited to the wedding at all, going through a long list of events he had missed in the past—birthdays, holidays, dance recitals, and the many visits he never showed up for. "All my life there was this latent resentment toward my father, mainly fueled by my mom. It was always 'He doesn't care about you,' " Samantha says. "I hated him for so long, and so around my wedding, I decided now it was my turn to hurt him. I said he didn't deserve to be there, that people would ask 'Who is that man?' And my father got really upset."

Soon, the question of whether her father would attend the wedding became the subject of family discussion. "My grandparents called me—they are really traditional, and they said my decision was so insulting. They never held my dad accountable for not being a good dad to me. He's the only child and so he's like God's gift to the world, this great guy. Even my mother—who loathes the man— said, 'If he can be civil and walk down the aisle with me, it would be nice.' It was an agonizing decision," Samantha recalls. "I think the clincher was when a friend said to me, 'If you don't invite him to the wedding, and it's something that he feels so strongly about, then you're basically closing the door on ever having a relationship with him.' And I finally agreed to let him come, but I had these ground rules of different events during the wedding that he could come to and not come to. The wedding was totally uncomfortable, but I'm telling you, from that moment on, being with him was really transformed; I don't know why."

In the past few years, Samantha and her father have been rebuilding their relationship layer by layer. "My birthday was last Friday, and my father left this message on my voice mail at work. I saved it, because it really touched me," she says. "First, he was saying happy birthday, which was sweet—this is from a guy who has never done that before; he's never celebrated my birthday. But then he was telling me that he found a videotape from 1981, when I was ten years old, and I'm carving a pumpkin with my brother, and he said something along the lines of 'I have so few memories of you as a child—it really meant something to me to find that tape.' And I thought, 'Wow, he really gets it. He knows he missed out.' "

For her part, Samantha is learning to appreciate having a long-absent father finally play a role in her life. "I talk to him frequently now, and we actually have so much in common personality-wise. I always think of the nature/nurture thing, because here's a guy who was not around for me growing up, yet we are so similar in both good ways and bad ways; even our taste in food is similar. Normally, you don't have that unless you've grown up with someone for eighteen years."

As Samantha explains, however, theirs is not exactly a typical father-daughter relationship groomed over the course of a childhood and now evolving smoothly into the child's adulthood. "To this day, one of my oldest childhood friends still says, 'I can't believe this is the same guy that I heard about growing up.' And it's weird, because my father will actually ask for my advice about women. And then he can give me way too much information—and I'm not going to gross you out, but way too much. I tell my husband, and he's like, 'Enough, I can't even hear it.' He says, 'Isn't that making you squirm?' And I say it does in a way, but in another way, I'm re-moved from it because my father's like a big brother or an uncle—he's not Daddy telling you about some woman he's sleeping with. It's such an untraditional relationship."

Unfortunately, making peace with one parent can cause a rift in our relationship with the other if he or she still carries resentment from the divorce; in this context, forming a closer relationship with a parent can be seen as switching sides. "I was always really tight with my mom and not really that tight with my dad," says twenty-five-year-old Frank. "My father was dealing with a lot of anger and respect issues while I was growing up, and while I wasn't scared of him, it was emotionally trying. But now that I'm trying to get closer to him, my mom and I argue about my relationship with my dad more than anything else. I think she would like it if . . . I not so much held a grudge but if I *remembered* more about the past, which I'm almost trying not to do. I'm trying to do the opposite, to move on, not only because my father's getting really old but because I need to have a relationship with my dad, and to do that, I have to let go of the anger from earlier on. And I think that's really hard on her because she was the one I would bawl my eyes out to when my father would pull his stunts, so she's internalized all that hurt."

Simply getting older can take care of most of the job of mend-ing frayed relationships with a parent. Says thirty-three-year-old Kenneth, whose parents divorced when he was four, "My child-hood, on the whole, was fairly painful. I don't regret any of it, and I am who I am because of what happened to me. But I definitely feel like, on my own level, there was a lot of pain and sadness and anx-iety. Since it happened when I was so young, I feel like I did miss out, at least in my own head, by feeling the burden of having to be more responsible. Not being carefree, just being exposed to so much conflict, and knowing that my parents' divorce was partly their fault. Now I've kind of arrived at a place where I can put it to rest." He adds, "It's always with you, but I used to be actively pissed at my father and my mother, and maybe it's part of getting older, but I guess I realized that people make some bad choices, and that's life. I've been able to let go."

I haven't quite reached that point of entirely letting go, but I'm trying. Together, my mother and I have started to venture into this darker territory of feeling. For the first time, she is beginning to tell me her version of events, from her marriage to my father to her affair to my parents' divorce. For the first time, I am beginning to express the hurt and anger I felt after she left, all the emotions that once hummed underneath our relationship of polite formality, unspoken and dangerous. There are many ways to let go, with some quieter than others, but as I've learned, it never happens in the span of a moment or the length of one conversation; rather, it comes in short bursts, in stops and starts.

Along the way, there are hard truths to face: I have to tear apart some of the myths I spun as a child and accept that, while my mother wasn't the selfless, nurturing one I wanted so desperately, she also didn't leave me without guilt and heartache. In breaking down these illusions, I have to acknowledge that I am no longer a wounded daughter, but an adult who is capable of making my own decisions and taking control of my own relationships. I am learning to view my mother in the present tense, to relate to her as a friend as well as her daughter, and to appreciate her efforts now without thinking back to a letdown in the past. On my last birthday my mother sent a birthday card, and she called me. Twice.

9

Finding Home

SHORTLY AFTER I MOVED into my first apartment—a space not shared with a roommate but mine alone—my father announced that he was turning my old bedroom into a makeshift gym and needed to drop off some of my belongings. On an early Saturday morning, while the sky was still dark, he drove up to New York and unloaded boxes of books, several garbage bags filled with clothing circa 1984, some vinyl records, and a small tribe of stuffed animals into my already cramped living room. We went out for breakfast, then he headed back to his home and I returned to mine. When I saw the piles on the floor waiting for me, I was overwhelmed by their mass, by the memories they summoned. I sat cross-legged beside them for hours, wading through the remnants of my childhood as if to say good-bye, and then packed all but a few treasured items for the Salvation Army.

I have now lived in the same apartment for five years. All my history is contained within its four walls. Framed photographs pepper the bookshelves, my desk, and the dresser; plants line the windowsill. Yet, although I have casually referred to my apartment as "home" for some time now, it is just starting to *feel* like home.

It's a new feeling, this feeling of putting down roots and surrendering to the familiarity of my surroundings by putting my faith in their stability, instead of constantly looking for something lost that I will never find.

For a long time, when I saw others who could find home so easily, who could invoke that kind of comfort and security wherever they were, I would observe them in wonder. I was never schooled in creating that kind of history. Even when all the pieces were there—a caring boyfriend, a good job, and close friends—I couldn't bring myself to fit them together into a picture that made sense. Something was always missing, and so, with a scattered intensity, the kind fueled by desperation rather than desire, I spent a couple of years hatching plans for escape. I played with the idea of quitting my job and going off to graduate school—maybe interior design, maybe law—taking off to backpack around the world, or holing up in an isolated cottage in the country. It didn't seem to matter at the time that my plans were sprouting off in opposite directions, or that my energies focused then fizzled as I explored all the different options that were available, and even a few that weren't. I was searching for a destination in the smooth horizon ahead of me, somehow convinced that I could cure my disquiet by simply switching the scenery.

I hadn't faced how my parents' divorce had affected me back then. Running away had always been easy for me, but making a home, and allowing someone to share it with me, was another matter entirely. After more than a year of living with my boyfriend I still couldn't say "our" rather than "my" apartment; it was, and sometimes still is, a struggle to fully let him into my life. But the closer I've come to accepting the fact I can't "go home," the more I have started to work on creating my own.

Although rocked by chaos as children, many of those I interviewed have spoken of constructing a stable foundation as adults. Remarks one twenty-nine-year-old woman, "I never had a home growing up. I had an address. My original family has disintegrated, but my sister and I have formed our own family, with her husband

and my boyfriend, mutual close friends, and our two dogs. We are determined to create a home of our own. That's part of the reason why I've been fiercely tenacious about staying put in the same city. The continuity has great meaning for me."

We each carry images of home that are a composite of observation, imagination, and emotion, but in grasping for a definition, we can't help but be drawn in by the clichés: *Home is where the heart is. There's no place like home. Home, sweet home.* We may associate "home" with place, but there's a universe of feeling behind this simple word. We use "home" to describe our state of mind: When we feel at home, we no longer wish to be anywhere else; there is no frustrating gulf between desire and fulfillment. We have achieved a sense of contentment with our lives.

Sitting in her high-rise office, behind a broad expanse of her desk, thirty-one-year-old Alice shows me a handful of photographs of her new house—which she recently bought with her fiancé—and their new puppy. The wedding is only a couple of months away, and her excitement is evident. She has a successful career and a loving partner, and they are about to embark on a life together in their new home. "I've managed to find happiness in my life," she says, but as she points out, her current happiness has come at the end of a path of discovery.

About three years ago, Alice was engaged to her boyfriend of six and a half years, and making preparations for their wedding. "We started dating in college, and we lived together after college, and then we got engaged while I was in graduate school," she says. "And he's a great guy. Everyone likes him." But, as she explains, while their relationship was comfortable and caring, it also missed a certain degree of passion. "As the wedding got closer, I started to feel an incredible amount of anxiety. I mean, I was having a full-scale anxiety attack, and everyone kept saying, 'Oh, it's just school, don't worry about it,' or that it was just the normal prewedding jitters," she remembers. "But I started to think about it, and I finally made the decision that I couldn't get married."

Her decision, she says, evolved over the course of a week, after many conversations with her parents. "I talked to my dad, and he was incredible, and I talked to my mom, and she was great. And they both said—which really rocked my world—that they had felt the same way before they got married, but they went through with it anyway. Hearing that just made me more certain, knowing the childhood I had, that I couldn't do it. So I called my wedding off a month before." She pauses. "And it was the greatest thing I ever did. I feel awful that it had to happen that way, but now I look at my life, and I can't believe I lived any other way."

Alice finished school, found a job, and for the first time lived in an apartment on her own. And she fell in love. In finding the courage to stop herself from entering into a marriage she didn't feel quite right about, she had also learned something about her family and herself. "Being a pleaser my whole life, I had always been afraid of what would happen if I didn't do the right thing, and here I had done the ultimate wrong thing, and everybody was still equally loving and supportive," she says. "It was a huge lesson for me to learn about the unconditionality of love. I learned you don't have to please everyone to have them love you, and they are going to love you for who you are."

After a childhood of accommodating the demands of two warring parents, Alice has gained the confidence to start making her own demands. "My goal is to start having holidays at my house— and whoever wants to come is welcome. That's the way I'm going to do it, and I feel pretty strongly about it," she says. "I'm tired of bouncing around. There have been losses along the way. I definitely never had the feeling of 'I'm home, and everyone is here and everything is right in the world.' I'm never going to have that feeling with them. I make visits, but they are more like targeted hits."

At her wedding, she is insisting that both her parents sit together at her table. "I think if I had gotten married five years ago, I would have had separate tables, but now I feel like, you know, this is my deal. I've had to adjust my schedule to their schedules and agendas for a long time, and for one day, everyone is going to be happy for us. That's how it's going to be." She smiles, and then concludes, "It took a lot of work for me to get to that level." By taking advantage of her experience as an opportunity for growth and change, Alice is entering into marriage on her own terms.

New Lessons: Marriage and Family

While sometimes our parents' divorces can leave us lacking the tools we need to navigate our own marriages, they can, on the other hand, also provide us with the determination and resolve to work on our relationships. Thirty-one-year-old Sylvia, who has been married to her husband for eleven years and has two children, explains how she has used the experience of her parents' divorce when she was thirteen to guide her behavior in her own marriage:

> I chose very young to learn from my parents' mistakes and not to repeat them, to always remember the pain caused by their divorce.
>
> It's sad that things in their marriage got so out of hand that they felt like they had to give up. So many things were said and done out of frustration on both their parts. Everyone was hurt, and I believe my parents regret that, but at the same time, they felt no hope. I feel wiser now, although it's still difficult to imagine how rough it really was for them. I see things they could have done better, and I try to apply those lessons to my own marriage. If something pleases or displeases me, I tactfully say what is wrong and encourage my husband to do the same. If my husband and I ever disagree, I go out of my way to try and communicate and compromise. It brings back horrible memories of my parents at times.
>
> I've seen firsthand how destructive selfishness and loneliness can be, and it's constant motivation for me to actively improve my relationship and head off any potential problems before they grow any bigger. I still feel pain as I remember

two people once in love now so weathered. My mom has never been the same, and I think my dad feels a lot of guilt for the way things were handled. I vow not to make the same mistakes my parents made. I would never do that to my children.

The critical variable in using the past in a constructive way is whether we stop to understand the problems that existed between our parents, so we can recognize and then change any destructive patterns we may have inherited from them. Once we have done so, we gain a valuable asset in transforming their experience into positive lessons for our own marriages.

Twenty-five-year-old Evan, whose parents divorced when he was nearly four years old, recently married a woman he had been dating for seven years. "It was nice to date for that length of time and feel comfortable and know that I probably knew her as well as I possibly could. Nothing was going to pop up and surprise me. Still, it's not 'Oh, once I'm married, everything will be fine,' " he says. "When you get married, there are going to be problems, and you're going to have to communicate about them. It's a real journey. I never had this romantic notion of marriage being this amazing, magical entity." With his parents' divorce as an example of what can go wrong, Evan is determined to maintain a level of honesty and openness in his marriage. "I tend to be a very good communicator. If there's any little problem, I tend to want to talk about it. I'm one of those," he admits. "I definitely focus on the quality of the relationship all the time—are things good or bad? And if things aren't good, why aren't they good? And what could I, or we, do about it? I have probably overcompensated in that respect, or at least made sure that communication is never an issue."

Conducting a marriage without a clear role model, though, can be a constant process of invention. As twenty-six-year-old Cynthia points out, her husband's mother has been divorced three times and both her mother and his father are remarried. None of these marriages, however, is one that either of them would want to emulate.

"So that's been challenging, because we have really tried to create a model of what it's going to be," she says. "My husband grew up in a house full of women, so I think we've kind of established a different model. I think we've tried to dispel a lot of gender roles in our marriage." Cynthia admits that at first she and her husband had some communication problems, partly stemming from their respective childhoods. "I have to talk about things, and sometimes we fight, and it took a while for him to realize that we could fight and not hate each other," she says. "But we got past that. And I think what I've learned from him is that, at the end of the day, we're friends, which my parents never were."

Although she strives for a different marriage from her parents, Cynthia also retains some of the lessons from their divorce. "As much as I love being married, and having someone to share my life with, I'm also very conscious of not feeling dependent, not feeling like I can't take care of myself," she says. "So, as a result, sometimes I take on too much, and I'm *too* independent. I always pay the bills, I just do, and we got into a stupid fight one day because I decided that he should pay the bills because men pay the bills." She laughs and shakes her head. "I'm very torn between taking responsibility for things and getting angry about it. I think I also feel torn between believing the stereotypes that were beaten into my head from birth about husbands and wives, and trying to avoid those stereotypes. I guess people like to have their roles defined for them to a certain extent, and during the adjustment period of marriage, it's a real challenge to define those roles on your own. You basically have to define yourself by what you don't want to be."

While we may understand why our parents divorced, as well as accept their shortcomings as parents, it can still be difficult to knock down the old emotional defenses that linger behind. Until she met her husband, Barbara, thirty-eight, was involved in a series of bad relationships once she left home at seventeen. After dropping out of college as a freshman, she took a job as a waitress for the next three years. "Those years were my most insane years. I was doing so many dangerous things, it's a wonder I survived. On the other hand, it was good, because I was able to get a lot of stuff out of my system. I had been in a relationship with a guy who was thirteen years older than me, and I basically showed up at my mother's house in his Chevy Impala one day and announced, 'I'm packing up my stuff,' " she says. "I eventually left him and landed with another guy, and we lived together for two years. He was a real out-of-control alcoholic, although I didn't know that at the time because I didn't have the language for it. I just thought he liked to party a lot. When things started to get really nasty with his alcohol and drug abuse, and I found out he was sleeping with someone else, I said to myself, 'I'm getting out of here.' I decided to get myself together. In a way, I had played out a worst-case scenario for a relationship, and was learning what not to do." Barbara returned to college, graduated with honors, and during her mid-twenties met and married her husband.

Now, after eleven years together, she and her husband have sustained a level of intimacy through both good and rough times. Barbara says that occasionally her old fear of abandonment can flare up, although she actively works to keep it at bay. "Sometimes I fear I will scare him away with my enormous need for reassurance. Also, I can be pretty controlling, and I know that can get to him sometimes, even though we joke about it. I think I probably learned early on not to expect to get my needs met in an intimate relationship, so I tend to not be really good about expressing them—why bother, right?" she explains. "I ask for a lot of mind reading on his part—I just like him to *know* and *do*. There are times when I resort to old patterns of behavior without realizing it. I assume the worst of him and act accordingly, in a kind of survival mode. I end up hurting him when I act that way, because it's as though I don't see him for who he has proven himself—time and time again—to be."

For the most part, though, Barbara has been able to chip away at the insecurity she carries with her from childhood and keep it from interfering in her everyday life. She has created stability, not only through her marriage but also through her career, her friendships, her creative outlets, and her constant efforts to improve ties with her family. "I think you have to be in a certain space internally to achieve this sense of home, either by yourself or with others. I may have experienced this fleetingly in the past, but now I feel I have achieved a sense of home in a sustained way," she explains. "Plus, we recently moved into a beautiful house that has allowed me to externally express what I feel inside—that is, through color and furnishings and details—and really create the visual manifestation of that comfort. But I don't get too dependent on material things to give me that feeling of safety. I enjoy the decorating, and I've been blessed with the resources to realize a certain kind of vision in my environment; but I always go back to the root of my happiness, which is maintaining a level of acceptance and satisfaction with myself, as well as maintaining the relationship I share with my husband. This relationship has really become my foundation. Honestly, I think I'm pretty blessed to be this happy."

Barbara's experience shows how a caring partner can play a vital role in helping us release a lot of the fears we bring into a relationship. Explains thirty-three-year-old Nicole, who has been married for two years: "My spouse is awesome. What works for us is communication and humor. I can't play my old games of sulking, crying, or picking fights. He doesn't respond to me except when we sit and face each other and talk. It's a great comfort to know I'm safe with him. But I think my true test of how my parents' divorce affects our marriage will be when we become parents someday. Until then, I'm grateful I have a safe person to learn and grow with." As Nicole points out, when we become parents, the quality of our own parenting looms around us, and once again, we must deal with the memories of the past.

Becoming Parents

As I write this, I am twenty-seven years old, two years older than my parents were when they had me, yet the thought of having children still seems like a possibility that belongs in the distant future.

Still, somewhere in a part of my brain devoted to fantasy, I have a very clear image of three little girls: my daughters. I envision family vacations during the summer by some anonymous lake, curled up in a hammock during hazy afternoons and catching fireflies at night. I think of noise, the wonderful bustle of activity that fills up the rooms, and then the quiet of their sleep. In my imagination, I can crowd the empty rooms of my childhood and erase the loneliness.

But that's fantasy. In reality, I'm pretty conflicted about the whole parenthood idea, partly because I value my freedom and independence, but mostly because the prospect of having a child brings up very specific fears: What if their father is not a good husband or a good father? What if we break apart? What if I find myself single, with three girls to care for all by myself? Although both my mother and father juggled the demands of parenthood with full-time careers, I suspect the stress of their loads helped to crack their union in two. I wonder if I would be up to the same task. The responsibility of shaping a childhood for my children is at once tempting and terrifying.

As I found, for those of us who don't have children and want them, the fear that we will have to raise them alone, that our relationships will crumble and we will be unable to provide the adequate parenting they need, often holds us back. When it comes to picturing our own families, many of us immediately jump to a worst-case scenario: We will get divorced and put our children through the same turmoil we experienced during our own childhood. That's why so many of those I interviewed expressed apprehension about having children of their own, afraid they would pass down a legacy of divorce to their children. As twenty-eight-year-old Kyra, whose parents divorced when she was five, explains:

> I used to think I wanted to have children. I love children, but I don't want to be responsible for hurting them or screwing them up psychologically . . . and I think there is a real possibility I might do that. At one time, I thought I

would go to a clinic and use donor sperm to have a child by myself, but now that I have been working for the past five years, I realize just how much my mother has done for me and how difficult it was. I don't know if I could do a good job. I think I'm too selfish and needy in my own right to be able to place another's needs above my own. Would I be able to raise a daughter without having my feelings for my father rub off on her? Could I protect and make her whole? And a son? I'm not sure that would be right either. If I raised him by myself, how would I do it? I have no idea. For me, love, marriage, raising children, are just romantic notions. I'm not sure if I think they exist, or should exist.

Even for those who are happily married, taking the step from spouse to parent causes anxiety; some put off having children until they feel secure enough in their relationships. Thirty-four-year-old Daphne, whose parents divorced when she was twelve, waited until she and her husband had been together for six years before getting pregnant. "It's funny now, I guess, but for the longest time I was fearful of having children. I worried that if my husband and I ever did get divorced, my child would go through the same pain I went through, and that fear held me off the whole child idea for quite a while," she explains. "If the marriage was a mistake, I wanted it to be our mistake—mine and my husband's—and not have a child suffer from it. Once I felt surer, we got pregnant. I remember when I delivered my daughter, and we brought her home, I told my husband that he was *really* stuck with me now." As a parent, Daphne is now actively trying to provide her four-year-old daughter with the type of childhood she never had. "I like to 'make memories' for her to think back on, so she can remember having a happy childhood."

This concern that we might put our child through divorce is usually paired with an equally powerful desire to give our children the childhood we never had. "I would like to have a large family," explains twenty-eight-year-old Tom, whose parents divorced when he was three. "I have dreams about this huge wooden table—and it's made out of a tree that I chopped down on my own land—cheesy, I know. It seats all of these different family members, and we're all passing around food and wine. And there are kids running around because they're sick of talking to the old folks, and that's me—I'm one of the old folks, with carving tools and everything. See, this is incredibly cheesy because I think I'm probably getting this image in my dream from an old *Waltons* episode, a show I used to watch on a religious basis."

Sophia, whose parents separated when she was a toddler, didn't meet her father until she was fifteen and grew up with a mother who was emotionally needy and frighteningly temperamental. Now twenty-nine, she is the mother of a two-year-old daughter. "The drive in my life is family," she says. "I didn't really know this about myself until I gave birth to my daughter, but I think I have always wanted to undo what I experienced growing up. I always knew I would overcome it because, even as a child, my singular desire in life was to be happy—to have an outgoing, happy life—and that is still my desire."

As with any major milestone, becoming a parent can bring about a powerful wave of emotion, especially as we start to identify with our parents as fellow parents. During Sophia's pregnancy, as she contemplated her upcoming maternal responsibilities, she suffered a surge of anger toward her own mother. "I was having really disturbing dreams about her: killing my mother, fighting with my mother, driving with her down the highway in the wrong direction," she recalls. "I spoke with a midwife who assured me these feelings were normal, that when women become pregnant they explore the mothering they had, and that helped me work through some of the issues that were coming up." Talking with her mother about the past also helped her address the source of her resentment.

Sophia describes her relationship with her mother during her growing-up years as conflicted and complex. "I was her mother," she says. "She would always tell me her problems. She would tell me way too much about her dissatisfaction with my father and her boyfriend. She was always angry, threatening us and shouting, and throwing shoes or plates, but then she also hugged us and said she loved us. When she turned on me I couldn't understand why. I was always afraid of her. She poured out her emotions to her kids, and it was crippling, and I think one of her biggest regrets now is that she didn't have her wits about her."

By exploring her relationship with her mother, Sophia was able to put together a picture of the kind of mother she wanted to be for her own daughter. "From the moment my daughter was born and they put her on my belly, I felt at that instant that she was a separate person. I always felt like my mother thought she could live her life through me. I was going to fulfill all the dreams that she couldn't fulfill herself," she says. "So I respected that my daughter is her own person from the beginning. She's mine, but she's not mine. Another thing is that I always make sure to listen to her, because I always felt like my mother didn't listen to me. Even as a newborn and infant, when my daughter would talk and explore her voice, I always viewed it as legitimate communication."

Now that she has her own daughter, Sophia feels a new bond with her mother and has come to rely on her for support and advice. While she has grown closer to her mother, though, parenthood has also caused Sophia to review her relationship with her father and his position on the periphery of her life. Her father has seen Sophia's daughter only once, four months after she was born. "He was in town twice last summer and didn't visit us, and that was mind-boggling to me. I have this amazing child, and knowing that my father left me at the same age, sometimes I can't imagine why my father didn't want me. How could he have rejected me?" she says. "I see how much my daughter loves her father and the expectations she has of him. She plays differently with him. It seems like yin and yang, the roles my husband and I play. I think it's really hard for a single parent to be everything to a child." She pauses. "But while my bewilderment over my father's abandonment has grown, I feel more and more that I don't need him, especially when all he brings into my life is pain. The thing I think I was craving from my father all these years I don't need anymore. I found it in my own life, and in my own family."

When History Repeats Itself: Learning from Our Own Divorces

Sometimes it's the experience of our own divorce that finally brings into focus any damaging patterns of behavior we may have inherited. For thirty-eight-year-old Malcolm, whose parents divorced when he was fifteen, too many years of observing his parents swap vicious insults, and occasionally engage in knockdown fights, had taught him to detach from his emotions and feign indifference when he felt angry or upset. Angry words from a partner were met, from his end, with silence. When faced with conflict, "I just walked out on it," he says, "sometimes for an hour or two, until my rage wore down. By the time I came back, I usually felt enough distance from the situation to deal with it coldly. When my wife would ask, 'Are you angry?' 'Are you sad?' 'Are you scared?' I certainly recognized the words, but they had no correspondence to anything I recognized in myself."

Malcolm had been dating his wife for almost three years when they decided to get married. He stepped into the union with few misgivings, believing that they were committed to each other. "Since we planned on staying together forever," he explains, "I thought, 'So why not?'" But looking back, he realizes that there were weaknesses in the relationship from the start. "I remember when we first met, agreeing with her that I didn't like deeply cynical people, even though I was one myself, and actually thinking, 'Oh, shit, if you want to get her, you're going to have to act not cynical.' That was the kind of relationship it was, and the kind of person I was in a relationship," he says. "I was such a dishonest person, so separated from my own feelings. Most of our interactions, it seems to me, were about my attempts to manipulate the daily situation to make things go the way I wanted them to. I put all kinds of efforts into packaging her in various ways to have her look or appear to be the kind of person I wanted to be seen with to win. I think I had this computer-dating notion of compatibility, whereas now, I think in terms of more important things, like worldview."

A few years into the marriage, things were not going well. Malcolm and his wife were arguing more, and he had secretly started to see another woman. Finally, they entered couples therapy together. "The affair came up in one of our therapy sessions, and at that point, she stood up, took her ring off, and threw it at me. Then walked out." Although Malcolm was distraught over the end of his marriage, he started to mourn with an intensity that indicated a deeper turmoil. "I felt like I had blown my golden opportunity. I had just started to get a glimmer of what was wrong with the way I had been living my life. It wasn't until I started to really look at our marriage that I realized we had very little in common, and we probably wouldn't have even had a first date if I had known what I know now."

With the help of therapy, Malcolm started a personal exploration, making a commitment to himself not to rush into intimate relationships until he gained more of an emotional footing. He focused on his work, on his friendships, and on rebuilding relationships with members of his family. Most important, though, he started to gain confidence in his abilities and insights. "Before, I had always looked toward other people for validation, and for the first time I actually felt like I was validating my own accomplishments," he says. "A lot of good things happened during that time, things that probably would not have happened if I had not stepped back and looked at my life. It was the first time that my opinion actually counted more to me than what other people thought. That was probably the most profound thing for me."

As Malcolm learned, until we recognize the invisible map provided by our parents, we may often find ourselves repeating their history in one way or another without being consciously aware of it.

But as Malcolm's story illustrates, going through our own divorces can give us the chance to reflect on our choices and to develop the skills that will help us enter into healthy relationships in the future.

For thirty-six-year-old Emily, her greatest fear in love has always been having her trust betrayed, and it was a fear she faced head-on when she divorced her husband three years ago. At twenty-four, Emily had married her boyfriend, whom she had been living with for a year. "It was actually his idea to get married," she says. "I was okay with just living together, but I remember afterward, it did feel kind of nice and different." A few years into their relationship, however, she started to suspect that her husband was having an affair with a woman he had met through work. "He introduced her as a 'friend,' " Emily recalls. "She came over to dinner one night and after that, I immediately felt uneasy about everything. Something about it bothered me." Later, Emily asked her husband about his relationship with this woman, but he maintained that they were just friends. "He never acknowledged what was going on, up until I asked him if he had slept with her. I can remember it suddenly popping into my head to ask him that outright, and it came out of the blue; there was this long pause, and he said yes, and then everything fell apart."

Her husband's infidelity was a double blow to Emily; her parents' divorce when she was eleven was set off by her mother's extramarital affair, and led to her father's demanding custody and the court's granting it to him. "Having to go through what I went through—the real significant betrayal that I had to deal with—I mean, I always knew what it was like from my dad; it's hard not to. But to have to go through it again, with my parents' example of what damage it can do. To find myself in this situation where someone I trusted and thought was pretty aware was doing this to me, that was the hardest part."

After she learned that her husband was having an affair, they remained married for three more years as they tried to reconcile. "He kept telling me one thing and acting a different way," she explains.

"He kept saying he was going to end his affair with this woman, and try to make things work with me, but then he would still see her. It dragged on for months. There were long periods of being in a holding pattern, and I think I tolerated it because he kept saying he wanted to work it out, which is what I wanted to do too. And partly because I thought my parents could have worked it out if they had wanted to, which I still think, but they didn't want to," she adds. "I think, from their divorce, I became much more willing to accept the responsibility for how my actions affect my partner, and that I am half of any situation. But it took a long time for me to realize that it takes two people who feel that way, and I can't do it all by myself." When it became apparent that her husband was unwilling to change his behavior, Emily, despite his objections, filed for divorce.

Although the experience was incredibly painful, in the process of having her worst fear come true, Emily mastered some important skills. "I practiced getting more and more articulate in expressing myself about trying to get him to change his behavior and accommodate me on some level," she explains. "I became very good at clarifying what I wanted."

In the past three years, living on her own, Emily has been able to create a home for herself, a place where she feels comfortable, with close friends nearby. "I never felt connected to a larger community, but right now I'm living in a co-op setting, and it's really what I need and want," she says. "There are a lot of kids around, and I watch how their parents parent them. There are single parents and parents who are together, and the kids seem to have a much better sense of self and how they fit into things than I did. I've always known who I was, but with all that's happened to me, I've learned where to draw limits and how to draw limits."

Old Lessons: Breaking Up with Children

Many of us can think of ways our parents could have handled their breakup better. As thirty-three-year-old Jane remarks, "Both my parents made terrible mistakes, and I hope that if they ever had a second chance to go through their divorce again, they would know better to do it differently."

Of course, most of our parents don't divorce each other twice, but for some of us who have—or will—split up, our own breakups offer us the opportunity to right the wrongs of the past with our own children. Thirty-one-year-old Amanda explains that in her early twenties, her insecurities drove her to enter into an unhealthy relationship and have a child; when she and her partner broke apart, he sued for custody of their daughter. Although she found herself in the same predicament as her parents, who spent her childhood clashing in court, she was determined not to repeat their mistakes. "I do not bad-mouth my daughter's father to her. We have not been to court in almost two years, and I let a lot go and try to get along for her sake," she explains. "I don't pit her against her father. I encourage a positive relationship, because I understand that she will love him irrespective of my opinion about him. Bad-mouthing him will only make her defend him and feel bad about herself."

When thirty-six-year-old Helen separated from her partner of ten years, leaving her as a single parent to their seven-year-old daughter, she looked back on her parents' divorce and identified with her daughter in two ways: as a parent and as a child whose parents had also divorced. Unlike her parents, Helen wanted to protect her daughter through this painful time. "I really wish my parents had been more honest with me," she says. "They said nothing. And my mother was very upset and nasty in the beginning—my father was every bad thing you could think of, and initially I believed her, I took her side. We never heard 'This has nothing to do with you kids, it has to do with us.' "

For Helen, who initiated the separation from her daughter's father, her relationship had reached the breaking point. Her partner had become more distant, not only with her but with their child as well. "My daughter would call me at work and say things like 'Daddy won't play with me.' And it would break my heart. I'm at work, though, and what am I supposed to do? So I would get on the phone with him, and he would basically brush me off," she says. "It became apparent to me that not having him around would be better than having him around but treating her and me this way. I would rather be alone than have someone here who isn't willing to listen. I didn't want to get to the same point where my parents were at—where you spend seventeen years of your life married to someone you can't tolerate; you used to love them, but you don't anymore."

Although she knew it was the right decision, breaking up with her partner was extremely difficult, especially for their daughter, who didn't take her father's departure well. "She blamed me in the very beginning," Helen recalls. "She would say things like 'Why did you send him away? If you weren't happy with him, *you* could have left. Having any daddy is better than having no daddy.' And, of course, that broke my heart, too, but I would try very hard to be honest with her. I didn't try to make it all sweet and pretty, because it wasn't, but at the same time I was careful not to bad-mouth him. I would say, 'Daddy and I just don't get along anymore, and it's not that I don't still love Daddy, because he's not a bad person.' I make sure to tell her that her father will always be a part of our lives, that he is welcome in our home, but if he gets angry, I'm not going to let him in until he calms down. I tell her that sometimes we will fight, but we're just fighting and we'll figure it out; and sometimes we won't fight, but just because everything's wonderful doesn't mean that we're getting back together."

In short, Helen has been able to say all the things to her daughter that she wishes her parents had said to her more than twenty years ago. "I remember that unbelievable disappointment—oh, look, Mommy and Daddy are talking to each other!—and that's a hard thing to deal with when you're young," she says. "You keep getting your hopes up, and when they get crushed, you don't know who to be angry at, who started the argument, who pissed on who. You get involved. So I try to help my daughter understand the situation in terms of her little friends. I'll say, 'You know you really like Carrie a lot, she's your best friend, but sometimes you argue and you don't see each other for a while? With grown-ups, it's the same.' Luckily, her father and I have been able to keep things pretty civilized between us."

Helen also points out that divorce today is a much different experience than it was for her growing up, which is helping her daughter handle some of the tough emotions she feels. "When my parents divorced, we were the lepers in the neighborhood," she remembers. "My friends were not permitted to come to the house, because there wasn't an adult around until evening. I actually lost a boyfriend over my parents' divorce. His father said right in front of me, 'That slut you're going out with—I don't want you seeing her anymore. She's growing up with her father and has no mother around. What kind of influence can he be? Say good-bye to her now.' And I never saw him again."

It's different for her daughter: The majority of her friends' parents are divorced, and so is her teacher at school. "My daughter is the norm now, and I don't know whether that is a good or bad thing," Helen admits. "But the fact that she is not an oddball makes it easier for her to be in an acceptable arena with her peers." Even at her elementary school, Helen says, her daughter's teacher made a point of calling in every parent and asking about the makeup of her students' home life. She adds, "Everyone is so much more aware."

Over the years, Helen has been able to embrace the strength and independence she developed when her parents divorced, and to use those qualities to provide her daughter with the emotional support she needs. "I work every day of my life, both with and without my daughter's father, to be all the things that make a place home." After her daughter was born, Helen flew her parents out to visit, determined to have pictures of her daughter with both her grandparents together. Her father brought her mother flowers. "It made me feel good to know that even after all the horrible things that went on, they could actually be mature," she says, then adds with a laugh, "For an hour or two at least."

Whether they are single, married, or divorced, I find hope in the stories of others who, over time, have been able to choose what lessons they take away from their parents' divorces and conduct their relationships using both knowledge and experience as positive guides. Their decisions and behavior are not dictated by the past, and their memories, rather than trapping them within, serve as some of the strongest building blocks in the homes they have constructed for themselves today. "After all the years of hating, all the years of hurting, I think I learned something from my parents' divorce," says one twenty-six-year-old woman. "I can use their divorce as a checkpoint in my own marriage. When the rough times hit, I can say, 'Okay, we have a choice. We can either behave like our parents or we can get through it by ourselves.' "

Unlike our parents, many of whom married young and thought marriage meant happily ever after, we grew up surrounded by the plots of failed marriages. We may enter into marriages cautiously, already grasping for ways to give our relationships staying power, but many of us have also adjusted our expectations and know that marriage involves more than a wedding and a license. "I've become a bit skeptical when it comes to 'traditional' marriage values—big weddings, the 'before' and 'after' marriage distinction, 'the most important day in my life' bullshit," says one thirty-seven-year-old woman. "In fact, I've come to believe that you don't have a clue what marriage is about until you've been in it for at least five or ten years, and shouldn't be allowed to have a big wedding until after you've celebrated your tenth anniversary or logged the equivalent amount of mileage in sharing traumatic events or other high-intensity, test-your-mettle kind of experiences."

As a result, many of us don't enter into commitment lightly. We live with our future spouses first, an option that decades ago was inconceivable. In understanding the obstacles our parents faced in their marriages, we come better prepared to work on the potential problems that arise in our own relationships, turning to communication rather than giving up. At the same time, we know that divorcing a spouse is sometimes necessary, but when we do, it is important to divorce responsibly, especially when children are involved. Many of us know firsthand how a contentious divorce can harm children, and we use this knowledge to protect our own children when we divorce.

We are each reinventing the terms "marriage," "divorce," and "family" in our own way. With insight and awareness, we have learned that we can make smart decisions about love, career, commitment, and lifestyle. In living with the legacy of our parents' divorce, we are, most important of all, creating our own legacy.

Epilogue: Lost and Found

A COUPLE OF MONTHS after my mother moved out, while rummaging through the closet, I ran across a set of homemade Christmas stockings I had cut out of cherry-red felt and sewn together only a year before. I remember it was an unseasonably warm Saturday afternoon, the sliding glass door in the family room open to let in a breeze. With stockings in hand, I sat down on the couch to examine them more closely. There were four in all—one each for my mother, my father, my sister, and me. Our names were written in green glitter cursive across the bottoms and the fabric was still crisp, not yet worn by use. I stacked one on top of the other, smoothing them across my lap. It was suddenly too much to bear, this inescapable proof that everything had changed, and so I lumbered to my feet, balled the stockings up in my fists, and shoved them to the back of the closet.

While packing up my belongings for college four years later, I accidentally unearthed those crumpled Christmas stockings again, covered in layers of dust and flecks of glitter. By then, I no longer knotted up at the sight of them, but handled the red fabric with a sense of alienation and a brief twinge of regret, which I quickly smothered. With little fanfare, I gathered the stockings together and threw them in the trash.

For some time, those stockings represented the pivot on which the narrative of my life turned. They were symbols of loss, and I didn't yet have the vocabulary for my experience to see them in any other way. But in taking the journey into memory, I have arrived at a different place than where I was the first—or even the second—time I encountered those stockings. When I think of them now, the memory is bittersweet. I remember my excitement at making them to celebrate our first family Christmas as four instead of three, just as I remember my painful realization that we would never share a holiday together again. I remember my father taking me to see a movie after I broke up with my first boyfriend, having slumber parties at my mother's house, and attending my sister's play in the first grade. In this place I inhabit now, there is room enough to see both the positive and negative outcomes of my parents' divorce and to accept them as a part of my life.

Over the past two years, friends, family, and acquaintances have all suggested that writing this book must be a "cathartic" experience. I have nodded in agreement when they've said this, murmuring, "Yes, yes, it is," partially because when I first started, I too believed that letting years of built-up emotion spill onto the page would provide a great release. I thought I could blow away the dust of this disintegrated center that was once my family, sending the particles to float in thin air and leaving behind only the answers I sought. But although I wanted and waited, the expected catharsis never arrived as scheduled.

In fact, writing this book has been difficult. After so many years of silence, it is not always easy to find your voice—a little scratchy in the beginning, rough in places in the middle, slowly growing stronger toward the end. After so many years of avoidance, it is not always easy to stop and face your past with a detached, scrutinizing eye. Sometimes the weight of the past has seemed unbearably heavy, ready to submerge me; but other times, it has seemed incredibly light, manageable, illuminating.

Occasionally the memories have formed instantly into words, my fingers almost racing faster than my mind over the keyboard. But most of the time, I have spent hours in front of the computer, fingers perfectly still, trying to figure out how to articulate feelings or an event in a way that would do it justice. Because when all is said and done, the words that we have at our disposal are terribly inadequate: Divorce. Abandonment. Conflict. These are drab words that hardly reveal the texture of memory that lies strung between their letters. And for each one of us, our parents' divorce is shaded in complexity and by nuances that I can't possibly isolate into paragraphs and phrases.

Although I wanted to find a simple way to characterize my parents' divorce and what happened after, instead I found many versions of their history and mine, a constant shape-shifting of how I perceived my parents' breakup and its effect on my own life: I am a girl who as a child adored her parents, viewing them as perfect and infallible, then was forever wounded when they let me down. I am a woman who discovered the value of independence and self-sufficiency, secure in the knowledge that I can take care of myself. I am a daughter whose parents love her, but made some mistakes along the way. Regardless, the experience remains intertwined in the fabric of my being and it is hard to separate the effects of their divorce from who I am today. "The thing is," points out one thirty-eight-year-old woman, "when divorce is part of the growing-up experience, it permeates all areas of experience, both at the time as well as in memory. So it becomes difficult to say which came first, the chicken or the egg."

I have no way of knowing what course my life might have taken if my parents had not divorced. I have no gauge for calculating the sum of that experience. I only know that their divorce has been a guiding force in shaping my life. I suppose that is why, in the end, the idea of catharsis falls flat for me: It implies an expulsion, a purification, a fiery explosion that cuts a clear path in front of you and leaves no ashes behind. Yet I can't erase or evict the impact of my parents' divorce, and like most of the people I interviewed, I would not want to.

Therefore, I like to think that writing this book has been a "reverse catharsis," if you will, a way to digest the past to root myself in the present. In the absence of utter revelation or relief, we have the ability to translate loss into power and clarity. To be an adult child of divorce is to be marked by contradictions and pulled by uncertainty, but it is also to gain an insight and maturity that others may not have acquired so young. Our parents' divorces offered us a crash course in understanding human frailties and the demands of personal responsibility; we may have learned these lessons before we were ready, and their instruction may have been tough at the time, but they were important lessons nonetheless.

When our homes split apart, we were often encouraged to seek security and recognition elsewhere. I heard stories of those who, in the absence of familial support, developed the determination to succeed, paying for their education by working full-time and pushing themselves to take risks they might not have otherwise taken. Rather than follow a path to oblivion, they consciously chose to surmount the obstacles presented by their parents' divorce. "For some reason—and I know there are worse cases than my family upbringing—my sisters and I all turned out quite well," says one twenty-nine-year-old man, whose parents divorced when he was twelve. "So even though I can say 'Woe is my life,' and I don't think I would wish it on too many people, I sometimes wonder if my parents had reconciled and become lovey-dovey, would we have turned out the way we did? Any step along the way, I could have been a druggie, I could have become some drunk. I could still be hanging out in my hometown doing nothing. But I didn't, and every step along the way, every hurdle that was thrown at me was a challenge. My parents' divorce taught me to deal with things myself, introspectively, from the good times to the bad times."

Probably the most unique challenge brought on by divorce was the need to alternate between the two worlds created by each parent. As one man put it, his parents' divorce made him feel "existentially well traveled." As travelers, we learned to adapt, adjust, speak a new language, adopt customs according to different lifestyles; in addition, we were exposed to different people and places. This can be an important asset once we step into the larger world. "I had two different identities growing up," says one thirty-three-year-old man. "My mother lived in a lower-middle-class, fairly urban neighborhood, and my father lived in the opposite extreme—a pretty, affluent suburb. After I left home, I kind of wore this split identity as a badge of pride, because it gave me the ability to coexist in these two worlds. As I got older, I realized that I could relate to many different people on a level that's hard to reach if you're only from one place. I feel good about it. I'm glad I had this experience, because my scope is not so narrow. When I meet people from different backgrounds, I don't feel uncomfortable with anyone in particular. I know a little bit about where they're from and what they're about."

Amidst the charges that parental divorce leads to higher rates of criminal behavior, substance abuse, and teenage pregnancy, those of us who emerged from our parents' divorces to become entrepreneurs, artists, lawyers, doctors, housewives, nurses, scientists, and actors are often overlooked. In a personal essay about his parents' divorce when he was twenty-seven, Walter Kim observed, "A lot of those teenage divorced kids I once knew sank and never resurfaced, but the ones who survived seem enviably vibrant to me. They're dynamic, open, unafraid. They play in the best new rock bands, write visionary computer software. The road less taken is where they're most at home." While I'm not arguing that divorce can limit a child's opportunities both emotionally and financially, the majority of us are indeed the "survivors." Many of us wouldn't trade in the knowledge we have now despite the hurt we went through to obtain it. "I was profoundly shocked and upset after my parents divorced," agrees one thirty-year-old woman, who is now a mother and a successful writer. "But now my life has gone in a direction that stemmed from events that happened after the divorce, so I can't say I wish it didn't happen because then I wouldn't be where I am today."

This is where we are today: In the wake of feminism, the counter-culture movement, the sexual revolution, and the phenomenon of divorce, fewer than one in five families fits into the "traditional" model, where a mother stays at home and rears the children and a father acts as the breadwinner. We are single parents, working mothers, stepparents, domestic partners, and men and women who choose to live alone.

We grew up during a time of dramatic change, and in homes that were far from "traditional"; and after growing up within this looser definition of family, we now have greater freedom to not only pick and choose what family means to us as adults, but also to change the way our families operate.

I grew up in a single-father home. My father came home from a long day of work, opened up a cookbook, and made us dinner almost every night. He constantly encouraged me to focus on school and to achieve academically, and I am forever grateful that I had such a father. I never felt the bind of traditional gender roles that sometimes exists in two-parent homes, and as an adult, I feel better equipped to make demands in my own relationship. My father provided me with an important expectation for the men in my life, while my mother, who has lived on her own since my parents divorced, offered me a role model for being a self-sufficient career woman.

Many women I interviewed, after growing up with single mothers who essentially raised and supported them, also say the typical gender barriers slipped away during their childhood. "Living with just my sister and my mother, I was forced to take on a lot of the traditionally 'male' tasks," remarks one thirty-four-year-old woman. "I learned to fix the VCR, catch bugs, hammer in nails, pay the bills. Now, I know that if I had to be alone, I could do it. I don't need a man to take care of me." We have more options than our mothers did, and whether we want to be alone or not, we know that it is possible to survive—even thrive—on our own.

While more and more people might be living alone, however, they are often surrounded by an extended network of friends they consider family. "For the first time in human history some Americans and other industrialized people have begun to pick their relatives—forging a brand-new web of kin based on friendship instead of blood," explains anthropologist Helen Fisher in *Anatomy of Love*. As children, when the old boundaries of family dissolved, many of us widened our circle to include stepparents, stepsiblings, other relatives, friends, and their families.

"One of my perspectives on life is that people can't define a relationship by title," says one thirty-two-year-old man. "Certainly my friends are as close to me as my family—they're like brothers and sisters. I stopped being upset when someone didn't fit their title a long time ago, and started to appreciate people for who they are. I consider all my friends my family, and maybe that's trite, and maybe everyone says it, but it's true. The line is blurred. My best friend since I was a kid—I've always loved his mother and father to death, and his father had a cyst a couple of years ago. They didn't know what was going to happen. It turned out to be benign, and he's fine now, but before he was going into surgery, I was speaking to my friend's mother and telling her, 'You two have always been like my second parents,' and she said to me, 'You are my third child.' It was a wonderful moment."

I started this book by focusing on what we've lost, and along the way, I've also found what we've gained: How we have created strong families, despite our parents' divorces; how we can use our ingrown caution about love to make careful choices in our partners; how we can use the independence we developed in childhood to forge ahead in our careers. Just as the loss shapes us, we can shape the loss. And it is a new and constant process, this shaping of loss.

Over the course of researching this book, I've spoken with people who have gotten engaged, gotten married, had children, and divorced. We are all caught up in the act of what Mary Catherine Bateson calls "composing a life":

> The process of improvisation that goes into composing a life is compounded in the process of remembering a life, like a patchwork quilt in a watercolor painting, rumpled and evocative. Yet it is in this second process, composing a life through memory as well as through day-to-day choices, that seems to me the most essential to creative living. The past empowers the present, and the groping footsteps leading to this present mark the pathways to the future.

It is with these tentative footsteps that I move into the future. How do I write a conclusion to a story that is still unfolding for so many of us, including me? I don't have a perfect ending to offer you. My parents still make unpleasant remarks and intimations about each other. I still have to figure out where I'm going to spend my holidays. I still haven't put on a white dress and walked down the aisle, moved by a renewed faith in love. I still wonder, if I ever have children, will their grandparents be able to sit together in the same room? I still feel twinges of sadness at the oddest moments, and I still have an armful of memories that hurt when I squeeze them.

But in remembering my own life and talking to others, I have also discovered hope. As a child I learned hard and fast that everything can fall apart; but as an adult I am slowly learning that everything can come together. And perhaps having this hope is the best ending of all.